CHRISTIANITY
A Complete Introduction

John Young is Canon Emeritus of York Minster and was a member of the General Synod of the Church of England for many years. He is an occasional broadcaster as well as the author of more than 30 books/booklets (which have been translated into several languages, including Chinese and Russian) and co-founder of *York Courses*, which publishes material to facilitate church discussion groups (www.yorkcourses.co.uk).

Greg Hoyland has been a lecturer in theology for over 25 years, after periods in teaching and, after ordination, in parish and youth ministry. He has written on the Christian Church and modernity, and on peace and reconciliation. He broadcasts regularly on local radio and occasionally on national radio and television.

For our grandchildren
Isaac, Anna, Beth, Jack and Niamh (Greg)
Robert, Mary, Emma and Jacob (John)

CHRISTIANITY
A Complete Introduction

Revd Canon John Young &
Revd Greg Hoyland

First published in Great Britain in 1996 by Hodder Education. An Hachette UK company.

This edition published in 2016 by John Murray Learning

Based on material previously published as *Christianity: An Introduction* and *Teach Yourself Christianity*

Copyright © John Young and Greg Hoyland 1996, 1999, 2003, 2008, 2010, 2016

The right of John Young and Greg Hoyland to be identified as the Authors of the Work has been asserted by them in accordance with the Copyright, Designs and Patents Act 1988.

The *Teach Yourself* name is a registered trademark of Hachette UK

Database right Hodder & Stoughton (makers)

British Library Cataloguing in Publication Data: a catalogue record for this title is available from the British Library.

Library of Congress Catalog Card Number: on file.

Paperback 9781473615786

eBook 9781473615779

1

The publisher has used its best endeavours to ensure that any website addresses referred to in this book are correct and active at the time of going to press. However, the publisher and the authors have no responsibility for the websites and can make no guarantee that a site will remain live or that the content will remain relevant, decent or appropriate.

The publisher has made every effort to mark as such all words which it believes to be trademarks. The publisher should also like to make it clear that the presence of a word in the book, whether marked or unmarked, in no way affects its legal status as a trademark.

Every reasonable effort has been made by the publisher to trace the copyright holders of material in this book. Any errors or omissions should be notified in writing to the publisher, who will endeavour to rectify the situation for any reprints and future editions.

Cover image © Shutterstock.com

Typeset by Cenveo® Publisher Services.

Printed and bound in Great Britain by CPI Group (UK) Ltd., Croydon, CR0 4YY.

John Murray Learning policy is to use papers that are natural, renewable and recyclable products and made from wood grown in sustainable forests. The logging and manufacturing processes are expected to conform to the environmental regulations of the country of origin.

Carmelite House
50 Victoria Embankment
London EC4Y 0DZ
www.hodder.co.uk

Also available
in ebook

Contents

Acknowledgements

Sixth edition

The reception of the five previous editions of this book has been gratifying and we are glad to report an alternative edition – in Russian. It is clear that a wide-ranging exploration of Christianity, in a paperback of reasonable size, is attractive to many people. We welcome the opportunity this new edition gives us of adding to the text, updating some information and contributing to the website (www.teachyourself.com). We're glad, too, to thank our editor Hilary Marsden, and to have this further opportunity of recording our gratitude and indebtedness to Iain Campbell of Hodder, and our colleague and friend Carrie Geddes. We are delighted that the former Archbishop of Canterbury, Rowan Williams, and Bishop Stephen Cottrell have commended this work, and we gladly record our thanks to them both.

John Young & Greg Hoyland, York, UK

Previous editions

On reflection, I am surprised at just how many people have been involved in producing one book of modest size. I am extremely grateful to them for reading drafts of the proofs and for making many valuable suggestions, and I hope they will not be embarrassed at being publicly associated with the finished work:

Dr David Barrett, Dr Peter Brierley of *Christian Research*, Fr Cyril Brooks OSB, Pastor Iain Collins, Fr Bill East, Nicky Enticknap, Nigel Forde, Revd Dr Michael Frost, Carrie Geddes, Christopher Idle, Jacquie Lawless, Duncan McInnes, Brother Patrick Moore FSC, Revd David Mullins, Revd Dr John Polkinghorne KBE FRS, Bishop Stephen Robson, David and Sheana Steels, Dr Alison Wray and Chris Woodcock.

My special thanks are due to three friends who agreed to write specific chapters and then bravely submitted themselves to my editorial control: the Revd Canon John Cockerton, the Revd Canon Dr John Toy and the Revd Canon Dr Peter Williams.

I wish to record my gratitude to Catherine Coe, my editor, for her patience, expertise and wise judgement. Above all, to Yolande Clarke, Linda Norman, Carolyn Prestwick, Barbara Thompson and Sharon Winfield, upon whom I came to depend for endless drafts and carefully researched information – one immense THANK YOU.

The author and publishers would like to thank the following for their kind permission to reproduce extracts from copyright material:

The Central Board of Finance of the Church of England for *The Mystery of Salvation*, Church House Publishing, 1995; HarperCollins Publishers Ltd for *Surprised by Joy* by C.S. Lewis; Darton, Longman and Todd for *School for Prayer* by Metropolitan Anthony of Sourozh (Archbishop Anthony Bloom); Hodder & Stoughton Ltd for *With Hope In Our Hearts* by David Sheppard and Derek Worlock; Newspaper Publishing plc for an article by William Rees-Mogg, *The Independent*, 21 December 1992; Oxford University Press for *The Oxford Dictionary of Saints* edited by David Hugh Farmer, 3rd edition, 1992; SCMPress Ltd for *Our Faith* by Emil Brunner, 1936, and *Introducing the Christian Faith* by A.M. Ramsey, revised edn 1970; SPCK for *The Way the World Is* by John Polkinghorne, *The Resurrection of Jesus* by Pinchas Lapide, *Who Was Jesus?* by N.T. Wright, *The Lantern and the Looking-Glass* by Nigel Forde, and *To Be a Pilgrim* by Basil Hume; Times Newspapers Limited for 'Odds on God's fine tuning' by Clifford Longley, *The Times*, 13 April 1991 © Times Newspapers Limited, 1991; the *Church Times* for the use of a letter by P.K.M. M'Pherson, © Church Times, 12 April 2002.

What they said about previous editions

'An exciting, engaging and intellectually serious book'
Dr Rowan Williams, former Archbishop of Canterbury

'I think it's brilliant!'
Bishop Stephen Cottrell

Beginnings

Christianity did not appear out of nowhere 'ready-made': it grew out of first-century Judaism (a faith which had been around for some two or three thousand years) centred on a Jewish teacher-prophet, Jesus of Nazareth. Palestine at the time was occupied by the Romans and Judaism was somewhat fragmented. There were different factions and sects such as the Pharisees, the Zealots and the Sadducees. Others, such as the Essenes, lived in remote walled communities in the wilderness (the Qumran community may have been one of these). Although these groups were often at odds with one another, one thing many of them did seem to share was the idea of a Messiah (*Christ* in Greek). One day this Messiah would come to restore their fortunes and rid them of Roman rule. What they could not agree on was what the Messiah would be like or when he (it was a very male-oriented world!) would appear.

The central figure

Into this confused context came Jesus, a carpenter's son, from Nazareth. He very quickly attracted a number of followers who began to see him as the promised Messiah. After his death and the events surrounding it, his early disciples had to work out the significance of his life and work. Guided by the Holy Spirit they began to re-examine their Hebrew scriptures (the Old Testament). They came to the conclusion that this was indeed the long-awaited Messiah. To begin with the early Christians continued as a sect of Judaism, but as time passed the relationship with traditional Judaism became increasingly strained. By the turn of the first century they were recognized – though still much resented and persecuted – as a separate religion. They seem to have acquired the name 'Christian' by around AD 40.

Developing beliefs

Christianity spread quickly throughout the Roman Empire, aided by the highly developed Roman transport and communication systems. As it spread geographically, it increased numerically. More significantly it moved beyond its Jewish roots to embrace people of all cultures – the Gentiles as the Jews called them. This required Christians to think through their faith in the light of the ways of life, languages and religious ideas of those cultures. How important was it to hold on to its Jewish heritage? Could its beliefs be expressed through other (non-Jewish) concepts? Was it necessary to understand Judaism in order to understand Christianity?

None of this was straightforward. Different communities developed slightly (sometimes significantly) different understandings of Christianity, circulating their ideas in letters and other writings. Many of these texts still exist and some of them were used to form the Christian scriptures, the New Testament. Over the course of the first 200 years Christianity developed its core beliefs, sometimes with considerable agreement, but sometimes with major disputes.

The Roman Emperor Constantine converted to Christianity early in the fourth century. He was responsible for calling together a great council in Nicaea (İznik in modern-day Turkey) where he forced the different groups to come together to agree on what they believed. This gave rise to the Nicene Creed, still used today in churches throughout the world as a summary of the core beliefs of Christianity.

Back to basics – the need for Reformation

Constantine's greatest decision was to make Christianity the sole legitimate religion of the Roman Empire. As a result of this, during the next 1,000 years the church became a key player in the world of politics, rivalling many of the secular powers. It became a great custodian of learning and culture and it achieved considerable status, power and wealth. It split into two major traditions: the Western church centred on Rome, and the Eastern (Orthodox) tradition centred on Constantinople (modern Istanbul), Antioch, Alexandria and Jerusalem. Some began to question whether the church (particularly in the West) had lost touch with the simplicity and vigour of the faith of its founder. These reformers – people like Martin Luther (1483–1546), Huldrych Zwingli (1484–1531) and John Calvin (1509–64) – argued that Christianity needed to return to its roots, to surrender its worldly attitudes and wealth and to preach again the simple gospel of the early church.

Global expansion

In spite of – or perhaps because of – these upheavals, the Christian church continued to grow. It expanded into Asia – China, the Indian sub-continent, Japan, Korea; it colonized the Americas north and south, and spread throughout the great continent of Africa, as well as reaching Australia and New Zealand. Today it is estimated that a third of the world's population can in some way or other be described as 'Christian'.

The word 'Christian' is used to describe an individual or communal faith but it also describes a cultural and philosophical heritage which many in the world claim. And it has continued to develop. Socially, scientifically, economically, politically, Christianity today inhabits a very different world from that of Jesus of Nazareth and his early disciples. As a result it has had to continue to adapt to new contexts and ideas. Areas where Christianity was once strong appear to be experiencing a decline. But other areas, such as China and the Middle East, are seeing quite remarkable growth. It remains a compelling and powerful faith in the modern world with a rich and diverse heritage. And it seems to possess an inherent ability to survive and thrive in the face of great change.

How to use this book

To some, this will be obvious. They will start at Chapter 1 and read through each chapter until they have finished. Others, however, may choose to approach the book differently. For example, some readers may be particularly interested in Christianity in the modern world and so will start at Chapter 14. Others might be especially interested in some of the key figures of Christianity and their links to art, music and architecture and so start reading at Chapter 10. Whatever their particular interests, we hope that all readers will read Chapters 1 to 5. These attempt to give some idea of the significance for Christians of Jesus Christ, and to provide a glimpse of what it means to be a Christian today.

Bible references are included in several places. These are given in the form of:

▶ the book's/writer's name, e.g. 'John'; 'Psalms'

▶ the chapter number

▶ the verse(s) number.

So 'John 3:16' refers to the Gospel according to John, chapter 3, verse 16. There are a few cases where books have the same name, such as Corinthians (of which there are two) or John's letters (of which there are three). These are written as, for example, '3 John 1: 2'.

Those who wish to look up these references are advised to use a good modern translation, such as the *New Revised Standard Version* (NRSV), the *New Jerusalem Bible* (an official Roman Catholic translation) or *The New International Version* (NIV). Most Bible quotations in this book are taken from the NIV and NRSV.

An attempt has been made to explain technical terms in the text itself. Reference has also been made to other chapters which refer to related issues. There is a short glossary at the end of the book, as well as an index.

In writing this book we have in mind two groups: students, and general readers interested in the many subjects covered. A wide range of books have been used in writing this volume and we are grateful for permission to quote from several. Many of these are included in the *Dig deeper* sections at the end of each chapter. Some of these are more academic and some of more interest to the general reader.

This *Complete Introduction* from Teach Yourself® includes a number of special boxed features, which have been developed to help you understand the subject more quickly and remember it more effectively. Throughout the book you will find these indicated by the following icons:

The book includes concise **quotations** from other key sources. These will be useful for helping you understand different viewpoints on the subject, and they are fully referenced so that you can include them in essays if you have to write one! It is always best to check the original for yourself but the full details are included in case you are unable to get your hands on the source.

The **case study** is a more in-depth introduction to a particular topic or example. There is at least one in most chapters, and they should provide good material for essays and discussions.

The **key ideas** are highlighted throughout the book. If you want a quick reminder of the important points or have only half an hour to go before your exam, scanning through these would be a very good way of spending your time.

The **spotlight** boxes offer interesting or amusing anecdotes to help bring the ideas to life.

The **fact-check** questions at the end of each chapter are designed to help you ensure that you have taken in the most important concepts from the chapter. If you find you are consistently getting several answers wrong, it may be worth trying to read more slowly, or taking notes as you go.

The **dig deeper** boxes give you resources to explore topics in greater depth than it is possible to go into in this introductory level book.

Part 1:

The central figure

Jesus Christ

In this chapter you will learn about:

▶ *the life of Jesus*
▶ *some of the teaching of Jesus*
▶ *the events at the end of his earthly life.*

Jesus has been the focus of more study, more controversy and more art than any other figure. He is the one who has 'chopped history in half': BC *before Christ*; AD *Anno Domini*, i.e. 'in the year of Our Lord' (sometimes called CE or *Common Era*). In today's world, millions of people – from every continent and nearly every country – claim some allegiance to him. Christians make up about one-third of the world's population.

Ralph Waldo Emerson, the American essayist, summed up the significance of Jesus when he said that his impact is not so much *written on*, as *ploughed into*, the history of the world. All this is remarkable enough. But when we consider the short and rather obscure life of Jesus, it becomes extraordinary. However, according to the Bible, there were clear indications of his greatness even before his birth.

The life of Jesus

According to St Luke's Gospel, the story began in the district of Galilee in Israel. A young woman, betrothed but not yet married to a man called Joseph, was visited by the angel Gabriel. He announced (hence 'the Annunciation' – beloved by medieval artists) that she had been chosen by God to give birth to a son who was to be called Jesus. Troubled as Mary was by this news ('How will this be, since I am a virgin?') she declared herself ready to do God's will: 'I am the Lord's Servant' (Luke 1:38).

The child was due to be born at the time of a Roman census. For Mary and Joseph this entailed a journey of about 70 miles from Nazareth to Bethlehem near Jerusalem. It was in Bethlehem that the baby was born. Matthew and Luke tell us that the child was visited by local shepherds and wise men from eastern lands and that a choir from heaven celebrated the birth. King Herod, on hearing from the eastern travellers of the birth of 'a king', tried to kill the infant Jesus. But Mary, Joseph and Jesus ('the holy family') escaped to Egypt and so fulfilled a prophecy (Matthew 2:15). Eventually they returned to Nazareth, where Joseph earned his living as a carpenter – a craft which he taught his son.

We are told little about the early years of Jesus, apart from one visit to Jerusalem when he was 12 years old. On that occasion Jesus went to the Temple, where he listened to the teachers and asked and answered questions: 'Everyone who heard him was amazed at his understanding and his answers' (Luke 2:47).

We learn nothing more for nearly 20 years, when Jesus was baptized by his cousin John ('the Baptist') in the river Jordan. John was preaching a new message of repentance and revival and challenging the establishment religion. He recognized in Jesus someone who would carry that message even further and as he baptized Jesus a voice from heaven declared, 'This is my Son, whom I love; with him I am well pleased' (Matthew 3:17). Then Jesus was led by God's Spirit into the desert where he fasted and wrestled with the devil for 40 days. This time of temptation was to fashion the shape of his ministry. Now he was ready.

After spending a night in prayer, Jesus called 12 disciples and set out on his travels around his small country. He began his ministry in his home area in the north, in the towns, villages and countryside around the Lake of Galilee. The four Gospels record some of his deeds and words. Jesus healed people with a wide range of diseases: a paralysed man, a man with leprosy, a woman who suffered from excessive bleeding, a man possessed by a demon. He even raised the dead (Luke 7:15; John 11:43).

He also showed power over nature: he turned water into wine, stilled a storm, and fed a huge crowd from five loaves and two fish. Miracle workers were common in first-century Palestine and the stories of Jesus's miracles in the Gospels are remarkably restrained, not performed as 'tricks' but to underline his authority. Jesus became known as a powerful and controversial teacher, who was willing to challenge established traditions. Time for rest, solitude and prayer was limited, but he 'often withdrew to lonely places and prayed' (Luke 5:16)

There is lively debate among scholars concerning the way in which the first Christians regarded Jesus of Nazareth. This is sometimes posed as a question: is the 'Jesus of history' the same as the 'Christ of faith'? Some scholars believe that the early Christians used Jesus's teaching freely, adapting it to their own purposes; even inventing sayings of their own. Others are convinced that the first believers treated his teaching with great reverence and took trouble to remember and record it accurately. They also point out that it would take someone of the stature of Jesus to invent the teaching of Jesus.

We must acknowledge that the early Christians were not just writing an historical record of the life of Jesus. For them it was the *impact* of his life rather than the *facts* of his life which mattered. The modern understandings of history and historical evidence are just that – modern. The facts about Jesus's life were well known at the time so 'proving' them mattered less. What was far more important was to grapple with making sense of who Jesus was. Their writings are not primarily concerned with history but with theology.

This can be frustrating for us. In the modern era there have been a number of 'quests for the historical Jesus' – attempts to recover the human story in more detail. The physician and missionary Albert Schweitzer was one of the early writers to explore this in the early 1900s. Other quests have followed.

While they raise interesting questions they have tended to reveal little. The New Testament does emphasize that Jesus was a real human being who understood the human condition 'from the inside'. They assert that he got hungry, thirsty and tired. He experienced the full range of human emotions, including joy, sorrow and desolation. But beyond this the historical details they include are not their main concern.

EARLY NON-CHRISTIAN REFERENCES TO JESUS

As far as the Roman authorities were concerned, Jesus was a small-time trouble-maker. They were forced to revise their opinion when the movement which bore his name grew rapidly – after his death. His followers were accused of many things: cannibalism, because they spoke of feeding on the body and blood of Christ in Holy Communion; atheism, because they did not accept the Roman gods.

▶ **Tacitus**, a Roman historian born in AD 55, describes (in his Annals) how the Emperor Nero blamed Christians for the burning of Rome. 'Therefore, to scotch the rumours, Nero substituted as culprits, and punished with the utmost cruelty, a class of men, loathed for their vices, whom the crowd styled Christians. Christus, the founder of the name, had undergone the death penalty in the reign of Tiberius, by sentence of the procurator Pontius Pilate.'

▶ **Pliny the Younger** (Roman governor of Bithynia, AD 110–113) complained of the problems caused by Christians who sang 'a hymn to Christ as to a god'.

▶ **Josephus** was a Jewish historian who defected to the Romans in the Jewish-Roman war which began in AD 66. He affirmed that Jesus was 'the Christ' who rose from the dead. There is no textual evidence against Josephus' remarkable testimony to Jesus. But many scholars assume that some key words were inserted later, because they cannot believe that Josephus would have written so positively about him.

▶ The Jewish **Talmud** (an ancient commentary on Jewish teaching) acknowledges Jesus as a Jew. His miracles, his teaching and his disciples are referred to, and he is described as a false teacher who was executed.

The teaching of Jesus

Christianity is based not only on ideas, but on events. At its centre we do not find a theory, but a person: Jesus Christ. Many people have a sentimental picture of Jesus. They view him as a rather anaemic character, more interested in flowers, birds and children than in the harsh world of adult reality. How different is the towering figure of the New Testament. We see there:

▶ someone marked out as a dangerous rebel by the authorities

▶ someone who drew large crowds

▶ someone who inspired others

▶ someone who comforted the disturbed and disturbed the comfortable

▶ someone of deep passion and decisive action

▶ someone who took the uncompromising road to martyrdom.

The Gospels assure us that Jesus *was* interested in children and in nature. And with the downtrodden he was very gentle. But the world he inhabited was a harsh world of power struggles, hatred, intrigue, brutality and revenge. The Gospels portray a dynamic figure who waged war against evil with the weapons of love, openness, honesty and forgiveness. His honesty was fearless. Against those greatest sins of pride, hypocrisy and indifference, his attack was blistering and devastating.

Jesus did not set out to be an 'original' teacher. As a Jew he stood in a tradition which was steeped in the Hebrew Scriptures (known to Christians as the Old Testament). He drew on those Scriptures, and his central demands – that we should love God with all our heart and our neighbour as ourselves – link two separate Old Testament texts (Deuteronomy 6:5; Leviticus 19:18). This was his genius: to make new connections, to bring fresh emphases, to take old ideas and give them new content, to reveal the deeper meaning which was latent within them, to dig behind the religious 'clutter' to get at what really mattered.

> 'the crowds were amazed at his teaching, because he taught as one who had authority, and not as their teachers of the law' (Matthew 7:28–29).

Jesus quickly established himself as a popular, unconventional and controversial teacher. The established leadership felt threatened. No doubt his striking authority had its roots in his dynamic personality. But it was emphasized by the content of his teaching.

The Gospel writers (called 'Evangelists' because that word means 'bringer of good news') preserved a lot of Jesus's teaching. They do not claim to be objective reporters. They are convinced of the immense significance of Jesus and want to convince others. St John makes this quite clear when he disarmingly admits that:

> 'these [signs] are written that you may believe that Jesus is the Christ, the Son of God, and that by believing you may have life in his name' (John 20:31).

> '*Had it not been for his teaching and of course his resurrection, Jesus would have been forgotten (or merely half-remembered) like most other Jewish figures of his time and outlook. As it is, Jesus of Nazareth remains one of the most revered figures from the whole of human history.*'
> J. Knight, *Christian Origins* (T.&T. Clark, 2008), p. 98.

At the same time, the Gospel writers insist that they are recording the truth about Jesus. There was no need to exaggerate, because Jesus was big enough already! Of course, they did not have recording equipment. They were dependent upon memories, stories and records. But Middle Eastern memories were good (and still are: many Muslims today can recite the entire Qur'an from memory). And there were enough eyewitnesses to act as a check on wild exaggeration.

THE SERMON ON THE MOUNT

An example of Jesus's radical teaching is contained in what has become known as the Sermon on the Mount (Matthew, chapters 5–7). It starts with a series of 'Beatitudes':

> 'Blessed are the poor in spirit for theirs is the kingdom of heaven.
> Blessed are those who mourn for they shall be comforted.
> Blessed are the meek for they will inherit the earth …'

The Sermon also contains:

▶ a breath-taking call to love and forgiveness: 'But I tell you: Love your enemies and pray for those who persecute you … For if you forgive those who sin against you, your heavenly Father will also forgive you' (Matthew 5:44; 6:14)

▶ an encouragement to faith in God: 'So do not worry, saying, "What shall we eat?" or "What shall we wear?" … your heavenly Father knows that you need them' (Matthew 6:31)

▶ an encouragement to pray: 'Ask and it will be given to you; seek and you will find; knock and the door will be opened to you' (Matthew 7:7)

▶ an uncompromising call to accept Jesus's teaching: 'But everyone who hears these words of mine and does not put them into practice is like a foolish man who built his house on sand' (Matthew 7:26).

'I do not believe there is a problem in this country or the world today which could not be settled if approached through the teaching of the Sermon on the Mount.'

Harry S. Truman (US President 1945–53)

THE KINGDOM OF GOD

Jesus spoke frequently about 'the kingdom of God' or 'the kingdom of heaven'. This idea is certainly found in the Jewish Scriptures. But Jesus put it at the *centre* of his teaching and illustrated (but never defined) its meaning with a series of brilliant, yet often puzzling, pictures and parables. In this way he made his hearers, and now his readers, think very hard.

'The kingdom of heaven is like treasure hidden in a field. When a man found it, he hid it again, and then in his joy went and sold all he had and bought that field. Again, the kingdom of heaven is like a merchant looking for fine pearls. When he found one of great value, he went away and sold everything he had and bought it.' (Matthew 13:44–46)

Jesus made it clear that his notion of God's kingly rule was very different from the popular views of his time. His country was under enemy occupation. The hated Romans were in charge and there were many Jews who looked for armed revolt. Their nation had a famous history of success on the battlefield; perhaps this teacher would be the new military leader? To those who wanted to go down that road, Jesus was a great disappointment: 'My kingdom is not of this world' (John 18:36). In his kingdom, disciples would turn the other cheek and leadership must be characterized by humble service.

▶ Miracles of the kingdom

Many miracles are recorded in the Gospels. They are not meant as persuasive 'tricks'. For the Gospel writers they are demonstrations of Jesus's power over sickness, sin, nature, demons and death. When his enemies accused him of healing by Satan's power, he replied, 'But if I drive out demons by the finger of God, then the kingdom of God has come to you' (Luke 11:20).

The miracles are 'signs of the kingdom'. God's kingly rule was present because Jesus was present. Indeed, John's Gospel calls them not miracles but signs. Jesus's ministry was also the sign of a future in which God's kingly rule would be fulfilled and consummated. One day the 'Son of Man' (see Glossary) will come 'in his Father's glory with the holy angels' (Mark 8:38). *Now* and *not yet* are held in balance.

▶ Parables of the kingdom

Jesus became famous for his stories or parables. A parable is a story which works on two levels; it is 'an earthly story with a heavenly meaning'. At one level it is an interesting tale with strong human interest. But the story has a deeper meaning and a personal application. Jesus's hearers are usually left to work this out for themselves. Some parables convey the notion of *growth*. Others convey a sense of *crisis*: decisions must be made, sides must be taken. Jesus's stories are usually about people:

▶ a woman who lost a coin (Luke 15:8)

▶ a woman who badgered a judge for justice (Luke 18:1)

- a man who built a tower (Luke 14:28)

- a farmer who scattered seed (Mark 4:3)

- a Samaritan traveller who cared for a man who was mugged and robbed (Luke 10:25)

- a young man who left home and squandered his money ('the Prodigal Son') before returning to a father who forgave him and a brother who resented him (Luke 15:11).

Two parables – the Good Samaritan and the Prodigal Son – are quite widely known beyond Christian circles. The former is not just an exhortation to compassion and kindness (though it is that). It is a strong attack upon racism and bigotry. Samaritans were widely despised by Jews, and vice versa. Jesus was taking a huge risk in making a *Samaritan* the hero, in contrast to the establishment figures of his own race and religion. Here were the seeds of conflict with the authorities which would end in his death by crucifixion.

The anguish of the Prodigal Son is captured powerfully by the sculptor Rodin, whose bronze figure of the Prodigal is in the Tate Collection. The parable of the Prodigal Son could equally well be entitled 'The Forgiving Father'. Again, the notion of God as Father was familiar to Jesus's contemporaries. But Jesus underlined its importance, stressing both the rule and the love of God.

Spotlight

Parables were a common form of teaching in the time of Jesus; for example, a Jewish rabbi used the parable of the fox and the fish. The fox suggested to the fish that he should jump out of the water onto the land to avoid the fisherman's net. The fish replied, 'The water is where I live. Though I *might* die here, if I leave the water I *will* certainly die.'

Jesus emphasized his own close relationship with God and taught that discipleship cannot be reduced to a set of rules. At its centre is a relationship with the living God, who is 'your heavenly Father' – to be loved and trusted. But a loving father is not a doting uncle. Much of Jesus's teaching is uncompromising in its moral and spiritual demands:

- turn the other cheek (Matthew 5:39)

- go the extra mile (Matthew 5:41)

- judge not or you will be judged (Matthew 7:1)

- forgive seventy times seven (Matthew 18:22)

- sell your possessions and give to the poor (Mark 10:21).

His teaching makes intellectual demands too. Jesus did not spoon-feed his largely uneducated audience; he respected their intelligence. He often said things that he did not mean! By exaggeration and paradox Jesus left, and leaves, his hearers thinking furiously, 'He can't really mean *that*. So just what does he mean ...?':

- let the dead bury their dead (Matthew 8:22)

- become like a little child (Matthew 18:3)

- cut off a foot rather than allow it to lead to sin (Mark 9:45)

- hate your father and mother (Luke 14:26)

- you must be born again (John 3:3).

A father's love includes discipline as well as encouragement. Hence Jesus taught us to *trust* God, to *love* God and to *fear* God – to hold him in respect and awe, for God is GOD. He emphasized that prayer, forgiveness, honesty, humility and generosity are all involved in accepting God's kingly rule in our lives. All this is summed up in the world's most famous prayer, given by Jesus in response to his disciples' request, 'Lord, teach us to pray':

> 'Father, hallowed be your name,
> your kingdom come.
> Give us each day our daily bread.
> Forgive us our sins, for we also
> forgive everyone who sins against us.
> And lead us not into temptation.'
> (Luke 11:2; see also Matthew 6: 9–13)

THE TEMPLE AND THE SABBATH

These were two of the foundation stones of Jewish society at the time of Jesus. He challenged the traditions which had grown up around them. It was Jesus's dramatic action in overturning the tables of the money-changers in the Temple precincts that led to his crucifixion, according to the influential American scholar E.P. Sanders. Jesus claimed to be greater than the Temple itself (Matthew 12:6), and greater than some important Old Testament characters, such as the prophet Jonah and King Solomon (Matthew 12:41–42). And he caused controversy by healing on the Sabbath. This drew the accusation that he disregarded the religious laws, because the Sabbath was a day of rest and healing the sick was regarded as work. In response, Jesus reminded his hearers that he was 'Lord even of the Sabbath' (Mark 2:28).

The end of Jesus's life: the Last Supper

The supper which Jesus ate with his disciples just before his arrest and crucifixion has been painted by countless artists – most famously by Leonardo da Vinci. At this meal Jesus instituted a new covenant 'in my blood'. 'Covenant' is an important biblical term. It describes an 'agreement' between unequal parties: God and his people. God was faithful *to* them; he required faithfulness *from* them. But the nation had failed and a new covenant was needed. Six hundred years before Jesus sat down to eat the Last Supper with his disciples, the prophet Jeremiah had promised that God would make a new, more glorious covenant. By his words and actions, Jesus indicated that the great day had arrived at last – and that he, Jesus, was the central figure.

We will explore the events which followed the Last Supper in more detail in Chapters 2 and 3. For now it leaves us with the big question which confronted many who met the earthly Jesus: was he more than just a man?

Jesus: more than a man?

The New Testament writers were concerned to record two key things: the impact Jesus had on peoples' lives; and who they thought he was – the Son of God. From the earliest days right down to the present, this has been the assertion of Christians. Enter a church service anywhere in the world and you may well hear the Nicene Creed. The congregation recite or sing these astonishing words:

'We believe in one Lord, Jesus Christ,
the only Son of God,
eternally begotten of the Father,
God from God, Light from Light,
true God from true God,
begotten, not made,
of one Being with the Father;
through him all things were made.
For us and for our salvation he came down from heaven,
was incarnate of the Holy Spirit and the Virgin Mary
and was made man.
For our sake he was crucified ...'

This Jesus, a real human being, is the focus of Christian worship. In Christianity he is honoured as 'Lord' and 'God' (John 20:28). This language of adoration is found throughout the New Testament. Even great words like 'Prophet' and 'Messiah' are not big enough for Jesus. The writers stretch language to its limits with terms like 'Son of God', 'Light of the World', 'Saviour', 'Emmanuel', 'Word made Flesh', 'Lord' and 'God'.

> 'There are three great questions for students of Christianity's beginnings: (1) what was it about Jesus which explains both the impact he made on his disciples and why he was crucified? (2) How and why did it come about that the movement which took off from Jesus did not after his death remain within first-century Judaism? (3) Was the Christianity which emerged in the second century as a predominantly Gentile religion essentially the same as its first-century version or significantly different in character and kind?'
>
> J.D.G. Dunn, *Christianity Remembered (vol.1): Jesus Remembered* (William B. Eerdmans Publishing Co., 2003), p. 3.

Where did these ideas come from? The first disciples of Jesus were God-fearing Jews; strict monotheists. Frequently they recited the *Shema*: 'Hear, O Israel: the Lord our God is one Lord' (Deuteronomy 6:4). Notice: *one* Lord. Most Jews refused to embrace the Roman gods or to acknowledge the Roman emperor as divine, for that would mean denying their belief in one God. So we can sympathize with those Jews who objected to the exalted view of Jesus which came to be held by his followers. The notion that a man could be divine held no great problems for most Gentiles. But for Jews it was unthinkable. *Yet some of them came to think the unthinkable.* At the same time they insisted that they were monotheists, who continued to be loyal to the one true God.

In a remarkably short space of time, the early Christians came to the startling conclusion that Jesus was divine as well as human. This resulted partly from their belief in his resurrection (see Chapter 3). But their conclusion finds its seeds in the teaching of Jesus himself: in his teaching about authority and the Temple and the new covenant which we noted earlier. Of course Jesus did not go around saying, 'I am God'. Indeed, he acknowledged his dependence upon God, his 'heavenly Father'. He was no usurper. But he did claim a unique relationship with God; he did claim a unique mission from God; and he did claim that he, and only he, was able to do things which it was proper only for God to do.

In this way Jesus himself laid the foundations for the kind of language used about him in the New Testament and, later, in the Nicene and other creeds. Over the years the distinctive Christian view of God emerged. He is three 'persons' in one God: Father, Son and Holy Spirit. This doctrine of the Trinity was not invented by the early Christians; it has its seeds in the teaching of Jesus himself. Those seeds can be seen throughout the New Testament.

▶ 'He is the image of the invisible God, the firstborn over all creation ... all things were created by him and for him' (Colossians 1:15–16).

▶ 'May the grace of the Lord Jesus Christ, and the love of God, and the fellowship of the Holy Spirit be with you all' (2 Corinthians 13:14).

▶ 'Your attitude should be the same as that of Christ Jesus: Who, being in very nature God, did not consider equality with God something to be grasped' (Philippians 2:5, 6).

▶ 'Thomas said to him [Jesus], "My Lord and my God!"' (John 20:28).

At the same time, the New Testament writers held that Jesus was a real human being. Their concern was to declare that God reveals himself through Jesus Christ – not to speculate on the innermost nature of God. Such speculation came later, as Christians pondered the relationship between Father, Son and Holy Spirit. The result of this mature consideration can be seen in the Nicene and other creeds.

Images of Jesus

Early Christian experience contained a paradox. Those who met him saw Jesus as 'one of themselves' – a real human being. But in their encounters with this man they also sensed they were encountering God in a new – and deeper – way. Through the years different cultures and peoples have tried to capture this. It is moving to find African artists painting an African Jesus, Indian artists painting an Indian Jesus, and English artists painting an English Jesus. Some artists have painted a female Christ. They are claiming that Jesus is one of them. He speaks to all people; he transcends cultures, nations and centuries. Jesus came not primarily as a first-century Jew but as a human being. He is able to cut through cultural differences; he shows people of all cultures and times what it means to be truly human.

But Incarnation – the belief that in Jesus Christ God became a human being – carries with it the necessity of particularity. In one sense, no one person can be universal. He or she must belong to one period in history, to one nation, to one culture, to one family and be of one gender. Jesus, in his particularity, was a first-century Palestinian Jew. In this sense he is, for most modern Western people, an uncomfortable figure, not easy to fathom. Perhaps too often, however, he is all too easy to understand.

Spotlight

Mark Twain once commented: 'It's not the parts of the Bible which I *can't* understand that bother me, it's the parts that I *can* understand!'

Key ideas

▶ Jesus led a short life, wrote no books and did not travel beyond his own small country.

▶ Despite this, Jesus's impact is immense and Christianity is the largest movement in history.

▶ Jesus is widely acknowledged as a great teacher.

▶ Jesus continues to be regarded as an inspiring figure by many influential, modern non-Christians.

▶ Central to Jesus's teaching was 'the kingdom (or rule) of God' with its stress on love and forgiveness.

▶ The values of this kingdom include humility, generosity and service – especially to the poor and marginalized.

Dig deeper

R.J. Bauckham, *Jesus: A very short introduction* (Oxford; New York: Oxford University Press, 2011).

M. Bockmuehl (ed.), *The Cambridge Companion to Jesus* (Cambridge: Cambridge University Press, 2001).

M. Higton and D.F. Ford, *Jesus* (Oxford: Oxford University Press, 2002).

Fact check

Note: in some cases more than one answer might be correct.

1 Jesus was born in:
   a Nazareth
   b Jerusalem
   c Bethlehem
   d Rome

2 The birth of Jesus is recorded in:
   a Matthew
   b Mark
   c Luke
   d John

3 The kingdom of heaven was:
   a a new political party
   b only to do with life after death
   c about getting rid of the Romans
   d a radical new way of living

4 Jesus's teaching emphasized:
   a anything for a quiet life
   b costly discipleship
   c love and forgiveness
   d rigid observation of religious rules and regulations

5 Jesus's earthly trade was probably:
   a a fisherman
   b a carpenter
   c an inn keeper
   d a baker

6 The Gospel writers were writing:
   a poetry
   b theology
   c personal testimony
   d fiction

7 The Gospels contain little information about the historical details of the life of Jesus because:
  a the Gospel writers didn't know anything about it
  b Jesus was not a real historical figure
  c they are concerned more with his teaching, actions and significance
  d they are theology as well as history

8 John the Baptist was:
  a an Old Testament prophet
  b the cousin of Jesus
  c the leader of a new sect
  d a Pharisee

9 Jesus performed miracles because:
  a it was a way of entertaining the crowds
  b they pointed to the coming kingdom of God
  c all the other preachers were doing them
  d he felt sorry for people

10 Jesus told parables:
  a to confuse the crowds who followed him
  b as a means of communicating truths about the kingdom of God
  c to undermine the Romans
  d in order to entertain the crowds

Crucified Saviour

In this chapter you will learn about:

- ▶ *the events surrounding the death of Jesus*
- ▶ *the significance of the death of Jesus*
- ▶ *some theories about 'atonement'.*

The final week

Towards the end of his three years in the public eye, Jesus faced a crucial decision. Should he return home to the safety of Galilee? Or should he go on to Jerusalem and to conflict? In his Gospel, Luke tells us that 'Jesus resolutely set out for Jerusalem' (Luke 9:51). That decision led to his death.

> 'Stronger still is the image of an innocent, silent man standing before the civil accusers and in his weakness appearing stronger than Caesar himself.'
>
> A.N. Wilson, *Jesus* (Random House, 2003), p. 6.

In Mark's Gospel we find a refrain on Jesus's lips: 'The Son of Man must suffer.' And in John's Gospel, Jesus refers to his death as his 'hour'. Everything he taught and did led up to his climactic death. This is seen most clearly in the dramatic events of the last week of his life. While the public ministry of Jesus lasted around three years (based on John's Gospel), that last week of his life accounts for a disproportionate amount of the Gospel writers' narratives. Matthew and Mark give almost a third of their Gospels over to the events around Jesus's death. In Luke and John it is even more – half of what they write is to do with the final phase of Jesus's earthly life.

The week began with his entry into Jerusalem. Jesus timed this to coincide with the great Jewish festival of Passover, when Jerusalem was teeming with pilgrims. His reputation ensured a large crowd. He rode on a humble donkey, fulfilling the prophecy of Zechariah 9:9.

> 'Rejoice greatly, O Daughter of Zion!
> Shout, Daughter of Jerusalem!
> See, your king comes to you,
> righteous and having salvation,
> gentle and riding a donkey …'

Here was no worldly king, coming in glittering style to impress and command. Here was the Prince of Peace, riding in great humility. The crowds greeted him with shouts: 'Hosanna', which means 'save now'. They scattered coats and palm branches on the road (hence

Palm Sunday). As he approached Jerusalem, Jesus wept bitterly over the city. For some days, he taught in the precincts of the Temple – a fabulous building erected by King Herod 'the Great', who had tried to kill him as a baby. Jesus made a direct attack on the attitudes and practices of many of the leaders of his people. He even drove out those who were trading in the Temple precincts. 'It is written', he said to them, 'My house shall be a house of prayer, but you have made it a den of robbers' (Luke 19:46).

To mark the annual Passover festival, Jewish people gathered in their homes to eat a celebration supper – a practice which continues to this day. This was the last supper which Jesus ate with his disciples; it was to become the most celebrated meal in history. After they had eaten, Judas – one of the 12 disciples – left the room and betrayed Jesus to the Jewish authorities. He was rewarded with 30 silver coins. The authorities plotted to arrest Jesus by night, away from the crowds. Although the other disciples swore undying allegiance, Jesus warned that they too would abandon him. His prophecy was tragically fulfilled.

After their meal, Jesus and the disciples sang a hymn and walked to a garden called Gethsemane on the Mount of Olives. Jesus knew what was coming. He prayed with deep emotion, asking that he might be spared the dreadful suffering which the next few hours would bring. But his prayer ended with these famous words, 'yet not my will, but yours be done' (Luke 22:42). Shortly after this, Jesus was arrested and interrogated through the night by hastily convened Jewish and Roman courts.

Rabble-rousers stirred up the people. No longer did the crowds cry 'Hosanna!' and 'Welcome!' Now they shouted 'Crucify!' Pontius Pilate, the Roman procurator of Judaea from AD 26 to AD 36, wanted to release Jesus but gave way to the popular outcry. To distance himself from this decision he washed his hands in public saying, 'I am innocent of this man's blood … It is your responsibility!' (Matthew 27:24).

Jesus was stripped. Nails were driven through his hands and feet. The cross was raised, and he was left hanging between two criminals. Soldiers gambled for his single worldly possession: a seamless robe. Later, his side was pierced with a spear to ensure that he was dead. As he was dying, Jesus uttered seven sentences which are recorded in the four Gospels. Among these is his astonishing prayer: 'Father, forgive them, for they know not what they are doing.' Crucifixion was more than a means of execution. It was a state-sponsored terror tactic, a humiliation. 'A most cruel and disgusting punishment', according to Cicero.

Spotlight

Medical opinion about the cause of death from crucifixion varies, including suggestions that it leads to pulmonary embolism, heart failure or asphyxia. As a form of execution it was practised by the Persians and Macedonians as well as the Carthaginians long before the Romans used it. It has continued as a form of execution into the present era in some states where the death penalty still exists.

Blandina was a Christian who had the misfortune to live in Lyons in Gaul (modern-day France) in AD 77. The authorities wished to stamp out the church. The job was straightforward: they had to persuade the Christians to disown their God and swear by the pagan gods. Eusebius, an early historian (*c.*260–*c.*340), recorded these events. Blandina, he reported, wore out her tormentors with her endurance. So they put her back in prison. Later, they brought her into the arena, together with a 15-year-old boy called Ponticus. After he had been killed, they put Blandina in a net and presented her to a bull. 'And so', wrote Eusebius, 'she travelled herself along the same path of conflicts as they [her fellow martyrs] did, and hastened to them rejoicing and exulting in her departure.'

The peace and serenity, and the sense of the presence of God, displayed by Blandina is characteristic of many Christian martyrs since the time of Stephen – the first Christian martyr – (Acts, chapters 9, 11 and 15). It is in sharp contrast to the death of Jesus himself. In the Passion narratives in the Gospels (e.g. Mark 14:32–15:47):

▶ We find a *lack* of serenity: 'He began to be deeply distressed and troubled.'

▶ We find a *lack* of peace: 'My soul is overwhelmed with sorrow.'

- We find a *desire for escape*: 'Abba, Father, everything is possible for you, take this cup from me.'

- We even find a *sense of abandonment* by God, as Jesus quotes the opening line of Psalm 22: 'My God, my God, why have you forsaken me?'

Jesus was no less courageous than the martyrs who followed him. He could have escaped to safe obscurity. Instead, he pressed on to Jerusalem, to his fatal confrontation with the authorities. But the striking contrast remains. *For those who died for Jesus Christ – a constant sense of the presence of God. For Jesus as he died – a sense of abandonment by God and of utter loneliness*. Many martyrs faced death willingly; Jesus shrank from it. This raises an important theological question …

Why did Jesus die?

The fact that those who followed Jesus to martyrdom drew their inspiration from his death raises a remarkable puzzle. It is a puzzle to which the New Testament gives a solution. The answer given there is that, for Jesus, there was an extra factor. The martyrs suffered physically, as did Jesus. But in Christian understanding Jesus also suffered spiritually as he experienced separation from God the Father for the first time in his life.

Theologically, Christians express this by saying that while martyrs bore *pain* for him, he bore *sin* for them: not only their sin but the sin of the whole world. And it is sin which separates from God – hence the cry of abandonment from the cross. All this was summed up by John the Baptist when he referred to Jesus as 'the Lamb of God, who takes away the sin of the world' (John 1:29).

Spotlight

Matthew 1:21 says, 'You shall give him the name Jesus, for he will save his people from their sins.' *Jesus* (*Yeshua* in Hebrew) is a version of the Hebrew name *Yehoshua*, usually rendered as *Joshua* in English. It carries the meaning of 'spaciousness' or 'freedom'. The name Jesus (Saviour) can mean 'the one who gives us room'.

Sin is often defined as moral failure – doing wrong things – but in Christianity (and Judaism) it means something deeper. The story of the Fall (told in Genesis 3) tries to capture something of this. Adam and Eve seek to go their own way, independently of God. In effect they say, by eating the fruit of the tree, that they can manage without God, that they know better than God. Moral failure *follows* this. As a result of their choice the story describes human beings as alienated from God, from each other, from themselves and even from the earth itself. It is a powerful story which seeks to explain the 'dis-ease' humanity feels in so many ways.

In Christian understanding the death of Jesus brings God and humanity back together. Jesus acts as a mediator between God and humanity – at the cost of his own life. The first letter of Peter conveys this with great power. Echoing the prophet Isaiah, Peter wrote: 'He himself bore our sins in his body on the cross … by his wounds you have been healed' (1 Peter 2:24).

The New Testament writers see the death of Jesus Christ as *the* solution to the human dilemma of alienation, 'lost-ness', guilt and meaninglessness. It is because of this that they place such emphasis on this event and devote so much space to exploring its significance. This same emphasis has been maintained within the Christian community over the centuries. The cross has become *the* central symbol of Christianity. Not only do we find a cross or crucifix within most churches, but many church buildings are designed in cruciform shape. The two great sacraments of the Church focus on the cross: *baptism* is 'into Christ', and especially into his death and resurrection and in *Holy Communion*, the bread and wine refer to the broken body and shed blood of Jesus.

THE MESSAGE OF THE CRUCIFIXION
The death of Jesus Christ takes us to the heart of the Christian understanding of salvation. It is, according to St Paul, of 'first importance' (1 Corinthians 15:3).

John Polkinghorne, former Professor of Mathematical Physics at Cambridge University, wrote:

Why was it necessary for Jesus to die to gain salvation? This is a deep mystery. Indeed, St Paul admits that the notion of a man dying on a cross to save the world, appears very foolish (1 Corinthians 1:18–25). *Mystery* in Greek does not the mean the same thing as a murder mystery or a puzzle. It refers to something which is ultimately beyond human comprehension but which has such a fascination for humans that they are drawn into *trying* to understand it. It carries the sense of something which is awesome and captivating, like the night sky filled with stars: the human mind cannot take it all in, but is compelled to try and grasp at least part of it. The mystery of the death of Jesus sheds light upon, and has brought meaning to, countless lives even if it cannot be fully understood. The New Testament probes the significance of the death of Christ at many points: we may attempt to sum up its significance under four headings.

▶ **The cross reveals the depth of human sin**

It was pride which opposed Jesus; it was greed which betrayed Jesus; it was jealousy which condemned Jesus; it was indifference which made many stand by and watch without doing anything. Cruel men flogged and mocked him. Then they led him out to die a shameful death in a public place called Golgotha, which means 'the place of the skull'. The crucifixion portrays the depths to which humanity can fall.

As Jesus died, the land was covered in daytime darkness. 'At the birth of the Son of God there was brightness at midnight, at the death of the Son of God there was darkness at noon'

(Douglas Webster, *In Debt to Christ*, 1957; p. 46). It was as though heaven itself was saying: this is the most dreadful day of all. But Christians believe that God took those evil actions and attitudes and used them as the raw materials from which to quarry salvation.

▶ The cross reveals the depth of God's love

Rather than using his power to dominate, Jesus chose to submit himself to human wickedness. So the power of God is seen in symbols of weakness: a borrowed manger for his birth, and a wooden cross at his death. Here is power kept in check; power handed over; power utterly controlled by love. Jesus's body was broken like bread and his life was poured out like wine, for the forgiveness of sins. One of the most famous of Bible verses begins: 'For God so loved the world that he gave his only begotten Son …' (John 3:16).

▶ The cross reveals the way back to God

In the Temple in Jerusalem, a large curtain hung between the most holy place and the rest of the building. It was a symbol of the separation between the holy God and the human race, resulting from our sin. As Jesus died, that curtain was torn in two from top to bottom. It was a dramatic sign of new access into the presence of God.

On the cross Jesus cried out: 'It is finished.' The Greek word (*tetelestai*) carries a triumphant ring. Not 'It's all over' but 'It is accomplished'. According to the Bible, only his death, the death of the Son of God, could break down the barriers of rebellion and indifference which separate us from God and from one another. So we call that terrible day Good Friday. That day was terrible, but the fruit of that day is beautiful.

▶ The cross reveals the demands of Christian discipleship

'Follow me', said Jesus. Then he took the road to crucifixion. As baptism indicates, following Christ always involves a sort of death. It means trying to hold Christian standards in a world which often rejects those standards. It means following

Jesus in a world which is often indifferent towards him. Jesus summed up like this: 'If any want to become my followers, let them deny themselves and take up their cross and follow me' (Mark 8:34).

Paradoxically, Jesus insists that the cross is also about *life*. He goes on to say, 'For those who want to save their life will lose it, and those who lose their life for my sake, and for the sake of the gospel, will save it.'

Explaining the Crucifixion: word pictures

The second of the Ten Commandments tells us that the early Israelites were forbidden to make graven images (Exodus 20). It was an essential instruction for a people surrounded by nations that fashioned images and worshipped idols. As a result of this prohibition, painting was an art form which did not flourish in ancient Israel. But other art forms did, especially music, architecture and literature – including poetry.

Much of the Bible is rich in pictorial language and many of the great Bible themes paint pictures on the mind. For example, in the Psalms, God is seen as a shepherd, a king, a judge, a rock, a fortress, etc. To make good sense of this we need to be aware of the way in which such verbal images 'work'. Calling God a rock does not mean that he is lifeless; it does mean that he is utterly dependable. One image needs to be balanced by another.

Bible language about salvation is highly pictorial too: 'from death to life'; 'from darkness to light'. The word 'salvation' is dramatic, suggesting rescue from danger. So is the English word 'atonement', which means 'at-one-ment' or reconciliation with God. So it is no surprise to find that language concerning the death of Jesus – of which there is a great deal in the Bible – is full of verbal images or pictures.

Consideration of some of these great images helps us to understand the significance afforded to the crucifixion in the Bible. Here are three of them.

1 St Mark records these words of Jesus: 'The Son of Man came not to be served, but to serve, and to give his life as a ransom for many' (Mark 10:45). A slave in the ancient world could be redeemed (set free) by a ransom price paid on his behalf. The Bible teaches that every person, regardless of culture, background, virtue or vice, can be set free ('redeemed') from sin, fear, guilt and death, by the death and resurrection of Jesus.

2 The Christian gospel is about reconciliation (2 Corinthians 5:19, 20). The death of Jesus built bridges across apparently unbridgeable gaps. To change the image, it knocked down two dividing walls (Ephesians 2:14):

✷ between the holy God and sinful human beings
✷ between Jews and Gentiles (non-Jews).

Elsewhere, the New Testament is even bolder. Christ's death brings together *all things* previously fragmented. Nature itself will be redeemed (Colossians 1:20; Romans 8:20–22).

The idea of atonement for sin runs throughout the Bible. The New Testament uses picture language to probe its meaning – employing words such as 'ransom', 'reconciliation', 'mediator', 'victor', 'saviour'. In the Old Testament we find an elaborate set of rituals based on the tabernacle and the temple. These found their focus in animal sacrifices. Those ancient practices have no practical significance for Christians today. They were the shadow; the death of Jesus was the substance – the fulfilment and summation of the entire sacrificial system. For on the cross, Jesus became the *one perfect sacrifice* and the *one true High Priest*. This is spelt out in detail in the New Testament letter to the Hebrews. The way back to God is open; through Jesus we may come to God the Father with confidence (Hebrews 10:19; Ephesians 3:12).

3 The prophet Isaiah wrote about the 'Servant of the Lord'. He was the 'Suffering Servant'. The earliest Christians made the connection: Jesus was that Servant. Indeed, Jesus saw his own ministry like that: 'the Son of Man … came to serve'

(Mark 10:45). This servant identified himself with the poor, the powerless, the stranger, and the marginalized: 'Whatever you did for one of the least of these brothers of mine, you did for me' (Matthew 25:40).

This emphasis is particularly important for our times, for more people have suffered in wars during the past century than in all previous centuries put together. The image of the suffering servant provides a vital clue as we face the sharpest of all questions for those who believe in a loving God. Where is God when we suffer? Where was he in the Nazi concentration camps and the Soviet labour camps? Where is he in the sweatshops of our world? Where is he when people suffer illness, torture, drought and famine?

This profound and difficult question was addressed powerfully by the German theologian Jürgen Moltmann. His answer was that *God in Christ is there in the anguish*, sharing the bitter pains of a suffering world. The crucifixion assures us that God does not sit on the sidelines; he gets involved. The Son of God did not only suffer for us; he suffers *with* us. In this way, he brings redemption and shows his love. The Bible does not offer us a theoretical solution to the question, 'Why does God allow suffering?' Instead, it offers us a God who suffers with us, and who redeems us through the cross.

'God was in Christ reconciling the world to himself' (2 Corinthians 5:19). It was God in Christ who died a degrading death. It was God in Christ who hung naked, exposed and helpless. That is the message of the cross. All this leads to a gospel of hope. Christians are confident that we human beings are not on our own in a cold, heartless universe. At the centre of all things is the crucified God – who brings life out of death, as the resurrection shows. Indeed, the most anguished and problematic words in the whole Bible point to this conclusion. 'My God, my God, why have you forsaken me?' cried Jesus from the cross, quoting Psalm 22:1. Rabbi Hugo Gryn pointed out that the opening line of a Psalm represents the whole Psalm to a devout Jew. And Psalm 22 ends in confidence and faith. Even the desolation, though desperately real, is shot through with light and hope.

Explaining the Crucifixion: theories of the atonement

None of this amounts to one definitive 'theory of the atonement': the Church has never declared an 'official' theory of the atonement to explain why Jesus's death is so significant. Just *how* the death of Jesus on the cross saves us is not spelt out in detail in the Bible. Ultimately it is a deep mystery – a mystery of love which conveys life and light. Throughout Christian history, theologians have tried to explain this mystery. They have set several ideas before us, based upon Bible images. Jesus is seen as:

▶ the perfect Penitent

▶ the Victor over the powers of darkness

▶ the One who paid the ransom to set people free from sin

▶ the Substitute who died in my place

▶ the Representative who died for all humanity

▶ the perfect Sacrifice for sin

▶ the One whose death satisfies the demands of holy justice

▶ the supreme Example of self-giving love

▶ the One whose death moves and inspires Christians to acts of loving service.

Each of these helps us to understand; none contains the whole truth. So it is not surprising that no single account has been adopted by the Church as *the* 'official theory' of the atonement. Indeed, the rather cold term 'theory' is often criticized as being inappropriate for this great act of passion, love and sacrifice. Perhaps, in the end, the significance of the death of Jesus can be understood only through pictures, parables and stories. One such story is *The Long Silence* (author unknown). It is set on Judgement Day, when people who have suffered terribly complain that 'God leads a pretty sheltered life'. To qualify as Judge, they say, God should be sentenced to live on earth as a man.

'"Let him be born a Jew and let the legitimacy of his birth be questioned. Let him be doubted by his family and betrayed by his friends. Let him face false charges and be tried by a prejudiced jury in front of a hostile crowd. Let him be tortured to death – and as he dies, let him feel abandoned and alone."

When this judgement was pronounced, there was a long silence. Nobody moved. For suddenly all knew that God had already served his sentence.'

Case study

There are a number of 'theories' of the atonement – explanations of how the death of Jesus 'saves' humanity. Each goes some way to explaining this – but each also raises questions. For example:

▶ the *ransom theory* (*Christus Victor* by Gustaf Aulen (1879–1977) summarizes this view). In this theory, Jesus 'pays the price' for humanity's sin – but to whom is that ransom paid? This theory argues that it is the Devil who demands the ransom but some argue this gives the Devil too much power and authority.

▶ the *moral influence theory* put forward famously by Peter Abelard (1079–1142). Jesus sets an example for humanity to follow, but critics argue that it suggests humanity can save itself and the death of Jesus is simply useful rather than necessary.

▶ the *satisfaction theory* espoused by Anselm of Canterbury (1033–1109). The *penal substitution theory* developed from the satisfaction theory and was favoured by reformers such as John Calvin (1509–64). Satisfaction and penal substitution are very similar. They refer to the idea that Jesus substituted himself in the place of humanity. In this theory, sin requires payment – 'satisfaction' – and Jesus pays that debt with his own perfect life, thus cancelling the debt.

Think about the merits and problems each one presents. Is it possible to hold more than one view at the same time?

The power of the cross

'Jews demand miraculous signs and Greeks look for wisdom, but we preach Christ crucified: a stumbling-block to Jews and foolishness to Gentiles ... For the foolishness of God is wiser than man's wisdom, and the weakness of God is stronger than man's strength' (1 Corinthians 1:22–25).

The apostle Paul wrote these words after his conversion to Jesus Christ. As Saul (he changed his name after conversion), he had persecuted the Christians. In those days he *knew* that the Christians were wrong, because he knew the Hebrew Scriptures. Deuteronomy 21:22–23 is clear: 'anyone who is hung upon a tree is under God's curse'. Jesus had been crucified – hung upon a tree – therefore he was accursed. So he could not be the Messiah, as his followers claimed. This was the logic which had motivated Saul's persecution of the church. Later, he came to see that the cross was indeed the place of a curse. But the curse which Jesus bore was *humanity's*, not his. So, with immense daring, Paul could write: 'Christ delivered us from the curse of the law, having become a curse for us' (Galatians 3:13).

> 'Estrangement from God has not only made us ignorant about ourselves, but also ignorant about God. We cannot repent because we do not know whom we have offended. Therefore, God will have to make himself known to us as the God of love who desires us to be reconciled with him ...'
>
> V. Brümmer, *Atonement, Christology and the Trinity* (Ashgate, 2005), p. 79.

So it was that Paul discovered and described the power of the cross in this vivid, perhaps shocking, way. Throughout the next 20 centuries, countless individuals would come to find its power by one route or another.

Crucifixion and death were not the end, however ...

Key ideas

▶ The death of Jesus is central to the entire New Testament.

▶ Christians believe that, through his death, Jesus accomplished something of eternal significance.

▶ Christians do not claim to fully understand how Christ's death achieved salvation.

▶ The New Testament seeks to unravel this mystery by using a wide range of word pictures – redemption, salvation, victory, reconciliation …

▶ In the Bible, the death of Jesus is always linked with his resurrection.

▶ There is no official 'theory of the atonement'. A range of ideas has been developed over the centuries, based on the rich language of the New Testament.

Dig deeper

V. Brümmer, *Atonement, Christology and the Trinity: Making sense of Christian doctrine* (Aldershot: Ashgate, 2005).

C.A. Evans, N.T. Wright and T.A. Miller, *Jesus, The Final Days: What really happened* (Louisville, KY: Westminster John Knox Press, 2009).

A.E. McGrath, *Theology: The basics*, 3rd edn (Oxford: Wiley-Blackwell, 2012).

Fact check

Note: in some cases more than one answer might be correct.

1 Towards the end of his three years in the public eye, Jesus faced a crucial decision. Which did he do?
   a Returned home to the safety of Galilee
   b Went on to Jerusalem and to conflict
   c Went into hiding
   d Negotiated a deal with the Romans

2 Christians see the crucifixion as:
   a the tragic end to the life of Jesus
   b the failure of Jesus's mission
   c the fulfilment of Jesus's mission
   d victory for the opponents of Jesus

3 The Last Supper was shared at which Jewish festival?
   a Pentecost
   b Passover
   c Rosh Hashanah
   d Tabernacles

4 Which Old Testament character, written about by Isaiah, did early Christians link with Jesus in his death?
   a King Uzziah
   b the Cherubim
   c the Suffering Servant
   d the Pharaoh

5 The crucifixion is:
   a an early Christian doctrine since abandoned
   b central to the Christian gospel
   c just one Christian doctrine among many
   d a story invented many years after Jesus lived

6 Crucifixion was:
   a rarely used as a means of execution
   b reserved for political criminals
   c a quick and easy death
   d a form of humiliation as well as execution

7 The Roman governor who oversaw Jesus's execution was:
  a Julius Caesar
  b Hadrian
  c Pontius Pilate
  d Quirinius

8 The Gospel writers:
  a only briefly mention the death of Jesus
  b see Jesus's miracles and teachings as more important than his death
  c devote considerable parts of their Gospels to the last days of Jesus's life
  d are puzzled by the death of Jesus

9 Saul, who later changed his name to Paul, did not originally believe Jesus could be the Messiah because:
  a he didn't believe Jesus performed any miracles
  b Jesus was not a real Jew
  c Deuteronomy 21:22–23 stated that 'anyone who is hung upon a tree is under God's curse'
  d he thought Jesus's death was faked

10 According to the New Testament:
  a only Jews can become Christians
  b only good people can become Christians
  c only really bad people can become Christians
  d Jesus died for everyone and anyone

Risen Lord

In this chapter you will learn about:

- ▶ *the events surrounding the resurrection of Jesus*
- ▶ *the centrality of the resurrection*
- ▶ *the implications of the resurrection.*

The Acts of the Apostles describes a visit made by the apostle Paul to Athens. As he spoke, some local philosophers asked, 'What is this babbler trying to say?' They were told that he seemed to be speaking about foreign gods, 'because Paul was preaching the good news about Jesus and the resurrection' (Acts 17:18). As they half-listened, Paul's hearers thought that he was talking about two deities, Jesus and Anastasis (the Greek word for resurrection), because Paul so frequently linked these two words together.

Spotlight

The Greek word used in the New Testament for resurrection – *anastasis* – became popular as a girl's name early on in the Eastern Orthodox Church. *Anastasia* continues to be used today around the world.

Also significant is the fact that the Gospels end not with the death and burial of Jesus, but with stories about the ways in which he appeared to his disciples. The Acts of the Apostles contains sermons which declare that God raised Jesus from the dead. The Letters, or Epistles, were written in the conviction that Jesus is alive.

The Gospels contain a number of accounts of the resurrection appearances of Jesus (see the Case study below). One of these stories – the appearance of Jesus to Mary Magdalene – contains two important features which occur frequently in the Gospel narratives recounting the resurrection. St John tells us (John 20:1) that Mary went to the garden tomb very early on the first day of the week, only to find the stone removed from the entrance. She alerted two disciples, Peter and John, who inspected the empty tomb and then returned home.

Mary remained and encountered an angel and a man. Thinking that the man was the gardener, Mary asked if he had moved the body. But according to the fourth Gospel, Mary was not talking to a gardener – she was talking to a carpenter. It was Jesus himself, risen from the dead. Jesus addressed Mary by name and she recognized him. He instructed her to tell his followers ('my brothers') about their meeting. Mary went to the disciples with her exciting news: 'I have seen the Lord.'

The two important features are that:

▶ the tomb was empty

▶ the risen Lord appeared to one (sometimes more than one) of his followers.

Case study

All four Gospels contain accounts of appearances of Jesus after his death:

▶ two Marys encounter the risen Lord (Matthew 28:1–10)

▶ the risen Christ commissions the 11 disciples (Matthew 28:16–20)

▶ three women are bewildered and afraid at the empty tomb (Mark 16:1–8)

▶ Jesus appears to two disciples on the road to Emmaus (Luke 24:13–35)

▶ Jesus eats with his disciples (Luke 24:36–39)

▶ Mary Magdalene encounters Jesus at the tomb (John 20:10–18)

▶ Thomas doubts until he meets Jesus (John 20:24–29)

▶ a miraculous catch of fish is followed by breakfast (John 21:1–14)

▶ Jesus encourages and commissions Peter (John 21:15–23)

▶ Jesus appears for 40 days before ascending to heaven (Acts 1:3–11)

▶ Saul has a vision of the risen Lord on the Damascus road (Acts 9:1–9)

▶ Jesus appears to more than 500 people (1 Corinthians 15:3–8)

What do you think are the main ideas the Gospel writers and the writer of Acts are trying to convey through these accounts?

The centrality of the resurrection

The resurrection is central to Christianity. It is not just *one* aspect of Christianity: it is the very essence of Christianity. A number of things illustrate this clearly. When asked for proof that Jesus was divine the early church did not turn, as some might think, to the Virgin Birth (a common misconception is that the story is saying Jesus had a heavenly father and an earthly mother) but to the resurrection. It was this that vindicated his claim to be God's Messiah. And the early church made Sunday, the first day of the week on which the resurrection happened, their principal day of worship – a great change for Jews. A third fact further illustrates the point. For over a thousand years of Christian history, Easter – the commemoration of the resurrection – was by far the most important festival in the church, even eclipsing Christmas.

It is impossible to remove a portion of the Christian jigsaw labelled 'resurrection' and leave anything which is recognizable as Christian faith. Subtract the resurrection and you destroy the entire picture. Without the resurrection of Jesus from the dead, it is unlikely that we would have any trace of his teaching, or anything else in the New Testament. It would have disappeared with the passing years, as would Jesus of Nazareth himself.

> 'Take Christmas away, and in biblical terms you lose two chapters at the front of Matthew and Luke, nothing else. Take Easter away, and you don't have a New Testament: you don't have a Christianity.'
>
> T. Wright, *Surprised by Hope* (SPCK, 2007), pp. 256–7.

In the early Church there was no preaching about Jesus except as the risen Lord. Nor could there be. For without the apostles' conviction that they had seen Jesus alive again after his crucifixion, there would have been no preaching at all. There would have been deep mourning for a lost friend and great admiration for a dead hero. No doubt his profound teaching would have been remembered and cherished by his small, loyal circle of followers. But when they died, he would have been forgotten. Significantly, the early Christian preachers were less concerned to expound his teaching than to declare his death and resurrection.

APPROACHING THE EVIDENCE

Resurrection is a difficult idea to grasp. There have been a number of attempts to 'rationalize' it. So we find assertions such as: 'Easter means: the cause of Jesus goes on' (Willi Marxsen); 'Jesus has risen into the Kerygma, i.e. the preaching of the Church (Rudolf Bultmann); or 'To believe in the resurrection of Jesus means to undertake the surprising risk to reckon with Jesus Christ as a present reality' (Meinrad Limbeck).

Spotlight

The use of 'resurrection' by the early church was deliberate. It does not mean resuscitation or revival. It carries the sense of 'the same but different'. So the resurrected body of Jesus was, at the same time, both familiar and recognizable – and yet strangely different. The Gospel writers convey this by the resurrection stories they tell.

Others, such as the late Dr Pinchas Lapide, felt that this was far too cautious. He is worth quoting as he was a Jewish theologian and historian. It is, he wrote:

> 'all too abstract and scholarly to explain the fact that the solid hillbillies from Galilee who, for the very real reason of the crucifixion of their master, were saddened to death, were changed within a short period of time into a jubilant community of believers. Such a post-Easter change, which was no less real than sudden and unexpected, certainly needed a concrete foundation which can by no means exclude the possibility of any physical resurrection.'
> (P. Lapide, *The Resurrection of Jesus*, 1983; pp. 129–130)

The assertion that a man who was dead and buried has been raised up from the grave is breathtaking: those who make such a claim must give their reasons. In this chapter, some important details from the narrative will be set out and their possible implications discussed. Readers may consider the evidence to be strong or weak. Certainly it is not overwhelming. There will always be some who will assert that something as extraordinary as resurrection simply could not have happened, however strong the evidence might appear to be.

The Gospel accounts of the post-resurrection appearances of Jesus are striking in this regard. They provide readers with space in which to doubt, to question and to explore. For they freely admit that the disciples themselves found the whole thing very difficult to accept. St Matthew tells us that at the end of the 40 days during which Jesus appeared, 'some doubted' (Matthew 28:17). St Luke tells us that even with the risen Lord present, the disciples 'disbelieved for joy' (Luke 24:41). It was simply too good to be true! The burning conviction which runs throughout the New Testament did not come easily.

> 'The reports of the [resurrection] appearances in the Gospels of Luke and John are fragmentary and complex. Yet they are also, in some ways, remarkably sober and matter-of-fact accounts.'
> R. Cooke, *New Testament* (SCM Core Text) (SCM Press, 2009), p. 466.

In any case, evidence can take us only so far. We may sympathize with 'doubting' Thomas, who reserved his judgement until he received convincing proof. But when he received the evidence which he requested, he did not simply say, 'So it *is* true.' Rather, he acknowledged the risen Christ as 'My Lord and my God!' (John 20:28). For Thomas, fact and evidence were followed by faith and commitment. With this in mind, we turn to consider some significant features of the story which require adequate explanation.

▶ No one produced the body

The Church began primarily not by the spreading of ideas, but by the proclamation that something had *happened*. The phrase most commonly used by the apostles was 'God has raised Jesus from the dead'. Those who wanted to discredit the apostles – and the Jewish leaders wanted to do that very much indeed – had only to produce one piece of evidence. All they had to do was produce the body of Jesus. If they had done so, we would never have heard of him or his followers. There would be no New Testament and no Church.

It is very significant that they did not do this. If the authorities had taken the body, or discovered it still in the tomb – because the disciples had lied, or gone to the wrong grave – they would have produced the corpse. This would have silenced all talk of resurrection. Instead, the authorities imprisoned, threatened and beat the disciples. And they circulated the report that the disciples had stolen the body. It is clear that the Jewish and Roman leaders had no idea what had happened to Jesus. Yet the stubborn fact remains: his body had gone.

▶ The tomb was not venerated

The empty tomb is strongly supported by the fact that the grave of Jesus did not become a place of pilgrimage. Tomb veneration was common at the time of Jesus; people would often gather at the grave of a prophet – as they do today. In surprising contrast, the earliest Jewish Christians did no such thing. The practice of venerating Jesus's tomb did start – but not until 200–300 years after the events surrounding the resurrection. The early disciples were emphatic that they honoured a risen Lord, not an empty tomb.

▶ The movement almost died

The Christian faith shares some common features with other great world religions. In particular, it looks back to a charismatic founder whose teaching is central for all his followers. In this it is like Buddhism, which traces its origins back to Gautama the Buddha; and Islam, which owes so much to the energy, vision and inspiration of Muhammad, the Prophet of Allah. But when all the similarities have been noted, the *differences* between Jesus and other great religious leaders are startling and puzzling. Three in particular are relevant to this chapter:

▶ Jesus died very young (Gautama the Buddha died *c.*483 BC, aged 80; Muhammad died in AD 632, aged 62; Jesus died *c.*AD 33, while only in his thirties)

- Jesus spent no more than three years in the public eye

- when Jesus died, the movement which he founded was in rapid decline.

Movements do grow and develop after the founder's death; we have ample evidence of this. It happens when the founder leaves a growing movement. And it happens when the founder's followers are in a buoyant frame of mind, because everything depends on their 'get up and go'. When Jesus died, these two factors were conspicuously absent. His followers were dwindling in number; those who remained were dispirited and afraid.

Yet somehow this demoralized group experienced a remarkable turnaround. Within a few weeks they were full of creative energy. They launched the biggest movement the world has ever seen, and one of the eventual fruits of this remarkable turnaround was the New Testament. In other words, it was the resurrection of Jesus which gave the teaching of Jesus to the world.

> 'When the early Christians spoke of Jesus being raised from the dead, the natural meaning of that statement, throughout the ancient world, was the claim that something had happened to Jesus which had happened to nobody else.'
>
> N.T. Wright, *The Resurrection of the Son of God* (SPCK, 2003), p. 83.

▶ No resurrection; no record of his teaching

Jesus's disciples gave two reasons for their own remarkable transformation, and these reasons have been celebrated ever since in two great Christian festivals.

- Easter: the first disciples claimed that God had raised Jesus from the dead. Because this happened on a Sunday, they transferred their 'special' day from the traditional Jewish Sabbath (the last day of the week) to the first day. This change is in itself a remarkable fact, requiring adequate explanation. For Christians, every Sunday is a 'mini-Easter' and never a fasting day, even in Lent.

- Pentecost (sometimes called Whitsun in the UK): the first disciples claimed that God had given them the gift of his Holy Spirit. They affirmed that it was God's Spirit within them who gave them boldness, joy and insight.

It is clear that Christians face a problem as they seek to convince an unbelieving world. But those who deny the resurrection of Jesus Christ also face a problem. They must find a satisfactory alternative explanation for the start and rapid rise of the Church in such unlikely circumstances.

▶ The disciples suffered for their preaching

'Then all the disciples deserted him and fled' (Matthew 26:56). In this short sentence, Matthew describes the behaviour of the disciples of Jesus following his arrest. He goes on to tell of the way in which Peter, for all his earlier boasting, denied all knowledge of Jesus. In the circumstances, such behaviour was completely understandable. However, a few weeks later those men were out in the streets, preaching that God had raised Jesus from the dead. These were the same men who had deserted him. They were the same men who had been shattered by his crucifixion. But as the Acts of the Apostles makes very clear, they were very different same men!

In place of bitter disappointment there was joyful confidence; in place of fear there was boldness. Instead of thinking gloomily that their leader was dead, they proclaimed that he had conquered death. In other words, they were transformed. The question is: what transformed them? They claimed that it was their experience of the risen Lord. Were they right? Were they mistaken? Or were they guilty of the most successful fraud in history?

From time to time during his ministry, Jesus spoke about his future death and resurrection. Perhaps his disciples embellished this idea into stories about a sequence of appearances by Jesus after his death? This possibility is undermined by one significant fact: history and human psychology teach us that people will suffer for deeply held convictions. However, few are prepared to suffer for an invention. We tell lies to get *out* of trouble, not to get *into* it. The whip and the sword soon uncover fraud. Besides, liars do not usually write high-calibre moral literature like the New Testament.

In any case, if the stories *were* inventions they were not all that good. A shared, deep conviction about Jesus's resurrection is clear from the Bible. But the details of his appearances vary considerably from Gospel to Gospel. It is unlikely that a conspiracy would have given rise to so many puzzles. It is even less likely that inventors would have given so much prominence to the testimony of women, for in ancient Jewish culture such evidence carried little weight.

We note too that the Bible gives no description of the resurrection itself. Nobody witnessed the moment when God raised Jesus from the dead. The records admit that nobody was there: the accounts start with the empty tomb and the appearances of the risen Lord. It is quite likely that inventors would have attempted a description of the resurrection itself. And it is unlikely that inventors would have given such emphasis to the fear, bewilderment and doubt which were such a central feature of the experience of the first disciples. Christians believe that the Gospel accounts carry 'the ring of truth.'

The willing suffering of the disciples also rules out the 'swoon' theory. On this view, Jesus did not die on the cross. Despite terrible wounds, he recovered in the tomb and escaped. The disciples nursed him back to health, or tried to and failed. This theory bristles with problems. Roman soldiers knew when a man was dead; and there was a guard on the tomb. But if we allow that somehow the disciples overcame these problems, the events which follow simply do not fit. Jesus would have cheated death; he would not have *conquered* it. No doubt the disciples would have been delighted, but they would have kept the whole thing very quiet. Publicity and preaching would have been fatal, for these would have resulted in a search. The authorities would not have made a second mistake.

Besides, to preach that God had raised Jesus from the dead – which is exactly what they *did* preach – would have been a lie. We are back where we started. The lash, the dungeon and the sword would soon have loosened their tongues. People will suffer and die for their convictions, but not for their inventions. A handful of frightened men would not preach boldly about the resurrection to the very people who had killed their leader. This would be far too risky, especially if they knew it was not true. People do not behave like that unless something tremendous happens to drive away the fear and disappointment.

The first disciples passionately *believed* that God had raised Jesus and that Jesus had appeared to them. Were they mistaken? Perhaps they saw a ghost, or suffered from hallucinations? Here the Gospel writers seem to present a conundrum. Some resurrection appearances have elements of a ghostly apparition about them. But in others (and sometimes in the same event) the physicality of the risen Jesus is emphasized. The appearance to Thomas is a good example. Jesus appears in a room without coming in through the door or windows. He simply seems to materialize; he behaves like a ghost. But then Thomas touches him – something not possible with a ghost. The early witnesses are struggling to explain an extraordinary event. The word 'resurrection' carries something of this. *Anastasis* can carry the sense of 'the same but different'. Human language strains to explain what they saw. What they believed was that God had raised Jesus from the dead.

▶ **Eyewitnesses were available**

Around AD 55, the apostle Paul wrote what has become a classic passage about resurrection (1 Corinthians 15:3–5). In this he states: 'For what I received I passed on to you as of first importance: that Christ died for our sins according to the Scriptures, that he was buried, that he was raised on the third day according to the Scriptures, and that he appeared …'. Scholars have detected an early Christian creed attesting faith in the resurrection embedded in this passage (hence the word 'received'). Some date this creed to within three to eight years of the crucifixion.

Paul goes on to list various eyewitnesses – people who had seen the risen Lord, who were still alive when he wrote and who could be questioned. This list includes a crowd of 'more than

500'. Free invention for purposes of propaganda could have been checked and contradicted.

▶ Jesus is called 'Lord'

As we noted in Chapter 1, the early disciples were Jews – devout monotheists who frequently recited the *Shema*: 'The Lord our God, the Lord is one' (Deuteronomy 6:4). Then they met Jesus or heard about him in sermons and conversations.

At no point did they abandon their belief in one God. It would have been unthinkable for them to become 'bi-theists' (believers in two gods). Yet their concept of God was greatly enlarged as a result of their contact with Jesus. So, while continuing to assert that God is One, they began to speak of God the Father and God the Son. Indeed, shortly after his death they had firmly placed Jesus, the man from Nazareth, on the Godward side of that line which divides humanity from divinity. They did not doubt that he was truly human, but they offered him their adoration and called him 'Lord'.

How can this amazing shift in attitude be explained? How can we account for the fact that those Jewish men and women (some of whom knew Jesus personally, and all of whom knew that he was a man who sweated and wept) addressed him as 'Lord'?

Jewish men and women would have been incapable of *deciding* to use the word 'Lord' in that way. Their entire upbringing was against it, because it carried a huge risk of being blasphemous. No, it was forced upon them – partly by the teaching of Jesus, but mainly by their conviction that God had raised Jesus from the dead. They quickly came to realize that if Jesus was Lord over death, he was quite simply 'LORD'.

▶ A continuing presence

One surprising feature of the reported resurrection appearances is that they were confined to a period of six weeks. After that they stopped abruptly. Yet the first disciples continued to speak and behave as though Jesus were still with them – not physically, but by his Spirit. Even more remarkable is the fact that this conviction came to be shared by others – at first by hundreds, then thousands, then millions – who had never seen Jesus, before or after his crucifixion.

This evidence is not confined to the past. The Christian Church down the years and into the present asserts that the continued 'presence' of the risen Christ is an on-going reality. Although of differing backgrounds, cultures, ages and temperaments, Christians continue in the shared belief that the risen Lord is alive and at work today.

Spotlight

'Resurrection pie' was a Sheffield dialect term in the early 19th century for a pie made from the previous day's leftovers!

Implications

Christians believe that the resurrection of Jesus from the dead has enormous implications. The New Testament sees it as a great new act of creation by God. It is 'a primal act of God, unimaginable and indescribable, like the creation, with which it is sometimes compared' (C.F. Evans). At least two implications are clear, and extremely practical.

▶ Death is dead

Theologically, Christians believe that the resurrection somehow means that death itself has been overcome. Mortality exercises a profound influence upon humans, producing a range of responses from fear to curiosity. Most reflective people occasionally feel the need to consider the fact that they will die, and the related need to attempt to make sense of life in the light of this inevitable but awesome fact. The words of Jesus, as recorded in the fourth Gospel, are startling:

> 'I am the resurrection and the life. He who believes in me will live, even though he dies; and whoever lives and believes in me will never die. Do you believe this?' (John 11:25, 26)

Here is the highest arrogance and folly, or the most profound wisdom. Which of these alternatives is true depends upon the truth or otherwise of the resurrection of Jesus himself.

In a moving passage, the Venerable Bede (c.673–735) reports that Edwin, king of Northumbria, gathered his warriors to listen to the missionary Bishop Paulinus. As Paulinus urged them to accept his teaching, a bird flew through the hall and out into the darkness. One of the nobles commented:

> 'The life of man is as if a sparrow should come to the house and very swiftly flit through. So the life of man here appears for a little season, but what follows or what has gone before, that surely we know not. Wherefore, if this new learning has brought us any better tidings, surely methinks it is worthy to be followed.'

▶ **Jesus is alive**

As we have noted, countless believers from all cultures and personality types testify to a sense of being 'accompanied' through life by a 'presence' which, though unseen, is very real (Chapter 6). This presence, they affirm, is a person – the risen Christ. They claim that he challenges, guides, encourages, inspires and renews them. Their experience is captured by the great (and controversial) Albert Schweitzer (1875–1965), a radical theologian and brilliant musicologist. He abandoned his outstanding academic career to train as a doctor, in order to go to west Africa as a missionary. Albert Schweitzer wrote, in *The Quest of the Historical Jesus* (1910):

> 'He comes to us as one unknown, without a name, as of old by the lakeside. He came to those men who knew Him not. He speaks to us the same word: 'Follow thou me!' and sets us to the tasks which He has to fulfil for our time. He commands. And to those who obey Him, whether they be wise or simple, He will reveal himself in the toils, the conflicts, the suffering which they shall pass through in His fellowship, and, as an ineffable mystery, they shall learn in their own experience Who He is.'

Key ideas

▶ The resurrection of Jesus from the dead is central to the Christian faith.

▶ The resurrection of Jesus is not just one part of 'the jigsaw'. Without it, there would be no jigsaw at all – no Church, no New Testament, no Christianity.

▶ It was belief in Jesus's resurrection which gave rise to the huge explosion of energy that kick-started the Christian movement.

▶ The resurrection of Jesus is not only about ancient history; it has huge implications for today.

▶ The resurrection points to another life beyond the grave – a richer, fuller life.

▶ The resurrection of Jesus has inspired thousands of individuals as they have faced persecution and death for their faith.

▶ Christians believe the risen Christ accompanies them through life by the Holy Spirit (Matthew 28:20), offering guidance, comfort – and challenge.

▶ The resurrection narratives were not inventions. The first Christians suffered for their beliefs, and people will suffer for their convictions – but not for their inventions.

Dig deeper

D. Catchpole, *Resurrection People: Studies in the resurrection narratives of the gospels* (London: Darton, Longman and Todd, 2000).

M. Levering, *Jesus and the Demise of Death: Resurrection, afterlife, and the fate of the Christian* (Waco, TX: Baylor University Press, 2012).

N.T. Wright, *The Resurrection of the Son of God* (London: SPCK, 2003).

Fact check

1 *Anastasis*:
   a   is the name of a female deity
   b   means *resuscitation* in Hebrew
   c   is the name given to Jesus after the resurrection
   d   means *resurrection* in Greek

2 The resurrection happened:
   a   several weeks after the crucifixion
   b   on the third day after the crucifixion
   c   at Pentecost
   d   immediately after the crucifixion

3 Who was the first to meet the risen Jesus?
   a   Thomas
   b   Paul
   c   Mary Magdalene
   d   Pilate

4 When asked for proof that Jesus was divine, the early church:
   a   cited the Virgin Birth (Jesus had a heavenly father and an earthly mother)
   b   pointed to the miracles Jesus had performed
   c   referred to his teaching
   d   pointed to the resurrection

5 The resurrection is celebrated at which Christian festival?
   a   Christmas
   b   Easter
   c   Pentecost
   d   Advent

6 Thomas said he would only believe that Jesus had risen from the dead if:
   a   he could hear his voice
   b   he could see his wounds
   c   he could touch his wounds
   d   he could see the empty tomb

7 The empty tomb:
    a immediately became a place of pilgrimage
    b was sealed up by the authorities
    c became the first Christian church
    d became a place of pilgrimage many decades after the resurrection

8 The resurrection appearances of Jesus:
    a continued for several years
    b ceased abruptly after about six weeks
    c only happened on the third day after his death
    d were witnessed by only a few people

9 Christians made Sunday their main day of worship because:
    a it was different from the Jews
    b it was the last day of the week
    c it was the day Jesus rose from the dead
    d they had to go to work on Mondays

10 Which of the following has *not* been offered as an explanation of the disappearance of the body of Jesus?
    a He had just fainted (the 'swoon theory')
    b His disciples stole the body
    c The authorities stole the body
    d The disciples went to the wrong tomb

The Bible: contents

In this chapter you will learn:

▶ *an overview of the Bible's 'story'*
▶ *about some of the key events in the life of the Jews and early Christians*
▶ *about some of the key books in the Bible.*

The 104th Archbishop of Canterbury, Rowan Williams, said at his first press conference:

> 'My first task is that of any ordained teacher, to point to the source without which none of our activity would make sense, the gift of God as it is set before us in the Bible and Christian belief.'

The Bible is for the Christian 'the Word of God'. It is the sacred scriptures of the Christian faith and has fulfilled that role for almost 2,000 years. For millions of people in the modern world the Bible brings direction, encouragement, challenge and comfort – a word from God for all seasons. But though many people know about it, fewer are familiar with the amazing story it tells.

An overview of the Christian Bible

> 'The book we know as the Bible is not so much a single book as a library. It is a collection of books, written by different authors, at different times, and dealing with a wide range of concerns.'
>
> G.W. Dawes, *Introduction to the Bible* (Liturgical Press, 2006), p. 6.

The Bible is made up of two major elements: the Hebrew scriptures referred to as the Old Testament by Christians, written mainly in Hebrew, and the New Testament, written entirely in Greek. Each of these is made up of a number of separate 'books' – though some are so short (e.g. some New Testament letters) that they hardly warrant calling 'books'. They were written by different people over many hundreds of years. Some of the material in the Bible almost certainly began life in the form of stories, songs or poetry.

These would have been passed on by word of mouth long before they were written down. The Bible did not begin life as a single narrative, but when all this material was gathered together there was some attempt at organizing it with a beginning, a middle and an end. So at a very simple level the 'story' begins with Creation – the first book is called

Genesis, the Greek word for 'beginning' – which records an understanding of how the heavens and the earth were made, where people came from and how God relates to the world. It moves through a series of historical periods which describe events in the life of the Jews and the early Christians, ending with the Book of Revelation which deals with the end of the world. We will look at how it came to be in this form in the next section but here we need to concentrate on a broad outline of that 'story'.

▶ Beginnings

As we have already seen, the Old Testament starts with the story of the Creation in the book of Genesis. Genesis does not attempt to give a scientific account of the creation of the universe, for it was written in a pre-scientific age. The focus of attention is not upon the 'mechanics' (the how) of creation, but upon the central fact that the universe was made, and is sustained, by the creative power of God. Its simple theological point is that we are not here by chance. Further, these early chapters of the Bible underline humanity's responsibility as God's stewards of the natural world.

The book goes on to tell the stories of Adam and Eve, of Cain and Abel, and of Noah and his famous ark. The stories in Genesis are *aetiological* narratives: that is, they tell stories of *causes* and *origins*. They were composed to answer the big questions which humans ask. They tell us about men and women who worked, worried, fell in love, laughed, suffered, married, betrayed, forgave, grew old and died. They are about people like us. The Bible deals with the great and abiding issues of life and death, sensitively and profoundly. It illuminates the human condition with deep insight and enduring wisdom.

▶ The founding father of a nation

A key figure in the book of Genesis is Abraham. He is an important character in three of the world's major faiths: Judaism, Christianity and Islam. As a result these are referred to as the *Abrahamic faiths*. He is really the founding father of the people who become known later as the Jews. He travelled from Ur of the Chaldees (in modern-day Iraq) northwards and westwards to Palestine, where he and his nomadic family settled.

Spotlight

The words of Deuteronomy 26:5, 'A wandering Aramean was my father', are thought to be one of the oldest texts recorded in the Bible and preserve an ancient 'cultic signifier' – a phrase that wandering tribesmen would use to proclaim their identity. 'Aram' is mentioned in a very ancient text which goes back to possibly as early as 1800 BC.

▶ A formative event

One of Abraham's descendants, Jacob, fathered 12 sons, the most famous being Joseph, who was sold as a slave to the Egyptians by his jealous brothers. When famine struck the land where Jacob was living, he and his family travelled down to Egypt. Joseph had not only been set free but had risen to be the second most powerful man in the land. These Hebrew people settled in Egypt, but over several generations they were enslaved and oppressed by the Egyptians. After many years, they escaped from the Egyptian pharaoh under the leadership of Moses.

This escape became known as the *Exodus* and it is celebrated today by Jews everywhere, in the Passover meal. A key verse used in the *Shabbat* meal is Deuteronomy 5:15 – 'Remember that you were slaves in Egypt and that the LORD your God brought you out of there with a mighty hand and an outstretched arm. Therefore the LORD your God has commanded you to observe the Sabbath day.' After wandering in the wilderness for 40 years they arrived in the Promised Land – where Jacob had lived all those years ago. The Exodus is a critically important event in the life of Judaism. It gave the Jews their collective identity, their law (which included the Ten Commandments given to Moses on Mount Sinai) and their land. The first five books (*Pentateuch* in Greek) of the Old Testament deal with this period.

The people of Israel settled in Canaan (later called Palestine) and lived in family groups in 12 tribes, named after the sons of

Jacob. Each tribe had its own elders and leaders. Periodically they came under attack by neighbouring nations and they rallied together under a single leader called a *Judge*. These included famous characters like Gideon and Samson. At least one of them was a woman – Deborah. In a male-dominated society it is significant how many women played an important role in Israel's history.

Spotlight

Joseph, according to the Andrew Lloyd Webber/Tim Rice musical, wore 'an amazing technicolour dream coat' or 'a coat of many colours'. Some scholars think this is a mistranslation of the Hebrew. It could simply mean 'a coat with long sleeves' or a coat with stripes!

▶ A united monarchy – but not for long

After some years of this ad hoc arrangement they eventually adopted a monarchy. Saul was their first king, followed by the most famous king, David. David was an unlikely choice at first sight. A shepherd, a poet and musician he illustrates a common theme in the Old Testament: God often chooses the unexpected. As the elders looked at the candidates for king, God said to them, 'Do not look at his countenance [outward appearance] and at his tall stature, for I have rejected him. For it is not as man perceives it; a man sees what is visible to the eyes but God sees into the heart' (1 Samuel 16:7). David appears to have been the youngest and least impressive candidate but was chosen to be king. Under David, who was a great military tactician, the Hebrew kingdom grew into an empire which was further expanded by his successor Solomon. Such growth and power inevitably led to conflict with neighbouring empires which were also seeking to expand. There were internal tensions as well.

The earlier tribal system created a 'north/south' divide. The ten tribes in the north felt that the two tribes in the south were privileged and more powerful. When Solomon died, his son Rehoboam proved inept at dealing with this situation and the northern tribes rebelled. This resulted in the kingdom splitting in two. Although they shared a common history, a common faith and a common cultural identity, the kingdom of Israel in the north and the kingdom of Judah in the south went their separate ways.

▶ Exile from the Promised Land

The northern kingdom of Israel existed as an independent state until 722 BC when the Assyrian empire in the east conquered it. The people were taken into exile, but in effect disappeared. Since that time there have been many groups who have claimed to be descended from the 'lost tribes of Israel'. It is a theme picked up in popular literature and films. In the biblical narrative these events are dealt with by some of the prophets, such as Isaiah.

The southern kingdom of Judah survived as an independent state for a further 200 years until 586 BC, mainly because of its alliances with Assyria. But eventually it too fell, this time to the Babylonians. This happened over a period of about 20 years, starting in 607 BC, but like the northern kingdom, many of its people were taken as prisoners or slaves to Babylon. Again there were prophets at work. Men like Jeremiah, Micah and Habakkuk spoke what they believed to be the word of God concerning these events. We also have one of the most famous psalms in the Old Testament from this time: 'By the rivers of Babylon we sat and wept when we remembered Zion [Jerusalem]' (Psalm 137:1).

▶ Return

Although this period did not last long – perhaps 70 or 80 years – the Exile was a critically important event in the life of the Jews. In the Exodus they had laid the foundations of their faith, nationhood and identity: in the Exile all this came into question. As a result of this experience they rethought much of their theology. One key doctrine which appears to have developed during this process was the idea of a Messiah (*Christ* in Greek), a great leader who would come and be a 'second King David'. This is the idea which links the Old Testament to the New in Christian thinking, for when Jesus of Nazareth arrived on the scene he was quickly believed by some to be that long-awaited Messiah. By the time of Jesus, the Roman Empire had taken over Palestine, ruling through the puppet-king Herod. The Romans were able to play off the different factions in Judaism against each other.

▶ Messianic hopes – and a new beginning

The New Testament tells Jesus's story in the Gospels, though it is important to remember that these are not simply biographies or histories in the modern sense of the word. They are theological accounts of who Jesus was and what he came to do. Central to that were the mysterious events around his death and resurrection. The Gospel writers and later the writers of the letters (*epistles*) seek to explain the significance of all this. The New Testament also tells the story of the beginnings of the Christian church in the book called The Acts of the Apostles.

▶ Some extra books

There is one last part of the Bible to mention. If you pick up a modern Bible translation, e.g. the New Revised Standard Version, you might find it contains a section between the Old and New Testaments called 'the Apocrypha'. This term refers to texts which were included in the ancient Greek translation of the Hebrew (i.e. Jewish) Scriptures known as *The Septuagint* (sometimes abbreviated to LXX, the Roman numerals for 70, as it was thought 70 scholars translated it). These were not in the original Hebrew Scriptures. They are sometimes referred to as *deutero-canonical* and though they were not part of the original Old Testament, they are accepted by the Roman Catholic and Eastern Orthodox Churches as Holy Scripture. Protestant Churches regard them as helpful, in that they cast further light upon biblical times, but not on a level with the 39 Old Testament and 27 New Testament books.

So this is the 'grand narrative' the Bible tells. It was not conceived in this way: the individual writers were not writing 'the Bible', as it did not exist as such when they wrote. The documents were written on scrolls by and for people of two communities of faith, the Jewish and the Christian, at different times and for different reasons. Over time, what they wrote came to be recognized as sacred scripture. We will look at how the Bible came into existence as a single book in Chapter 5.

Some key books: the Old Testament

The very early parts of the story we have just looked at are in the first five books of the Old Testament. This is sometimes known as *the Pentateuch*. More commonly in Judaism it is called the *Torah* ('the Law'). It takes the story of the Jews up to their entry into the Promised Land. The arrival in the Promised Land and the years up to the founding of the monarchy (around 1000 BC) are covered by the books of **Joshua, Judges** and **Samuel**.

The books of **Kings** and **Chronicles** take the story from the death of King David right through the Exile (in Babylon) to the Return to the Promised Land. They cover around 400 years of history and several parts repeat material written elsewhere. We also have some insights into the exile in Babylon and the return to their own land through the great prophetic writings in the Old Testament. **Isaiah**, for example, which may have been written in a number of stages by different authors, talks about the eighth-century invasion by the Assyrians and ends with the return from Babylonian exile some 200 years later. **Ezra** and **Nehemiah** are two separate books in the Christian Bible but only one in the Hebrew Bible. They tell the story of the Return and the rebuilding of Jerusalem.

The period between the Return and the arrival of Christianity is not dealt with as a story in quite the same way. But we are given insights into that time from some of the later prophets and the Writings. **Daniel**, famous for the story of his encounter in the lion's den, for example, is set around 170 years before the birth of Jesus.

Case study: Myth

In everyday speech the word 'myth' denotes an untrue story, designed to mislead. In contrast, when academics describe an ancient story as 'myth', they are heaping praise upon it! Myths are enduring stories which carry profound and abiding truths, which cannot be portrayed in any other way. Hence the 'Creation myths' or the 'myth of Noah's flood' are stories conveying powerful – and true – messages about God's love and constancy, the inevitability of judgement, and the glory of nature. To take these tales literally – whether to dismiss them as childish nonsense or to build an anti-scientific view of the world – is to make a fundamental mistake.

Some key books: the New Testament

The New Testament contains four Gospels, summaries of the life, teaching, death and resurrection of Jesus. The first three Gospels are often referred to as the *synoptic Gospels*, which literally means 'with one viewpoint'.

Mark is widely regarded as the earliest Gospel, although it is placed after Matthew in the Bible. It was probably completed around AD 65, some 30 years after the death of Jesus. Written in fairly rough Greek, it breathes dynamic action: 'immediately' is one of Mark's favourite words. He includes some Aramaic words (Chapter 5) and takes care to explain Jewish customs for Gentile readers. Jesus is seen as the One who has authority over sickness, sin and chaos.

A quarter of Mark's 16 chapters focus on the death of Jesus. This Gospel ends on an enigmatic note, with the women visiting the tomb in which Jesus was laid. The tomb is empty and they are overawed by forces and events which are beyond their understanding. Mark's account ends abruptly and there is debate about a possible lost ending. A 'longer ending' was written later and is included in most Bibles as Mark 16:9–20.

Matthew is a longer account than Mark's, written from a Jewish perspective. The writer gathers the teaching of Jesus into five sections, consciously echoing the Pentateuch – the five books of 'the law of Moses' at the beginning of the Bible. Jesus is seen as a new and greater Moses. But despite his Jewish background and emphasis, Matthew records the visit of the Gentile wise men from the East to the infant Christ. In this way he makes it clear that Jesus is the Saviour of the *whole world*, not just the Jewish people. This Gospel also ends on a universal note with 'the great commission' in which Jesus commands his followers to make disciples from 'all nations'. The final sentence contains an inspiring promise by Jesus, which sustains and encourages Christian believers in every generation: 'I will be with you always, to the end of the age (Matthew 28:20).'

Luke, probably a Gentile (non-Jewish) doctor, picks up this theme of the universal significance of Christ. Luke underlines the concern of Jesus for women, for the poor and for the marginalized – his Gospel carries the parables of the Good Samaritan and the Prodigal Son. He stresses the importance of prayer and the activity of the Holy Spirit. Luke's Gospel is the first of a two-part work; **the Acts of the Apostles** is also from his pen.

John: it is widely agreed that the fourth Gospel was written last. A reflective account of the impact and importance of Jesus, this Gospel revolves around certain miracles of Jesus, described by John as *signs*. These are linked with *discourses* which highlight the significance of Jesus through a sequence of 'I am' sayings. Thus the healing of a blind man is linked with 'I am the light of the world'. The raising of Lazarus from the dead is linked with Jesus's breath-taking statement 'I am the resurrection and the life'. 'Eternal life' is a frequent Johannine phrase. This term means 'everlasting life'; it also carries the meaning of a new quality of life in this world, given to all who put their trust in Jesus Christ.

Case study: the fourth Gospel

John's Gospel is often referred to as 'the fourth Gospel'. Nowhere in the Gospel does the author reveal himself (it would have been a man). The problem is compounded by the fact that John was a very common name, so there are several possible candidates. Irenaeus (c.AD 115–142) stated that it was John the disciple who wrote the Gospel when he was a very old man. Papias (AD 70–163) confusingly talks about 'the Elder John' as the author. It is not clear if he is referring to the same John that Irenaeus names as author.

Other suggestions are that the Gospel was written by John Mark, one of Jesus's disciples and a companion of Paul. Or it may be a piece of *pseudepigraphal* writing. That's a technical word meaning the author is anonymous but takes the name of someone famous or important to add authority to their writing. This was a common and accepted practice at the time (and earlier).

Each argument has its merits and its problems. Hence the term 'the fourth Gospel' is often used. Knowing the identity of an author matters today in a way it did not in ancient cultures. Why might this be – and does it matter?

In the fourth Gospel the enormous significance of Jesus is underlined. John makes it clear that Jesus breaks through and transcends all the usual categories. Even great words like 'teacher', 'prophet' and 'Messiah' are not significant enough to capture him. He is 'Lord', 'God' and 'the Word made flesh'. Yet John shows Jesus as a real human being. He thirsts, grows tired and experiences deep emotions, including sorrow and joy.

Following the Acts of the Apostles there are 21 letters (**epistles**) in the New Testament, written by a range of authors. Although they are placed after the four Gospels in the Bible, many of them were written before the Gospels were completed. Some are very brief; others are more comprehensive. Several bear the names of, or are linked to, apostles: **Peter** (two letters); **John** (three letters); **James** (one letter); **Jude** (one letter). One lengthy letter is anonymous (the letter to the Hebrews).

Paul wrote most of the letters in the New Testament (13 carry his name). Following his conversion on the Damascus road (told in Acts 9:3–9), he poured his vision and energy into planting churches in the countries surrounding the Mediterranean. He regarded the preaching of the good news of Jesus Christ and the formation of Christian communities as events of enormous, cosmic significance. Paul believed that God was creating nothing less than a new humanity.

> *'[By] the late second century, there was a consensus that the Gospels, Acts and letters [of the New Testament] had the status of inspired Scripture.'*
> A.E. McGrath, *Historical Theology: An Introduction to the History of Christian Thought* (2nd edn, John Wiley & Sons Ltd, 2013), p. 27.

Yet he was well aware of the fragility of the whole enterprise. All the early churches of the New Testament were small: 50 members would be considered large. They were surrounded by powerful pagan influences which many converts continued to find attractive. Paul seems to have had an unshakeable belief that the enterprise was secure; ultimately it was *God's* work. But he realized that these churches and individual Christians were very vulnerable. So he wrote letters to these small communities in which he challenged, encouraged and argued, displaying intense passion and great tenderness.

He dealt with *doctrinal questions* such as the importance of 'justification by faith', and the cosmic significance of Christ. He dealt with *ethical questions*, seeking to strengthen ties of faith, love, family life and Christian fellowship. Paul was a trained Jewish scholar who employed the Hebrew Scriptures in the service of Christ, boldly and creatively.

Frequently he focused on the significance of the death of Jesus, the implications of the resurrection of Jesus and the power of the Spirit of Jesus. His thought is complex, but if there is a single key it is this: *'God was in Christ reconciling the world to himself'* (2 Corinthians 5:19). This theme of reconciliation is vital for an understanding of the Christian faith. According to Paul, through Jesus, God knocked down all the barriers which divide:

▶ the barriers which sin erects between disobedient humanity and the holy God

▶ the barriers between races, social classes and the sexes: 'There is neither Jew nor Greek, slave nor free, male nor female, for you are all one in Christ Jesus' (Galatians 3:38).

The last book in the New Testament is the **Book of Revelation**. This is a particular type (*genre*) of writing called *apocalyptic literature*. It is full of symbolism and imagery concerning *eschatology* – the 'end times'. It deals with heaven and hell, with final judgement and the defeat of Satan. It reads rather strangely to modern ears though it does give some insight into the life of the early church. The book contains 'letters to seven churches' in chapters two and three. These give us insights into the state of some of the early church congregations.

Spotlight

Verse for verse, St Luke wrote more of the New Testament than St Paul. His two 'books' are the Gospel which bears his name and the Acts of the Apostles.

Key ideas

▶ The Bible throws light upon the deep questions and complexities of life in every age.

▶ Although the Bible is an ancient book it deals with the 'constants' in human life – relationships, love, hate, war, forgiveness, the created world ...

▶ To take the Bible seriously does not involve taking all of it literally.

▶ The Hebrew (Jewish) Scriptures are called the 'Old Testament' by Christians.

▶ The New Testament is directly about Jesus Christ and the life of the early church.

▶ The Bible contains various kinds of literature – law, history, parable, poetry. Overall, it is the story of God's love and faithfulness.

▶ The Bible is regarded by Christians as a 'living' text through which we can hear the word of God. It is 'God breathed' (2 Timothy 3:16).

Dig deeper

J. Barton, *The Bible: The basics* (London; New York: Routledge, 2010).

I. Boxall, *The Books of the New Testament* (London: SCM, 2007).

J. Holdsworth, *SCM study guide to the Old Testament* (London: SCM, 2005).

Fact check

Note: in some cases more than one answer might be correct.

1 The Old Testament was originally written mostly in ...?
  a Latin
  b Hebrew
  c Greek
  d English

2 The New Testament was written in ...?
  a Hebrew
  b Latin
  c Aramaic
  d Greek

3 The Exodus was the story of:
  a the flood
  b the journey back from exile
  c the escape from Egypt
  d the establishing of the monarchy

4 The Passover celebrates:
  a the Creation
  b the Exile
  c the Exodus
  d the establishing of the monarchy

5 Which of the following was *not* a king of the united kingdoms of Israel and Judah?
  a Solomon
  b Isaiah
  c David
  d Saul

6 The northern kingdom fell to:
  a the Persians
  b the Romans
  c the Greeks
  d the Assyrians

7 The southern kingdom fell to:
   a the Assyrians
   b the Babylonians
   c the Romans
   d the Persians

8 Which of the following is *not* one of the synoptic Gospels?
   a Matthew
   b John
   c Luke
   d Mark

9 Myths are:
   a stories told for children
   b enduring stories which carry profound and abiding truths
   c stories which are not true
   d factual accounts of what happened

10 The Apocrypha is:
   a sometimes referred to as *deutero-canonical* material
   b normally situated at the end of the Bible
   c accepted by the Roman Catholic and Eastern Orthodox Churches as Holy Scripture
   d completely rejected by Protestant Churches

The Bible: sacred scripture?

In this chapter you will learn about:

▶ *the formation of the Bible*
▶ *the impact of the Bible*
▶ *the Bible in the modern world.*

Words and scrolls

As we noted in Chapter 4, the Bible did not appear as a complete and ready-made document at one point in time. What we call the Bible came together almost 2,000 years ago, but it contains some material which possibly started its life at least 1,000 years before that. And it started out as separate scrolls. The way it arrived at its current form is a long and complex story.

Jesus of Nazareth and his first disciples (all Jews) were conscious of standing in a long and noble tradition. It was a tradition in which the Scriptures had a central place. In his Gospel Luke tells us that Jesus went into the synagogue in his home town of Nazareth, where the people had gathered for worship on the Sabbath. He took a scroll of Hebrew Scripture and read from the prophet Isaiah:

> 'The Spirit of the Lord is upon me, because he has anointed me to preach good news to the poor. He has sent me to proclaim freedom for the prisoners and recovery of sight for the blind, to release the oppressed, to proclaim the year of the Lord's favour' (Luke 4:18,19).

Jesus returned the scroll to the official and declared: 'Today has this prophecy been fulfilled in your hearing.'

That incident draws attention to some interesting facts. The Bible was originally written on scrolls, not in a book. Books as we know them today probably did not arrive on the scene until the fourth century AD. The sacred scriptures at the time of Jesus were written on separate scrolls and kept in a special box or cupboard in the synagogue, to be taken out when they were needed. They fell into three groups – the scrolls containing the *Law* (the Pentateuch – Genesis, Exodus, Leviticus, Numbers and Deuteronomy); those containing the *Prophets* (such as Isaiah, Jeremiah and Ezekiel along with the 12 minor prophets); and the *Writings* (e.g. Job, Psalms or Proverbs). By common practice these books were regarded as the holy books of the Jews – their 'canon'. Interestingly, they did not formally settle on these books until well into the Christian era – possibly around AD 95. Was this a move prompted by the arrival of this new sect of Judaism called Christianity? The Christians very quickly started writing and circulating material and the Jews probably wanted to stop these writings being thought of as sacred scripture.

A new invention

In a society where few could read or write, it was only the most important material that was written down. Many of these scrolls were communal property and were read out to the assembled company. But a lot of material was passed on by word of mouth. It wasn't until the book form came along that the decision had to be made about which order to put the documents in. As we saw in Chapter 4, the order was determined by the content of each scroll rather than the date they were written. It is probable, for example, that some of the prophecy of Isaiah was written before Genesis, but as Genesis tells the story of the beginning of the world it was placed first in the book. The order didn't matter when they were written on scrolls! Once they were in a book between covers, the order was fixed.

When Jesus of Nazareth began his public ministry the stories about him circulated by word of mouth. Accounts of his teaching and miracles spread initially by being _told_ rather than _written_. Teaching, preaching, storytelling; hearing, remembering, repeating: these were crucial elements in the spread of the message of Jesus and his early followers. The oral and the written accounts intermingled at an early stage.

Eventually the first disciples grew old, or their lives were in danger from persecution. The need for a written record of the actions and teaching of Jesus became urgent. In a remarkably short time, the four Gospels which stand at the beginning of the New Testament came into being – written in Greek, which was widely understood.

Jesus and his first disciples were almost certainly tri-lingual. They spoke Aramaic, and a few Aramaic words are scattered throughout the New Testament. They understood Hebrew, the language of their own Jewish Scriptures. But to communicate widely they also needed Greek, the language spoken and written throughout the Roman Empire.

What is in and what is not: forming the canon

The first few Christian centuries gave rise to a considerable volume of literature. So two questions arise: *why* and *how* did these particular 27 books come to comprise the New Testament? In the early church, the term 'Scripture' originally referred to writings from the Old Testament. But the second letter of Peter refers to Paul's letters as 'Scripture' and very soon Christian writers, such as Justin Martyr (*c.*AD 100–165), were referring to 'the New Testament'. For some time there was debate about whether certain books should be included (for example, hesitations were expressed about Hebrews, 2 Peter and Jude). In the Armenian Church, the inclusion of the final book, Revelation, was resisted until the 12th century.

Some other early writings, such as the *Didache* and the *First Letter of Clement*, were serious contenders for inclusion. There was also some disagreement about the order of the books. The four Gospels and Paul's letters were accepted as authoritative by the end of the second century. In AD 367, Bishop Athanasius wrote a letter in which he listed the 27 books of the New Testament as being canonical, i.e. 'official' Scripture.

The second question concerns the criteria used for deciding which books should be included in the 'canon' of the New Testament. Presumed authorship by an apostle was one strong reason for including some books; but not, for example, the Gospels of Mark and Luke (although the early Bishop Papias [*c.* AD 60–130] asserts that Mark received his material from St Peter. It has also been suggested that Mark was the young man who fled naked at the arrest of Jesus in the Garden of Gethsemane (Mark 14:51–52). Presumed apostolic authorship of some of these documents would be questioned by some biblical critics, several centuries later.

There was never a formal meeting of the church at which the final composition of the Bible – which books were in and which were not – was agreed upon. Indeed, right up to the Reformation there was dispute around some of the books in the New Testament. Martin Luther in the 16th century wanted to get rid of the Letter of James as well as Revelation, Hebrews and Jude. What appears to have happened is that over the years Christians *recognized* rather than imposed authority on the 27 books which today make up the New Testament.

> 'Although many of the New Testament books are in use and being quoted from an early stage, the earliest surviving list of all 27 books together is in an Easter festal letter of Athananasius, written in 367.'
>
> I. Boxall, *The Books of the New Testament* (SCM, 2007), p. 228.

Reading the Bible: biblical criticism

We turn now to examine some of the tools and approaches which scholars employ in their study of the Christian Scriptures. The word 'criticism' has two meanings. In everyday speech, to criticize is to say something negative (however constructive the outcome may be). In the arts, however, it is a neutral term. Film critics are not always critical. They may say that a film is poor or superb, and go on to give their reasons: such critics are simply using their critical faculties. Whether they praise or condemn, they are seeking to make a careful analysis leading to an informed judgement.

Biblical 'critics' do not stand in judgement on the Scriptures. Rather, they seek to deepen understanding by bringing knowledge and discernment. Indeed, *all* who read the Bible seriously find themselves involved in this enterprise. Sooner or later we are bound to ask such questions as:

▶ Why does Luke include the shepherds in his birth narrative but not the visit of the wise men (included only in Matthew)?

▶ Why are there apparently two stories of creation (Genesis 1 and 2)?

- Why does Matthew have a Sermon on the Mount and Luke a Sermon on the Plain?

- Why are six chapters in the book of Daniel (chapters 2–7) written in Aramaic when the rest is in Hebrew?

- Why do different evangelists record different post-resurrection appearances of the risen Lord?

We are intrigued by the possible reasons for these and other differences, which engage our critical faculties. In pursuing such questions, scholars developed many tools. Here are six which developed during the 19th and 20th centuries and still have some influence on the way the text is understood. Others have since arisen which we shall mention later.

Case study

Which of the following is the most appropriate understanding of 'criticism' as used in Biblical studies?

- marked by a tendency to find and call attention to errors and flaws: 'a critical attitude'

- at or of a point at which a property or phenomenon suffers an abrupt change, especially having enough mass to sustain a chain reaction: 'a critical temperature of water is 100 degrees C'

- characterized by careful evaluation and judgment: 'a critical reading', 'a critical dissertation', 'a critical analysis of Melville's writings'

- urgently needed; absolutely necessary: 'a critical element of the plan', 'critical medical supplies', 'vital for a healthy society', 'of vital interest'

- forming or having the nature of a turning point or crisis: 'a critical point in the campaign', 'the critical test'

- being in or verging on a state of crisis or emergency: 'a critical shortage of food', 'a critical illness', 'an illness at the critical stage'

- of or involving or characteristic of critics or criticism: 'critical acclaim'.

▶ Textual criticism

This activity is designed to establish, as closely as possible, what those who wrote the biblical texts actually recorded on their scrolls. Textual critics work with the numerous early copies available to them. They note and seek to resolve differences, and attempt to provide translators with accurate Hebrew and Greek texts.

Existing ancient documents have survived a hazardous journey down the centuries. They were written and copied by hand (a slow and laborious process) and were liable to damage or destruction by fire, water, rough usage or simple neglect. So it comes as no surprise to learn that the world's museums and libraries contain only:

- ▶ eight ancient copies of Thucydides' History
- ▶ ten ancient copies of Caesar's Gallic War
- ▶ two ancient copies of the Histories of Tacitus.

By ancient copies we mean that there is a gap of about 1,300, 900 and 700 years respectively between the originals of these famous historical documents and the copies which have survived. In contrast, hundreds of ancient copies of the Gospels can be found in the world's museums and libraries. So it is evident that there is a rich harvest of ancient biblical texts for scholars to work with.

Hundreds of early copies of parts of the New Testament are available to scholars. Two complete copies of the New Testament are dated around AD 350 – less than 300 years after the original. One is in the Vatican Library; the other in the British Museum. The latter was bought from the Soviet government on Christmas Day 1933 for £100,000. The earliest undisputed find, a fragment from St John's Gospel, is dated around AD 130 and is held in the John Rylands Library in Manchester. Recently (2012) a fragment of Mark's Gospel was discovered which some scholars are arguing dates from the first century.

▶ Source criticism

This was first applied to the Pentateuch in the 18th century. Later it was applied to the New Testament, especially the Gospels. The things which Jesus said and did were remembered and passed on by word of mouth: some material was written down. In the course of time, the Gospel writers drew on a variety of oral and written sources, none of which has survived in its own right. Many scholars have tried to unravel this process in an attempt to discern the various sources which fed into the completed gospels. Two questions are of particular interest:

▶ Was there a document (now lost) containing collected sayings of Jesus? (Scholars refer to this as Q, probably from *Quelle*, the German word for 'source' – although even this is disputed!)

▶ What is the relationship between the three synoptic Gospels? For centuries it was thought that Mark abbreviated Matthew's Gospel, but most modern scholars believe that Matthew and Luke drew on Mark's Gospel, which was written first.

Spotlight

Translating can be tricky! Do you go for a *literal* translation of what the original says or try to translate the *sense* of it? Here are some examples of challenges from translating everyday phrases:

▶ The Kentucky Fried Chicken slogan 'finger-lickin' good' comes out in Chinese as literally 'eat your fingers off'.

▶ The Czech phrase used to mean 'to beat about the bush' is 'to walk around hot porridge'.

▶ Saying 'of course' in Korean is expressed by the phrase 'it's a carrot'.

▶ The German equivalent of 'as clear as crystal' is 'as clear as potato dumpling water' – but originally it meant *difficult* to understand (as in the English 'as clear as mud').

And there are some odd problems which emerge for translators of the Bible.

▶ Early Christian missionaries in Korea had to invent a word for 'God'!

▶ 1 Samuel 24: 3 says 'Saul went into the cave to relieve himself.' One modern translation renders it as 'Saul went into the cave to go to the men's room.'!

▶ Form criticism

Form critics are concerned with the various forms of material in the Bible: miracle stories and sayings of Jesus, for example. They are also concerned with the *Sitz im Leben* ('situation in life' in German) of the various units.

In the fourth Gospel, we read that Jesus said and did far more than could be recorded. Why then was *this* episode recorded but not *that*? And why does Luke (for example) include material omitted by Mark? Possibly one writer had access to different information about Jesus from the others. Possibly they had different interests. Possibly too, because the communities for which the different authors originally wrote had particular concerns (hence *Sitz im Leben* – 'situation in life' – a consideration of the circumstances of the early Christian communities for which the Gospels were first written). If Jesus addressed issues of importance to these churches, it would be natural for the Evangelists to record those particular words and deeds.

Form criticism flourished in Germany in the mid-20th century. Some form critics were very radical – assuming that the early church would readily invent sayings which they attributed to Jesus. Other scholars disputed this. John Robinson spoke for these in *Can We Trust the New Testament?* (1977):

> 'There seems to have been a reverence for the remembered speech and acts of Jesus which provided an inbuilt resistance to the temptation to make him merely their mouthpiece or puppet.'

Spotlight

The world's libraries and museums have far more old copies of the Scriptures (part or whole) than of any other ancient book. The Bible, and especially its four Gospels (Matthew, Mark, Luke and John), has been subjected to closer and more intense scrutiny than any other book in history.

▶ Redaction criticism

This was a reaction against methods based on analysis and dissection. True, the Evangelists used a range of sources, but they did not 'cut and paste'. *Selection is interpretation* and they were skilful editors (i.e. redactors) and purposeful theologians. The four Evangelists were highly creative – weaving their sources into genuine works of art. Redaction criticism considers the complete text, the particular concerns of each writer, and the different emphases which he wished to make.

▶ Narrative criticism

This is concerned with the Bible as a sequence of stories within an overall story. It takes seriously the universal appeal of story, in its various forms. *Why Narrative?*, edited by S. Hauerwas and L.G. Jones (Wipf and Stock, 1997), and *Telling the Story* by Andrew Walker (SPCK, 2004) develop this.

OTHER CRITICAL APPROACHES

The focus of these kinds of criticism is on the production of the text. When was it written? Who wrote it? How did they write it? Why did they write it? While these questions remain important, interest in recent years has shifted to the *readers* of the text. This is sometimes referred to as 'reader response' theory or criticism. It takes into account the fact that when we approach a text we see it through particular 'lenses'. We bring to the text a whole set of assumptions, experiences and agendas. Being aware of these is important to ensure we do not read inappropriate things into the text. At the same time, listening to these 'voices' can enrich the reading of the text.

There are a number of examples. For many years biblical scholars were mainly men (church leaders were men) so the predominant reading of the biblical text assumed a male perspective. But what does the text say to women? How might it be read from a feminist perspective? Similarly, for a long time biblical scholarship was in the hands of white Western males. What if you are Black, Asian, Inuit or Caribbean? How does the text speak then? More recently Queer Theology has focused on how gender orientation affects the reading of the text, and the voice of people with disabilities is making an increasing contribution to biblical studies.

> 'Instead of focusing on the text's author and the complicated issue of authorial intent, biblical scholars should concern themselves with the text's reader, and the role of the reader in the production of meaning.'
>
> E.W. Davies, *Biblical Criticism: A guide for the perplexed* (T.&T. Clark, 2013), p. 12.

Non-canonical material

There are a number of other texts from the early church in existence which did not make it into the Bible. For example, the Apocryphal Gospel of Thomas is a Coptic document which was discovered near Nag Hammadi in upper Egypt in 1945. It is a short work, containing 114 sayings attributed to Jesus, with no narrative setting and few roots in history. Some of these sayings resemble Jesus's words in the New Testament Gospels; many do not. The material does not pre-date the Gospels in the Bible (the 'canonical' Gospels) and was not originally called a 'Gospel'. There were others:

▶ the Gospel of Peter, probably written around AD 100–150 and very hostile to the Jews

▶ the Gospel of the Hebrews, in circulation early in the second century

▶ and even the Gospel of Judas!

Nothing in these 'Gospels' threatens to shake long-accepted views of the origins of Christianity, despite the claims of sensationalist writers hoping for a best-seller!

Case study: Apocryphal Gospels

'At the age of five, Jesus fashioned 12 sparrows from clay on the Sabbath day. This was reported to Joseph who asked, "Why are you doing these things which ought not to be done on the Sabbath?" Jesus clapped his hands and called out to the sparrows, "Be off!" At this the birds flew away chirping.'

This charming story comes from the Infancy Gospel of Thomas. It reminds us that the four Gospels in the Bible were not the only early documents about Jesus. Other non-biblical writings include the Gospel of Nicodemus, the Acts of Pilate, the Gospel of Peter, the Gospel of Judas and the Gospel of Thomas.

The Gospel of Thomas is the best known. The brief extract below gives a flavour of this document, which was used by a Gnostic community.
'These are the secret words which Jesus, the living one, spoke and Didymus Judas Thomas wrote down …
And he said: "Whoever finds the interpretation of these words will never face death.
"Love your brother as your own soul; guard him like the apple of your eye.
Split the wood; I am there. Lift up the stone and you will find me there."'

THE DEAD SEA SCROLLS

As we have noted, from time to time an archaeological find or a new theory makes headlines because it gives rise to sensational claims which appear to disprove established ideas. One famous example is the Dead Sea Scrolls, universally agreed to be an extremely important discovery. These scrolls were from the library of a Jewish community based at Qumran on the north-western shore of the Dead Sea, between 150 BC and AD 68. Their discovery in 1947 was described by Professor W.F. Albright as 'the greatest manuscript discovery of modern times'.

Wild claims were made for the scrolls. In particular, a few writers suggested that there were strong similarities between Jesus and the original leader ('The Teacher of Righteousness') of the community which wrote and preserved the scrolls. It was argued that Christianity had its roots in the teaching of this Jewish sect, which flourished before Jesus was born. A group of scholars working on the scrolls denied this. They issued a statement asserting that: 'Nothing that appears in the scrolls hitherto discovered throws any doubts on the originality of Christianity.' There is a marked contrast between:

- the community at Qumran (where the scrolls were found) and the early Christians

- the Teacher of Righteousness and Jesus.

This contrast was later confirmed by two Jewish scholars, Geza Vermes and Yigael Yadin. The position is summed up by the British archaeologist Professor Alan Millard: 'The differences between the Teacher of Righteousness and Jesus are huge.'

This does not detach Jesus from his culture. There *are* similarities between Jesus and other Jewish teachers of his day. As we have seen (Chapter 1), Jesus was unique in approach and stature but he did not set out to be 'original'. He gladly accepted many of the rich traditions of his nation and was aware of standing within the flow of its history.

Pursuing links between Jesus and the Teacher of Righteousness may have ended in a cul-de-sac, but the Dead Sea Scrolls do have some bearing upon the Bible: both Old and New Testaments.

- The scrolls increase our confidence in the text of the Old Testament. At least part of every Old Testament book (except Esther) has been found in the scrolls. They are about 1,000 years older than any other text of the Hebrew Scriptures so far discovered. Careful comparison shows just how successful Jewish scribes were, over the centuries, in their desire to pass on faithful and accurate copies of the Scriptures. Magnus Magnusson rightly spoke of 'the essential integrity of the scribal tradition'.

- The scrolls illuminate the world of the New Testament, for they were written between 150 BC and AD 68. Before the scrolls were discovered, some scholars believed that John's Gospel was a free composition, written in the second century under Greek influence. If so, it had no strong roots in history. But when we put the Dead Sea Scrolls alongside the fourth Gospel, we see how very Jewish St John's work is. Contrasts like 'light and dark' and 'life and death', which abound in John's Gospel, were thought to be Greek in origin. But the Dead Sea Scrolls show that these contrasts are at home in first-century Jewish thought. So the fourth Gospel fits well into the Jewish background which it describes; it has a secure basis in the history of that period.

AFTERTHOUGHT

In 2007 Professor Michael Jursa of the British Museum deciphered an ancient cuneiform inscription on a clay tablet dating from 595 BC, confirming a payment by Nabu-sharrussu-ukin, 'chief eunuch' at the court of King Nebuchadnezzar. He commented, 'A throwaway detail in the Old Testament turns out to be accurate and true. I think that means that the whole of the narrative [of the prophet Jeremiah] takes on a new kind of power.'

The Bible today: the Word of God?

For centuries, belief in the inspiration of Scripture by God was uncontroversial and widespread. Just what was meant by such phrases as 'the Word of God' and 'inspired Scripture' was not a real issue, until Enlightenment thinking gave rise to biblical criticism. In today's Church, various views are held concerning the precise nature of divine inspiration. Debate centres around questions such as:

▶ What does the Bible teach about itself?

▶ How did Jesus view and use the Hebrew Scriptures?

▶ How did the New Testament writers use the Old Testament?

▶ Does 'inspired' necessarily mean 'infallible'?

▶ Must 'inspired' always mean 'inspiring'?

▶ Did God inspire the writers and/or the text itself? Does the Holy Spirit also inspire the reader to understand the true meaning?

▶ Is the Bible 'the Word of God'? Or does it contain the Word of God?

In this regard two important Bible verses are often quoted:

▶ 'All Scripture is inspired [literally 'breathed'] by God and profitable for teaching, for reproof, for correction, and for training in righteousness' (2 Timothy 3:16–17). This indicates the practical nature of the Bible. It is for guidance and obedience. God's word speaks to the human condition: it shines in a dark world which desperately needs light. The concept of revelation (self-disclosure by God) is vital to Christianity. Christians believe that the Bible reveals otherwise hidden truths about God, about life, and about the way of salvation.

▶ 'No prophecy ever came by the impulse of man, but men moved by the Holy Spirit spoke from God' (2 Peter 1:20–21). This shows that inspiration by God does not rule out full human participation in the communication of his message. Debate about the precise nature of inspiration continues. But all churches believe that they are called to live under the Bible's authority. Interpretation and application can and do vary, but the Bible is – or should be – decisive for Christian belief and behaviour.

The two verses quoted above were of course written before the Bible as Christians know it today existed. For example, though there is some dispute about the date Paul wrote 2 Timothy (if indeed it *was* Paul), it was probably before Matthew, Luke and John wrote their gospels. So is it legitimate to apply what he says in that verse to the whole of the Bible? Christians have argued that a theology *of* the Bible needs to be in accord *with* the Bible and to draw on material written over a lengthy time span to build that theology.

> 'We can only clarify what we think the authority of the Bible is once we have an idea of what the Bible itself is.'
> W. Strange, *The Authority of the Bible* (Darton, Longman and Todd, 2000), p. 103.

INSPIRED? INSPIRING?

'Inspired' does not always mean *inspiring*. Some of the Bible is intrinsically boring. Tables of family names and detailed rules and regulations for sacrifices to be offered in tabernacle and temple do not make exciting reading! Nor is every part of equal importance. Some of the rules for worship in the Old Testament have no authority over Christians, because those rules have been fulfilled and superseded by Jesus Christ.

However, these passages are necessary if we are to understand the overall message. And, of course, some passages are wonderfully inspiring. Who cannot be stirred by the storm scenes in the Acts of the Apostles? Who can fail to be moved by the suffering servant in Isaiah 53, the Passion narratives, and the great hymn about love in 1 Corinthians 13? Who is not comforted by Psalm 23? Whose heart is not lifted on hearing the Sermon on the Mount? Whose will is not challenged by the call to forgiveness in the Lord's Prayer?

Some passages which seem at first sight to be of little direct relevance, contain underlying principles with continuing application. Few Western Christians face the question of 'meat offered to idols' discussed by the apostle Paul (Romans 14; 1 Corinthians 8). But the need for empathy, mutual support and consideration of the effects of our behaviour on others is never out of date. These issues are at the heart of that debate.

It is because the Bible 'speaks' in this way that it is read at the bedsides of the sick and dying and on occasions of great joy such as weddings. And many Christians meditate upon a Scripture passage daily and find with the psalmist that it is 'sweeter than honey'. To use another image from the Bible itself, it is a lamp which gives light to their path through life – encouraging, inspiring and challenging by turns.

Although it is an ancient text it is still *the* best-seller, continually in print.

TRANSLATIONS

An estimated 6,900 languages and major dialects are spoken around the world. But many of these are spoken by minority groups who are often competent in at least one other mainstream language. At the beginning of 2008, the number of languages with a translation of some or all of the Bible reached 2,426. In 2006 the complete Bible was available in 429 languages and the New Testament had been translated into a further 1,144. This means that at least part of the Bible is available to the vast majority of nations, tribes and clans.

The first book to be printed using moveable type was the *Gutenberg Bible* in 1456. This was the Old Latin version by Jerome (AD 342–420) called the *Vulgate*. The world's presses continue to print hundreds of thousands of copies of the Bible, which remains the world's best-seller (even though copies are often given away free of charge). English translations abound; among the most famous are:

▶ Tyndale's translation, which was based on Hebrew and Greek manuscripts. It is incomplete because William Tyndale was executed in 1536 before he finished his great work. It formed the basis for the Authorized Version (see below). Melvyn Bragg asserts that Tyndale's work is 'probably the most influential book that's ever been in the history of language – English or any other'.

▶ The Geneva Bible, which was dedicated to Queen Elizabeth I, who came to the throne in 1558. This Bible introduced the verse numbers that are now in universal use. Before this, only chapter divisions had been available.

▶ The Authorized Version (also known as the King James Bible) of 1611, which established itself as the English edition for 300 years. It is still in use but many regular Bible readers use modern editions. These are easier to understand and based on more numerous and accurate sources.

Moving stories are told of churches where Bibles are scarce. The Scriptures are treasured, memorized, copied and circulated with great care and love.

Key ideas

▶ The Scriptures were originally written on scrolls.

▶ The 66 books in the Bible were written over a period of more than 1,000 years.

▶ The Old Testament was written in Hebrew; the New Testament in Greek, with some Aramaic words in both.

▶ Christians believe that God's Spirit guided the human authors, whose backgrounds, personalities and formal education (or lack of it!) shine through.

▶ The Bible has been subject to more careful scrutiny than any other book in history.

▶ The copies of the Bible we have are more numerous, and much closer in time to the originals, than all other famous ancient documents.

▶ The Dead Sea Scrolls also illuminate the world of the New Testament.

▶ The Bible has been translated into all the world's major languages – and (in whole or part) into hundreds of minority languages.

Dig deeper

E.W. Davies, *Biblical Criticism: A guide for the perplexed* (London: T.&T. Clark, 2013).

M. McClintock Fulkerson and S. Briggs (eds), *The Oxford Handbook of Feminist Theology* (Oxford: Oxford University Press, 2013).

S. Moyise, *Introduction to Biblical Studies*, 3rd edn (London: T.&T. Clark, 2013).

J.W. Rogerson and J.M. Lieu, *The Oxford Handbook of Biblical Studies* (Oxford: Oxford University Press, 2006).

V.G. Shillington, *Reading the Sacred Text: An introduction to biblical studies* (London: T.&T. Clark, 2002).

Fact check

1 The Bible:
- **a** was written by the disciples of Jesus
- **b** was written as a book 2,000 years ago
- **c** was written over long period of time by many different writers
- **d** was put together by St Paul

2 Biblical criticism refers to:
- **a** finding all the mistakes in the Bible
- **b** highlighting the contradictions in the Bible
- **c** the verses where people are told they are sinners
- **d** seeking to make a careful analysis leading to an informed judgement about the biblical text

3 The 'canon' of scripture is:
- **a** a list of the most popular books in the Bible
- **b** the books recognized by the community of faith (early church) as authoritative and inspired
- **c** using the Bible as ammunition in evangelism
- **d** the first five books of the Bible

4 The books in the Bible:
- **a** are arranged in the order in which they were written
- **b** are arranged in alphabetical order
- **c** were only put in their present order when the book form was invented
- **d** are arranged according to length

5 The Dead Sea scrolls:
- **a** pre-date the Old Testament by about 500 years
- **b** were from the library of a Jewish community based at Qumran on the north-western shore of the Dead Sea, between 150 BC and AD 68
- **c** tell the story of Jesus
- **d** are a commentary on the Bible written by Jewish scholars in the first century AD

6 The first Bible printed using moveable type was:

   a the Geneva Bible

   b Tyndale's translation

   c the King James Bible

   d the Gutenberg Bible

7 The number of languages with a translation of some or all of the Bible is around:

   a 500

   b 1,000

   c 2,500

   d 3,000

8 Which of the following statements about the Gospel of Thomas is incorrect?

   a It is a Coptic document which was discovered near Nag Hammadi in upper Egypt in 1945.

   b It is a short work, containing 114 sayings attributed to Jesus, with no narrative setting and few roots in history.

   c Some of the sayings it contains resemble Jesus's words in the New Testament Gospels, while many do not.

   d It can be found at the end of the New Testament.

9 How many books are there in the New Testament?

   a 20

   b 33

   c 27

   d 25

10 In the only recorded sermon preached by Jesus in a synagogue he took his text from:

   a Genesis

   b Deuteronomy

   c Isaiah

   d Jeremiah

Part 2:

Christian belief and practice

Beliefs and creeds

In this chapter you will learn about:

▶ *Christian creeds*
▶ *the nature of God*
▶ *Christian experiences of God.*

The creeds

As mentioned at the beginning of this book, Christianity did not arrive 'ready-made'. The early disciples – all Jews who had a life-changing encounter with Jesus and the events surrounding his life, death and resurrection – had to work out what it all meant. This required their revisiting a number of long-held beliefs and practices. Unsurprisingly, in the early years there were differences in their understanding and theology, especially as Christianity expanded to include people of other religious and cultural backgrounds. Various attempts were made to formulate this new faith in what are called creeds (from the Latin *credo*, 'to believe'). The earliest was probably very basic – 'Jesus is Lord' (Romans 10: 9). Although this looks simple it was in fact full of significance. To the Jews, calling Jesus Lord was tantamount to saying he was God and for the Romans that he was Caesar. Both statements were very radical, religiously and politically, and could lead to trouble!

Other fuller creeds followed. They often came about as a result of refuting what Christians saw as erroneous (*heretical*) beliefs. For example, the 'Apostles Creed' was probably formulated in Rome partly to counter the ideas of Marcion (AD 85–160) who rejected the Old Testament and its God. Marcion was the son of a bishop and a leading member of the church around the middle of the second century. He developed what is sometimes referred to as a 'di-theistic' theology, a belief in two Gods. For Marcion the God of the Old Testament was simply a tribal God of the Jews, a vengeful and violent deity. God in the New Testament on the other hand – the God of Jesus – was kind, loving and forgiving. As well as wanting to get rid of the Old

Testament, Marcion wanted to cut out any references to it in the New Testament. He proposed a much shorter set of Christian Scriptures made up of only a Gospel and an edited collection of some New Testament letters. He was denounced as a heretic by the church in Rome.

Similarly the Arian controversy (or 'controversies' – there were several points of dispute) in the fourth century led to the formulation of the Creed of Nicaea in AD 325. This creed was reworked some 50 years later as the Niceno-Constantinopolitan Creed. It is usually referred to as the Nicene Creed and is still used in many churches around the world today. Arianism challenged the idea of the Trinity (see below), believing that both Jesus and the Holy Spirit were in some way inferior to God the Father. The original Creed of Nicaea ended with a statement condemning any who held such views as heretics.

> 'We may say that far from merely summing up the things of God, [the creeds] are an invitation to explore the wonders to which they point.'
>
> A. McGrath, *Faith and the Creeds* (SPCK, 2013), p. 59.

Key beliefs

The creeds spell out some of the key theological ideas of Christianity. They try to express in words what Christians believe about the nature of God. Central to that understanding is the idea of the Trinity, that God is 'three persons in one God'. This doctrine is linked with the Christian view of *revelation*. God is too good and too great for the human mind to comprehend. But in God's mercy God chooses to be revealed in creation, through prophets and poets, and through Scripture. Supremely God is revealed in Jesus (Hebrews 1:2) and by the Holy Spirit (Galatians 5:22). It would have been impossible for the Jewish disciples of Jesus – with their tenacious belief that 'the Lord is One' – to *invent* this idea of One God as Father, Son and Holy Spirit. They were *forced* to this belief through their experience of Jesus, and the events of Easter and the first

Christian Pentecost. This understanding of God as 'Three in One' was not worked out by lonely academics in libraries, but by men and women making sense of their experience in active lives and dangerous times.

The majority of the Nicene Creed deals with this Trinitarian belief. Each of the first three sections deals with an aspect of God. The first describes God as 'maker of heaven and earth' as well as all things 'visible and invisible'. It tries to capture the idea that God lies behind all forms of life and reality.

The second section goes on to describe the incarnation (literally 'to en-flesh'). It is the idea that God is not some distant deity who lives in a remote heaven but a God who is active and present in the real, concrete world of human existence. So in the Son (the second person of the Trinity) God 'came down from heaven and was *incarnate* [our italics] by the Holy Spirit and the Virgin Mary and was made man'. It emphasizes the idea that salvation – being saved from sin – is accomplished through the suffering and death of a human being. The creed goes on to describe Jesus as having suffered on the cross. He 'was buried and [on] the third day … rose again'. He then 'ascended into heaven' where he sits at the right hand side of God the Father: a place of authority, exaltation and judgement. The third part of the creed refers to the Holy Spirit, the 'life giver'. The Holy Spirit is believed by Christians to be that aspect of God which lives in the heart and mind of the Christian, guiding, inspiring, reassuring and challenging them.

Trinity is a complex idea. The early disciples were not educated or trained theologians playing at philosophy: they were trying to make sense of a very profound set of experiences. They held firmly to the belief that there was only one God but they had clearly experienced God in three particular but different ways. Expressing this in words had to avoid implying there are three Gods but at the same time not suggest that God appears in different forms at different times (*modalism*). One way of thinking about it is to suggest that at the heart of God lies both *individuality* and *relationality*. If God is love (a common assertion in Christianity), who did God love before the world existed? To say God loved himself or herself (human language struggles to talk about a genderless God!) suggests a kind of narcissism – a God absorbed in self-love. But to think of God as a 'community' of individual beings totally united allows for relationships within God. This is one reading of what might be meant in the creation story in Genesis which says that humans were 'made in the image of God' (Genesis 1:27). Humans are at their most fulfilled when they are individuals in community. 'I need to be me and I need to belong'.

The creed picks up on this idea of individuality and relationships. After the Trinitarian affirmations about the nature of God, it concludes with a brief section expressing belief in the church, baptism and life after death. The church is a community of individuals who believe in Jesus. The creed goes on to describe it as 'one, holy, catholic and apostolic'.

We will look at the Church in more detail in Part Three of this book but at this point we need to note that this phrase says important things about the nature of the Church. It is more than an institution. It is *holy*. This is not saying it is perfect or morally beyond reproach but that it is a body set apart by God for a special purpose. *Holy* means 'set apart by God for a particular purpose'. The Church's task is sharing the good news ('Gospel') of Jesus. It is to be the agent of God in the world, doing God's will and demonstrating God's love and mercy.

It is *catholic*. This does not refer to a particular denomination, such as the Roman Catholic Church, but literally means 'worldwide'. The Church has spread to every corner of the globe and is represented by every nation on earth. In this sense it belongs to the whole world. And it is *apostolic*. All churches are built on the foundation of the message of the first Christians, the apostles. What they preached has been handed down through the generations (the literal meaning of 'tradition') so that there is an unbroken historical link back to the life of Jesus himself. The Church is made up of those who have been baptized (see Chapter 7 for more on this) and the Nicene Creed includes this as an article of faith.

Spotlight

The story is told of St Augustine encountering a small child on a beach. The child was digging a hole, filling his bucket with seawater and emptying it into the hole. 'What are you doing?' asked Augustine. 'I'm emptying the sea into this hole', replied the boy. 'You'll never do it!' gasped Augustine. 'I'll have finished before you've fully understood the Trinity!' replied the boy.

The Christian doctrine that there are 'three persons in one God' developed over the first few Christian centuries. But the building blocks are found in the New Testament and in the experience of the early disciples. As they reflected on the significance of Jesus, they became aware that he was 'the man Christ Jesus' (1 Timothy 2:5) and 'My Lord and my God' (John 20:28). On the day of Pentecost they were filled with the Holy Spirit. They understood these experiences as actions or manifestations of the One True God, Creator and Redeemer of the World. This understanding of God as 'Three in One', the doctrine of the Trinity, makes God accessible. He is not locked away from us in heaven. God has become one of us in Jesus; he continues to live within us by his Spirit.

The last part of the creed deals with life after death. Every religion is concerned with life. But every religion is also concerned with death. Each religion makes its own distinctive emphasis as its adherents grapple with deep and profound questions raised by human mortality. Traditional Christian theology speaks of the 'four last things': death, judgement, heaven and hell.

In 2007 Pope Benedict XVI issued an Encyclical on eternal life, *Spe Salvi*, in which he addressed questions of judgement, purgatory, hell, faith, hope and heaven. Taking St Paul's letter to the Romans as his starting point, Pope Benedict wrote about the Christian virtue of hope: 'The one who has hope lives differently; the one who hopes has been granted the gift of a new life.'

The 'four last things'

▶ Death

The Christian faith sets its face against escapism. Even in the joy of a wedding service, the couple are reminded that the promises they make are 'till death us do part'. This note contrasts sharply with Western culture in general, in which many people are shielded from the harsh reality and supreme mystery of death. Thomas Hobbes (1588–1679) could say that life is 'solitary, poor, nasty, brutish and short'. In his world, most families knew the sorrow of death, including the death of a child. Relatives would observe the dying process, for most people died at home, and many, including children, would have seen a dead body. Today, most people are not exposed to such experiences, and some do not attend a funeral until their adult years. Furthermore, our life expectancy is much longer. The biblical 'three score years and ten' (itself rather generous in those days) would seem a meagre ration to today's many octogenarians!

Almost all these changes are for the better. But they do push into the background the necessity to consider death. This point has been made by many people, not just Christians. The existentialist philosopher Martin Heidegger insisted that we are not authentically human unless and until we have considered our own mortality. This can be seen as morbid, but it need not be. Indeed, it can be enlightening and liberating.

In the modern world, many people would prefer a quick death, because it is the *process* of dying which is widely feared. Significantly, Dame Cicely Saunders, a Christian doctor with vast experience of care for the dying and founder of the worldwide hospice movement, spoke of the value of time and space in which to contemplate eternity, and to take practical steps to 'close the book' on this life. This will include saying 'thank you' and 'sorry' as well as ensuring that a valid and up-to-date will has been made.

▶ Judgement

The New Testament contains this terse statement: humans are 'destined to die once, and after that to face judgement'

(Hebrews 9:27). The creed picks up this theme when it says that Jesus Christ 'will come again to judge the living and the dead'. Alongside its joyful stress on resurrection, the Bible teaches that humans are accountable to God. Christianity teaches that one day people will be called to account for the way they have used their gifts, opportunities and energies. Above all, each will be required to account for the way they have behaved in relation to the poor, the needy and the marginalized (Matthew 25:31–46).

Spotlight

Mark Twain, the American writer and humourist, caught the Christian emphasis on realism when he quipped, 'No one gets out alive'!

But despite the reminder of Judgement and the call to consider human mortality, the Christian funeral service includes a strong note of hope – even joy. For the gospel gives assurance of God's grace and forgiveness. This does not mean that tears and grief are out of place. Far from it; the bereaved are encouraged to mourn. There is a moving example of this in the New Testament. Following the death of Stephen, the first Christian martyr, we read that 'godly men buried Stephen and mourned deeply for him' (Acts 8:2). Their tears were not for Stephen, who died with a radiant faith and who was 'on another shore and in a greater light' (Eric Milner-White). They wept for themselves. Their spokesman and close friend had been taken from them. They would miss him deeply, and so they grieved.

▶ Hell

When Jesus taught about hell, he had in mind an actual place – the valley of Hinnom (Jesus would have used the Aramaic word *gehinnam* – Greek *Gehenna*; Hebrew *ge Hinnom*). This valley, south-west of Jerusalem, was where pagan worshippers once sacrificed children to Molech (Leviticus 18:21). This practice was hated by the prophets, and Jeremiah spoke of it as a place of shame and punishment by God. In the first century BC, Jews were using this valley of shame as a metaphor for the place of everlasting punishment for the wicked. By Jesus's day it had become a rubbish dump.

By the Middle Ages, the notion of hell had become very literal, very picturesque, and very frightening! This can be seen by looking at depictions of hell in stained glass, watching the medieval mystery plays or reading Dante's *Divine Comedy*. Dante's classic text (*c.*1300) portrays hell as nine circles at the centre of the earth. On the gate at the entrance is the inscription, 'Abandon hope, all ye who enter here'.

Teaching about hell continued down the years. On 8 July 1741, Jonathan Edwards preached a sermon entitled 'Sinners in the hands of an Angry God', which contains the following passage:

> 'It would be dreadful to suffer the fierceness and wrath of Almighty God for one moment; but you must suffer it for all eternity. There will be no end to this exquisite horrible misery ... You will know that you must wear out long ages, millions of millions of ages, in wrestling and conflicting with this almighty merciless vengeance.'

Jonathan Edwards was not a bloodthirsty monster; he was equally eloquent on the great themes of mercy, forgiveness and divine love. Indeed, his preaching on hell was motivated by love; he had an overwhelming desire to warn those whom he feared would be lost, unless they were given a clear warning. His words were not unusual in the 18th century, and there are modern preachers who would say much the same thing in much the same way. In general, however, the 20th century saw a move away from such harsh ideas, which do not square easily with the notion of the love of God, so clearly and frequently spelt out in the New Testament. Various views have been put forward.

▶ 'Universalists' argue that the love and grace of God must ultimately conquer every human heart. In the end, *all* will be saved.

▶ Others disagree. Yes, it is clear from the Bible that 'God desires everyone to be saved' (1 Timothy 2:4). But God's will can be frustrated by human choice. They point out that of the 12 occurrences of the word 'Gehenna' in the New

Testament, 11 are on the lips of Jesus. Jesus was particularly harsh on those who led 'little ones' astray (Luke 17:2).

▶ Today's theologians wish to dispense with medieval literalism. They remind us that Jesus was using picture language based upon an actual rubbish dump in the valley of Hinnom. Hell does not literally involve fire and darkness (which are mutually exclusive!). Those who believe that we cannot reject the concept of hell simply because we do not like it, sometimes speak about 'separation from God', freely chosen.

▶ The above point has been put with dramatic force. On the Day of Judgement, four words will be spoken: 'Your will be done'. Addressed by us to God, they assure us of heaven. Spoken by God to us, they have an awful finality. If we insist on enthroning ourselves at the centre of our personal universe, God will allow this to happen. To change the image: the prison door is open but we must decide to walk out if we are to be free.

▶ Some theologians speak of 'conditional immortality'. In their view, hell does not involve eternal punishment; it means ceasing to exist.

▶ Some stress the outrage that we feel in the face of naked evil. Hitler, Stalin, Pol Pot, the leaders of IS and al-Qaeda have caused untold suffering; should they 'get away with it'? And what about less well-known people who spread misery throughout their lives? At the very least, would not extinction, if not actual punishment, be a just outcome? Others ask why these people behaved as they did. Cruel or indifferent adults may have lacked love in childhood; many child abusers have themselves been abused. Perhaps 'to know all is to forgive all'?

▶ On the other hand we might ask, 'Would Hitler be happy in heaven?' Without a massive change of heart, would he not find it intolerable to spend eternity worshipping 'Jesus the Jew'? And might not bitter, self-centred people dislike and despise the love and openness which characterize life in heaven? A change of heart is precisely what the gospel requires. Christians call this *repentance*. In giving human beings a measure of real choice, God knowingly places limits on his own power. To over-rule our fundamental freedom of choice is something which God will not do.

▶ There is no evidence that Hitler repented before he died. Might it be possible for him to repent *after* his death? The notion of a further opportunity to respond to God's love after death was developed by some Protestant theologians in the 19th century – but resisted by others.

▶ Jesus's descent into hell

We need to add two brief postscripts to this idea of hell. In the Apostles' Creed we find the mysterious phrase 'he [Jesus] descended into hell'. The 20th-century Swiss Roman Catholic theologian Hans Urs von Balthasar took this as a major theme. He raised the question: what happened between the death of Jesus on Good Friday and his resurrection on Easter Sunday? His answer? 'The outreach of God [through Jesus] to the furthest possible limits of human lost-ness' (1 Peter 3:18–22; Ephesians 4:9–10). Commenting on this in a 2009 interview, Archbishop Rowan Williams said:

> 'So wherever you are, however lost you are, however much darkness there is around you, you have not got beyond the reach of God because if God is Father and Son then the embrace of God can go right round and bring you back …
>
> 'I was visiting Uganda when I was invited to preach in the condemned section of Lisiro Jail in Kampala, to about 300 people under sentence of death. Well, there are congregations and congregations – and this wasn't one of the easier ones. And all I could think of to say was – there is nowhere where Jesus is not. And if there's nowhere where Jesus is not, there's nowhere where God's transforming openness is not …'

▶ Purgatory?

Purgatory is seen as a 'staging post' between this world and heaven, providing further opportunity for sanctification. The idea is found early in the history of the Church. The stress on torment in Purgatory was developed in the Middle Ages. With this came the notion of multiple 'Masses for the dead' and 'indulgences', from which concepts many were glad to be released at the Reformation.

In general, Catholics believe in purgatory and Protestants do not. But the lines are not distinct. Most Protestant denominations believe that the change which comes at death is instant: 'in a flash, in the twinkling of an eye' (1 Corinthians 15:52). The life of heaven lies just beyond death. Roman Catholics continue to believe in a period of preparation and purification before heaven. It is not a place of punishment nor does it afford a 'second chance' for initial repentance.

▶ Heaven

The distinctive feature of Christian thought as it faces the brevity of life and the reality and meaning of death, is *resurrection*. Because of his firm belief in this, St Paul claimed to look forward to the world to come, asserting that to die is 'to be with Christ, which is better by far' (Philippians 1:23). In his *Journal*, Pope John XXIII wrote that his bags were packed and he was ready to go. The 20th-century journalist Malcolm Muggeridge picked up this theme. He suggested that dying is rather like checking out of a seedy boarding house and being welcomed into a glorious palace, with all expenses paid!

Christians deny that this is wishful thinking, for the Christian hope is grounded in the love and forgiveness of God, and it is based upon the resurrection of Jesus Christ. Easter celebrates the wonderful fact that Jesus was too good and too great to be held by death. God raised him from the grave.

Some ancient 'nature religions' focused upon belief in a dying and rising god, for example Osiris (Egypt) and Baal (Canaan). By enacting and reciting their great myths, they sought to ensure that a season of barrenness would once again give way to harvest and fertility. But there is a striking contrast between those religions and the Christian faith. In fertility religions, resurrection operated at a *mythological* level: it was *story*, not history. Christians believe that in Jesus Christ, the 'myth became fact'. What 'happened' annually in those nature religions, *actually happened* once for all in Jesus Christ, according to the Bible. The idea became an event – erupting into history and transforming the future. This is the Christian claim and it is for this reason that Easter is the supreme Christian festival. In the New Testament, Jesus's resurrection is described as the 'first fruits' of a great harvest.

This does not mean that facing death is necessarily easy for Christians. Derek Worlock, former Roman Catholic Archbishop of Liverpool, died of lung cancer in 1996. He wrote honestly and movingly about his pain and his faith (D. Sheppard and D. Worlock, *With Hope in Our Hearts*, 1995).

> 'I remained cold as a stone spiritually and desperately troubled by nightmares … Our own sufferings and difficulties can seem cruel and pointless unless they are related to the work of salvation. In our hearts we know that properly directed, they can be a way in which we are drawn into the life and purpose of our Saviour. That is never easy for us but it is part of our faith.'

Spotlight

When Cardinal Basil Hume, a former abbot of Ampleforth, rang to tell his friend Abbot Timothy Wright that he was dying of cancer, the abbot said, 'Congratulations! That's brilliant news. I wish I was coming with you.' The cardinal was relieved by his brother monk's response: 'Thank you, Timothy. Everyone else has burst into tears.'!

Beyond belief? Christian experiences of God

Christianity is more than a set of formal creeds. Those creeds represent the distilled understanding of Christian beliefs rather than dry checklists of 'impossible things to believe before breakfast', as the White Queen said in *Through the Looking Glass*. They capture the key beliefs of the faith of those who have encountered God.

The Bible is full of people who had profound experiences of God. Celebrated examples in the Old Testament are:

▶ Abraham, who heeded a call from God to leave his home in order to 'go to a land which I will show you' (Genesis 12:1). This is frequently recalled throughout the Bible as a key example of obedience and trust.

▶ Moses, who encountered God in a burning bush, where God revealed himself as 'I am who I am' (Exodus 3:14).

▶ Isaiah, who received a vision of the blazing holiness of God in the Temple in Jerusalem. He had a deep sense of his own unworthiness, and received a call from God to be a prophet to his people (Isaiah 6).

As with the Old Testament, so with the New. Its pages describe numerous examples of people encountering God – sometimes with joy, often with awe and fear.

▶ At the first Christian Pentecost, the Holy Spirit came in power upon 120 followers of Jesus (Acts 2). They became bold and were able to communicate with those who had gathered in Jerusalem for the Jewish festival, even though the visitors spoke a wide range of languages.

▶ The apostle Peter, a devout Jew, was wrestling with the question of Gentiles (non-Jews) and the gospel. Was it possible that they could be welcomed as full members of the Church without first becoming Jews? As he prayed, Peter had a vision in which he was commanded by God to eat food which was 'impure' according to the Jewish law. He protested but a voice replied, 'Do not call anything impure that God has made clean' (Acts 10:15). Peter came to realize that he had the answer to his question: the gospel is for everyone, regardless of race. That realization by one praying man was a defining moment for the history of the world.

▶ John, the author of Revelation, was in exile on the isle of Patmos when he had a vision of the risen and ascended Christ. So awesome was the sight that he 'fell at his feet as though dead'. Jesus encouraged him with words of gentleness and an instruction to 'write what you have seen' (Revelation 1:17–19).

Similar experiences have been recorded throughout Christian history. Some have become famous; others are known to only a few. Here are some which illustrate the breadth of the Christian experience of God.

Conversion

St Augustine of Hippo (modern-day Annaba, in Algeria) was born in north Africa to a pagan father and Christian mother. He wrestled with the Christian faith for many years. In AD 386 he was in his garden when he heard a child singing the words, 'Take up and read'. He picked up the Scriptures and read these words from Paul's letter to the Romans:

> … not in sexual immorality and debauchery, not in dissension and jealously. Rather, clothe yourselves with the Lord Jesus Christ, and do not think about how to gratify the desires of the sinful nature (Romans 13:13–14).

That moment was a turning point for Augustine, and for the Church. From then on, he employed his formidable intellect in the service of Christ.

Malcolm Worsley was a thief. On the day of yet another release from prison, a prison officer remarked, 'You'll be back, Worsley.' That officer was right; Malcolm did return, but as a member of staff! For in prison, Malcolm had been converted to Christ. He trained to be a probation officer, and worked with people who are dependent on drugs. In 1996, Malcolm was ordained in the Church of England.

Metropolitan **Anthony Bloom** was different from Malcolm Worsley in almost every way: education, personality, upbringing and culture. In turn he became a surgeon, a member of the resistance movement in the Second World War and leader of the Russian Orthodox Church in Britain. He too had a remarkable experience which gave shape and direction to his future life.

As a teenager he wanted to prove to himself that Christianity was untrue, so he read St Mark's Gospel. (He chose St Mark because it is the shortest, and he didn't want to waste time on the exercise!) He wrote, in *School for Prayer* (1970):

> 'Before I reached the third chapter, I suddenly became aware that on the other side of my desk there was a presence. And the certainty was so strong that it was Christ standing there that it has never left me. This was the real turning point. Because Christ was alive and I had been in his presence I could say with certainty that what the Gospel said about the crucifixion of the prophet of Galilee was true, and the centurion was right when he said, "truly he is the Son of God".'

There are two further points to note about conversion. The first is to consider the phrase 'conversion of life'. Many writers on Christian spirituality (see Chapter 9) insist that conversion is a process rather than a 'one-off experience'. Though the initial experience marks a change in direction in life, there follows the daily experience of changing attitudes, practices and behaviour. Second, Christian discipleship does not depend upon dramatic experiences. From the New Testament we learn that Timothy (a younger colleague of the apostle Paul) came to faith gradually through the influence of a Christian home (2 Timothy 1:5; 2 Timothy 3:15). Research suggests that a minority of Christians have a dramatic conversion experience. The way into faith is less important than the outcome. David L Edwards makes this point clearly and helpfully (*What Anglicans Believe*, 1974; pp. 65–6):

> 'That is why everyone is challenged to respond to God through Jesus Christ in *a personal turning* (which is what the word 'conversion' means). You have to meet Jesus yourself, and to accept him as your friend and as your Lord ... In many Christian lives, this turning or conversion reaches a climax which can be dated. People can remember the exact time when they accepted Jesus Christ as Lord and Liberator, often after intense struggles to escape from the pressure of his love. But it is not necessary to be able to date your conversion like that ... What *is* essential is

that everyone should have his or her personal reasons for being a Christian. You cannot inherit Christian faith as you can inherit red hair or a peculiar nose. You cannot copy Christian faith as you can copy hairstyle or an accent. And you cannot get it completely out of books, as you can get a knowledge of history.'

If David Edwards is right, then the phrase 'born-again Christian' must be used with care. It is true that Jesus told Nicodemus, a Pharisee, that 'no one can see the kingdom of God unless he is born again' (John 3:3). And, of course, conversion experiences do give a dramatic sense of new beginnings: people like St Augustine and Malcolm Worsley were indeed 'born again'. The danger is that those who come to faith more slowly and less dramatically can feel themselves to be spiritually inferior. Another translation of that phrase is 'born from above' (i.e. by the Holy Spirit). In this sense, all who put their trust in Jesus Christ are 'born-again Christians', whether they turn to him in an instant or gradually over a period of time. But, however it starts, this turning to Christ must continue throughout life.

Case study

Look at the Nicene Creed and the Apostles' Creed, used by the vast majority of Christians around the world. The Nicene Creed is longer and fuller than the Apostles' Creed but there are other differences as well.

▶ Sometimes they say 'we believe', sometimes 'I believe'. In what ways might this be significant? Does it mean one is more appropriate for individual use and the other for collective use? Or are they interchangeable?

▶ What significant details does the Nicene Creed add to the description of God – Father, Son and Holy Spirit? Is the Apostles' Creed weakened without them?

▶ What significant details does the Nicene Creed add to the description of the life of the Christian? Is the Apostles' Creed weakened without them?

Key ideas

▶ Christianity did not arrive 'ready-made'. The earliest disciples, who were all Jews who had a life-changing encounter with Jesus and the key events in his life, death and resurrection, had to work out what it all meant.

▶ The creeds spell out the key theological ideas of Christianity. Creeds try to express in words what Christians believe about the nature of God.

▶ Christianity is more than a set of formal creeds. The creeds capture the key beliefs of the faith of those who have encountered God.

▶ Central to Christian belief is the idea of the Trinity, that God is 'three persons in one God'. This doctrine is linked with the Christian view of *revelation*.

▶ Traditional Christian theology speaks of the 'four last things': death, judgement, heaven and hell.

Dig deeper

J. Astey, *Christian Doctrine* (London: SCM Press, 2010).

C.E. Gunton, *The Christian Faith: An introduction to Christian doctrine* (Oxford: Blackwell, 2002).

I.S. Markham, *Understanding Christian Doctrine* (Oxford: Blackwell, 2008).

Fact check

1 To the Jews, calling Jesus 'Lord' was tantamount to saying he was:
   a   a Roman
   b   God
   c   a member of the ruling Jewish elite
   d   a rabbi

2 For the Romans, calling Jesus 'Lord' was tantamount to saying he was:
   a   a Pharisee
   b   a Zealot
   c   a member of the ruling Jewish elite
   d   Caesar

3 The Apostles' Creed was probably formulated partly to counter the ideas of:
   a   Paul
   b   Caesar
   c   Marcion
   d   Judas

4 Central to Christianity is the idea of the Trinity. This means:
   a   there are three Gods
   b   God appeared three times
   c   that God is 'three persons in one God'
   d   God has three different names

5 Marcion:
   a   was a Jewish scholar who opposed Christianity
   b   believed the God of the Old Testament was simply a tribal God of the Jews
   c   believed the God of the New Testament was a vengeful and violent deity
   d   thought the Old Testament should be the sacred scriptures of Christianity

6 Which of the following is *not* used in the Nicene Creed to describe the Church?
   a 'holy'
   b 'sinless'
   c 'apostolic'
   d 'catholic'

7 Apostolic:
   a means invented by the first disciples
   b means built on the foundation of the message of the first Christians, the apostles
   c is a title given to Jesus
   d means 'ancient'

8 Arianism:
   a emerged as an idea in the Reformation
   b argued for a shorter version of the New Testament
   c argued that both Jesus and the Holy Spirit were in some way inferior to God the Father
   d invented the idea of the Trinity

9 'Catholic' means:
   a Roman
   b traditional
   c worldwide
   d Protestant

10 Which of the following is *not* one of the 'four last things'?
   a Heaven
   b Hell
   c Judgement
   d Purgatory

The sacraments

In this chapter you will learn about:

▶ *the New Testament background to the sacraments*

▶ *the significance of baptism and Holy Communion*

▶ *other sacraments and symbols.*

What is a sacrament?

Christianity is a sacramental religion. That is to say, physical objects and actions convey spiritual truths. The two central sacraments are **baptism** – the rite of Christian initiation – and **Holy Communion,** by which God nourishes and sustains our spiritual life in fellowship with other believers.

In times of conflict, a nation's flag assumes great significance. Indeed, people are sometimes willing to die rather than deny their national emblem. Viewed in one way, this is absurd. Who in their right mind would exchange life for a little bit of coloured cloth? But to those on the inside of that experience it is completely understandable. They see a 'little bit of coloured cloth', but they also see, represented in their flag, the past history of their nation and all that it stands for at its best. This notion of ordinary objects taking on deep significance is a helpful picture to hold in mind as we consider the sacraments of the Church.

> 'Sacraments are actions through which the power of God is conveyed to us. God not only became human once, but continues to meet us on our human terms by divine self-giving, through words and actions.'
>
> J.F. White, *Sacraments as God's Self Giving* (Abingdon Press, 2001), p. 31.

To call Christianity a 'sacramental religion' is to say that certain actions (eating, drinking, pouring) and physical objects (wine, bread, water) 'speak' powerfully about spiritual truths. This insight is found throughout the Hebrew Scriptures and in the Gospels. Later, the Church attempted various definitions. One of the most famous can be traced back to Augustine of Hippo: 'a sacrament is an outward and visible sign of an inward and spiritual grace'.

Another way to think of a sacrament is to say that it *evokes* something. It does more than simply represent or point to it: it somehow makes that thing present in the here and now and imbues it with particular importance and significance. And it reinforces what it represents. A hug is a sign of affection: it means something. But in giving someone a hug it also strengthens the relationship. In the same way a sacrament strengthens the relationship with God.

Christianity has two central sacraments: baptism and Holy Communion. Both of these are representations of events in the life of Jesus Christ, but with a specific and personal significance for Christian worshippers today.

In the New Testament, the Greek word *mysterion* ('mystery') refers to a truth which was hidden but is now revealed in Jesus Christ – and especially through his death. In the ancient Latin Bible (Jerome's Vulgate: fourth century) this term was translated as *sacramentum*; it is from this that we get the English word 'sacrament'. In the (Eastern) Orthodox traditions the Greek for *mystery* is still used rather than the Latin.

> '[What] makes the Christian sacraments unique is not so much something inherent in the doing of them, some 'specialness' in the action, but the uniqueness of Jesus Christ in his dying and rising.'
> R. Williams, *On Christian Theology* (Blackwell, 2000), p. 197.

Baptism

THE BAPTISM OF JESUS

The Gospels tell us that John the Baptist (the cousin of Jesus) 'preached a baptism of repentance for the forgiveness of sins' (Mark 1:4). Crowds went to be baptized in the River Jordan; among them was Jesus. John expressed reluctance to baptize the One who was so much greater than he. But Jesus insisted and John agreed. When Jesus came up out of the water, 'he saw the Spirit of God descending like a dove and lighting on him. And a voice from heaven said, "This is my Son, whom I love; with him I am well pleased"' (Matthew 3:16,17).

John's was a baptism of repentance for sin and this raises a question for Christians, for the New Testament teaches the sinlessness of Jesus (1 Peter 2:22). He was the one human being who had no need to repent. But in submitting to baptism, Jesus was not declaring his own sinfulness; he was endorsing John's ministry. He was also identifying himself with the people.

Jesus could have stood with John, calling the people to repentance. Instead, he associated himself with the people; a fitting start to the ministry of the One who would be called 'friend of sinners' and who would die on a cross between two criminals.

BAPTISM IN THE CHURCH

Baptism features strongly in the New Testament, and in subsequent Christian history, as a vital aspect of Christian initiation. But Christian baptism is a much richer concept than John's baptism. For, as John declared, Jesus would 'baptize with the Holy Spirit'.

The Acts of the Apostles gives several examples of people being baptized, among them an Ethiopian official (Acts 8:38) and a Philippian jailor, together with his family (Acts 16:31–34). These show that a lengthy period of preparation was not required. Following confession of faith in Christ, baptism was the immediate next step. In the years following the New Testament period, a lengthy preparation and 'apprenticeship' became common, with most baptisms taking place at Easter or Pentecost. Those being prepared for Christian initiation were called *catechumens* or the *catechumenate*, terms still in use today. This lengthy time of preparation may in part have been a defence against infiltrators. It must be remembered that for the first 200–300 years of its existence Christianity was an illegal religion, an underground movement which had to meet in secret. The possibility of infiltration by those who would stamp it out was ever present, and so lengthy periods of teaching, preparation and scrutiny were used to expose such opponents.

WATER

A key passage for understanding Christian baptism is found in St Paul's letter to the church in Rome. He describes baptism as a burial! (Romans 6:4) Baptism links believers with the crucified Saviour – it illustrates the call of Jesus to 'take up your cross'. This call to 'die to self' is a central aspect of Christian discipleship and it is signified in baptism when candidates go under the water. But baptism is also a symbol of resurrection; the candidates come up out of the water, signifying that they have received new life in Christ.

Water has many other rich associations in the Christian tradition. It signifies that a person has been washed clean from sin. And it points to a promise of Jesus – that he will give the 'water of life' (John 7:38). Baptism also reminds those present of God's great saving act in the Old Testament in bringing the people of Israel safely through the divided sea, pursued by their Egyptian captors (the Exodus). They remember too, that Jesus referred to his impending death as 'a baptism' (Mark 10:38). The sacrament or ordinance of baptism evokes all these associations. Christian baptism is modelled on the baptism of Jesus by John the Baptist in the river Jordan. Water is usually poured onto the candidates. Or the candidate might be immersed in water by the officiating minister. Baptism is administered in the name of the Father, Son and Holy Spirit.

Spotlight

A font is a receptacle for holding water for use in baptism in some churches. The word comes from the Latin for 'fountain'. Many fonts are made of stone and placed near the door of the church to signify entry into the Christian faith.

LATER DEVELOPMENTS

Different customs have grown up around baptism. These differences, the subject of some controversy between the Churches, focus on:

▶ the candidates for baptism

▶ the mode of baptism

▶ who may baptize.

Nobody is too old for baptism and all churches baptize adults who come to faith in Christ. But many churches baptize babies too, usually on the understanding that they will be given a Christian upbringing. These churches assert that infant baptism speaks clearly of the grace of God – indicating that his love is for all, even those who cannot consciously respond to it.

> 'The sheer gratuitousness of the grace of salvation is particularly manifest in infant Baptism. The Church and the parents would deny a child the priceless grace of becoming a child of God were they not to confer Baptism shortly after birth ... For all the baptized, children or adults, faith must grow after Baptism' (Catechism of the Catholic Church).

Note: This modern catechism (1994 and 2000) – the first for 400 years – will be quoted frequently in this chapter. These quotations will be referred to as 'CCC'.

While it is usual for baptism to be administered by a priest or ordained minister during a church service, churches encourage lay people to baptize where there is danger of death. Some Protestant Christians, notably Baptists and Pentecostalists, believe that baptism should be reserved for believers. Parents take newborn babies to church for a special act of thanksgiving and dedication to God. But baptism by water, in the name of the Father, the Son and the Holy Spirit, is delayed until the children grow up and request it for themselves. The baptism service then becomes a powerful act of personal witness to faith in Jesus Christ.

This approach does have attractions even for some churches which traditionally baptize infants. One problem for many churches is 'nominal' Christianity. Parents who have little contact with the Church and no real intention of raising their children in the Christian faith, nevertheless desire a 'christening' (a popular term for baptism) to celebrate the birth. Churches are torn between a desire to welcome everyone into the life of the Church, however fleetingly, and a concern to assert that the Christian faith has content and 'bite'.

The importance of personal choice and radical discipleship as inescapable features of Christianity, are emphasized by those who practise *believers' baptism*. Many Christians who hold that there are good reasons for infant baptism nevertheless welcome the fact that the centrality of personal commitment to Christ is focused so clearly by their Baptist and Pentecostal brothers and sisters. But they point out that those baptized in infancy also have to make a personal choice as they grow up. They should be encouraged to view their baptism as a call to follow Christ.

DIFFERENT MODES OF BAPTISM

Many churches baptize by *affusion*. This means that the minister pours water on the head of the candidate (child or adult) and administers baptism 'in the name of the Father, and of the Son and of the Holy Spirit'. Other churches baptize by *immersion*. Immersion is almost always the mode of baptism employed by churches which restrict baptism to believers. Their church buildings often contain a 'baptistery' – a sunken area which contains enough water for candidates to be fully immersed. Some churches offer both modes of baptism. Baptisms are sometimes held in the sea, or in a river or swimming-pool. Eastern Orthodox Churches baptize infants by immersion. The baby is immersed three times (reflecting the Holy Trinity).

To settle these different approaches, baptismal practice in the New Testament has been closely studied. But it is not spelt out in enough detail to put the issues beyond doubt, and some would argue that this gives validity to a range of practices. The Bible certainly records the baptism of entire households. While it seems likely that such households would have included babies and children, this is not explicitly stated. But there is clear evidence that infant baptism was practised from the second century onwards. As for the *mode* of baptism, some paintings depict Jesus standing in the river Jordan while John the Baptist pours water over his head – a neat way of solving the *either/or* problem!

In practice, there is widespread mutual acceptance among Christians of the baptism administered by other churches. Even when individuals change allegiance and move from one denomination to another, most churches do not insist on 're-baptism'.

Spotlight

In medieval times, infant baptism was often by total immersion which is why ancient fonts in churches are so large. There are many stories of the water freezing in winter and the priest or sexton having to break the ice before the ceremony could take place!

Indeed, Ephesians makes it clear that there is only 'one baptism', just as there is only 'one Lord' (Ephesians 4:5). So most Christians would argue that 're-baptism' is a theological nonsense.

However, some individuals, on experiencing a profound conversion experience, feel the need to express their new-found faith in baptism, despite having been baptized as infants. Many Baptist and Pentecostal churches encourage this. And as these churches believe that infant baptism is not real baptism, some *insist* on believers' baptism for would-be members, even if they were baptized ('christened') as infants. However, this is not universal.

Holy Communion

Holy Communion is modelled on the last supper which Jesus ate with his disciples before his betrayal and crucifixion. Bread is broken and wine is poured by the officiating minister, then shared with the congregation (sometimes just the bread is shared – referred to as communion 'under one kind').

Jesus spent the week leading up to his crucifixion in Jerusalem. The Jewish Passover festival fell during that week – when Jews ate (as they still do today) a special family meal to celebrate their escape from Egypt. They view this event as a great saving act of God. The appropriate Scriptures are read (from the book of Exodus) and various dishes are eaten in a specified order.

On the night before his crucifixion Jesus ate this meal with his disciples. When he broke the bread, he also broke with tradition, for he added the mysterious – and shocking – words,

'*This is my body*.' He then took wine and added, '*This is my blood*.' As he gave the bread and wine to his disciples, he went on to say, '*Do this in remembrance of me*.' That instruction has been joyfully obeyed throughout the centuries. The Last Supper was to become the first of many, many more.

From the beginning, a fellowship meal in remembrance of Jesus Christ, and especially his death, resurrection and promised return in glory, was a central feature of the Christian Church (Acts 2:42). It soon became less of a meal and more of an act of worship, in which the eating and drinking became nominal and symbolic. Regulations gradually developed as to who might preside at the meal, who might participate in it and in what circumstances. The main celebration was held on Sundays, for the Christian community kept that day special (rather than the Jewish Sabbath, or Saturday), to honour the Lord's resurrection.

> 'As a sign points to its object, and as a sacrament effects what it signifies, so the Eucharist brings about the encounter with Jesus.'
> T. O'Loughlin, *The Eucharist: Origins and Contemporary Understandings* (Bloomsbury, 2015), p. 30.

Descriptions of the Last Supper are found in five places in the New Testament. An account is found in each of the synoptic Gospels (Matthew 26, Mark 14 and Luke 22), in John 13 and in Paul's first letter to Corinth (1 Corinthians 11:23–32). Paul includes a note of warning. Members of the church were abusing the Lord's Supper. He made it clear that to eat the bread and drink the wine 'in an unworthy manner' was a very serious matter. From then on, Christians were encouraged to prepare themselves by prayer – and sometimes by fasting too.

Paul also links the Lord's Supper with the return of Christ in glory, 'For whenever you eat this bread and drink this cup, you proclaim the Lord's death until he comes' (1 Corinthians 11:26). This connects with the Gospel accounts, where Jesus tells his disciples that he will not drink wine with them again until 'I drink it anew with you in my Father's kingdom' (Matthew

26:29). This theme is picked up in some modern liturgies with the affirmation:

> Christ has died:
> Christ is risen:
> Christ will come again.

The fourth Gospel includes the Last Supper but does not describe the breaking of bread and sharing of wine. Instead, it describes how Jesus took a towel and washed his disciples' feet as an example of humble service. But John does use sacramental language. Following the miraculous feeding of the 5,000, he records a discourse in which Jesus says, 'I am the bread of life ... Your ancestors ate the manna in the wilderness, and they died ... I am the living bread that came down from heaven. Whoever eats of this bread will live forever' (John 6:48–51).

ONE MEAL, MANY NAMES

Jesus's words about remembrance were frequently repeated when believers met to 'break bread' together. Other words, spelling out the significance of Jesus's death, also became part of the liturgy of Holy Communion. Gradually, full liturgical texts were developed for these gatherings around the Lord's Table. Various names for this sacrament or ordinance have come into common usage over the centuries, as follows.

▶ Holy Communion

This title stresses the fellowship aspect of the service or meal. Sharing the bread and wine fosters communion between the worshippers and God, and between those present. Holy Communion is a corporate experience. Believers are encouraged to think not only of 'making my communion' but of sharing one loaf and one cup at the Lord's Table, with their brothers and sisters in Christ.

▶ Eucharist

This title comes from the Greek word for 'thanksgiving'. It is a reminder that when Jesus took bread at the Last Supper, he 'gave thanks'. It also focuses upon the fact that this is a sacrament of the gospel. Christians who gather at the Lord's

Table wish to express their gratitude to God for his saving love. The focus of the service is upon Jesus, the crucified Saviour and risen Lord. But believers are required to express their gratitude, not only with their lips but with their lives. At the end of the Eucharist, worshippers commit themselves afresh to serve God in the world. Worship is only a temporary withdrawal from the pressures of life and the duty (sometimes joyful, sometimes difficult) of loving service.

▶ **The Lord's Supper**

This title reminds us of the origins of the sacrament; it was a meal shared between Jesus and the original 12 disciples.

▶ **The Mass**

Holy Communion in Roman Catholic churches is in the language of the people. But this is a recent development: an initiative taken at the Second Vatican Council (1962–5). Before that, this service was in Latin, as it had been for centuries. At the end of the Latin Rite, the priest dismissed the people with the words: *Ite, missa est* ('Go, you are dismissed'). The word 'Mass' – the commonest word for Holy Communion among Roman Catholics and some Anglicans and Lutherans – derives from this phrase. The term contains a challenge. As the Catholic catechism puts it, 'the liturgy in which the mystery of salvation is accomplished concludes with the sending forth (*missio*) of the faithful, so that they may fulfil God's will in their daily lives' (CCC).

▶ **The Breaking of Bread**

This term comes directly from the New Testament and speaks for itself. A famous verse (Acts 2:42) makes clear that breaking bread together was one of the key features of the early church.

ONE SACRAMENT, DIFFERENT THEOLOGIES

Over the centuries, differences in emphasis and in understanding of what happens in Holy Communion emerged – especially as theologians wrestled with the meaning of the phrases 'This is my body' and 'This is my blood'. Strong differences over possible interpretations have been expressed. On the one hand are those who see the breaking of bread and sharing of wine as a powerful means of recalling the focus of salvation. A highly significant change takes place. It occurs within the hearts and lives of the worshippers, as they consider afresh God's love revealed in the life and death of his Son.

On the other hand are those who believe that something vital happens, not only in the hearts of the worshippers, but to the bread and wine too. This is sometimes referred to as **transubstantiation**. This is the belief that when the priest says the prayer of consecration over the bread and wine, these actually become the body and blood of Christ. In 1551, the Council of Trent put it like this:

> 'After the consecration of the bread and wine, our Lord Jesus Christ is truly, really and substantially contained in the venerable sacrament of the holy Eucharist under the appearance of those physical things.'

This spells out a belief in the *Real Presence* – Jesus present in the elements of the sacrament in a real, not simply symbolic, way.

Those who take this view do not deny that the communicants eat actual bread and drink real wine. They employ the Greek philosopher Aristotle's distinction between 'substance' and 'accident'. 'Substance' refers to the essential nature of a material; 'accident' to its outward appearance (colour, shape, taste). In this view, the accidents of the bread and wine remain – they still look and taste like bread and wine. But the substance changes to that of the body and blood of Jesus Christ.

The 16th-century Reformers criticized the idea of transubstantiation, although they did not agree among themselves on every detail. Martin Luther held to **consubstantiation** – the view that the substance of both bread and the body of Christ are present together. When placed in a fire, iron glows because iron and heat are *both* present. A simple analogy like this helps as we consider the Eucharist, said Luther, who emphasized that the fact of Christ's presence is more important than any explanation or theory. Others pointed to the nature of the language used by Jesus. They argued that he was using the vivid language of metaphor. 'This is my body' means, 'Pay close attention. This bread represents my body which is broken for you.' Bread it remains, but it is set apart for a holy and special purpose.

This was a very sharp debate. What people believed about the Real Presence in Holy Communion could determine whether they lived or died in 16th-century Europe. Mercifully, much of the heat has now gone out of the argument. Many today think that it matters less whether all Christians believe in precisely the same way.

Case study

Dom Gregory Dix (1901–52) was an English Benedictine monk who wrote an important book in 1945 on Holy Communion called *The Shape of the Liturgy*. He put forward the idea that the service had a particular 'shape', informed by four actions.

▶ *Offertory*, referring to the presentation of the bread and wine to be used in the sacrament

▶ *Consecration*, when the bread and wine are offered to God and a special prayer is said setting them apart for this special purpose

▶ *Fraction*, referring to the ceremonial breaking of the bread to represent the broken body of Jesus on the cross

▶ *Communion*, when the bread and wine are shared by those taking part in the sacrament.

However ornate or complex the service of Mass or Holy Communion might be, or however simple, Dix argued that these four actions lie at the heart of every celebration.

Some modern Catholic theologians have reworked old ideas and coined new words. Edward Schillebeeckx, for example, speaks of **trans-signification** – the view that the consecration of the bread and the wine is primarily concerned with a change of meaning.

Church leaders have made efforts to understand each other better and to draw closer together. The World Council of Churches convened an inter-Church conference in Lima in 1982 to consider baptism, Eucharist and ministry. The Anglican–Roman Catholic International Commission (ARCIC) began in 1970 and ensured that high-level discussions between Roman Catholics and Anglicans continued for some 35 years. It has been succeeded by the International Anglican–Roman Catholic Commission for Unity and Mission (IARCCUM). Churches in the modern world have drawn closer in understanding, but full inter-communion with other Churches is still not permitted by the Roman Catholic leadership.

Most denominations welcome members of other Churches to the Lord's Table. In contrast, the Roman Catholic Church officially forbids its members to receive Holy Communion in other Churches (though some do), and will not offer communion to non-Catholics. So Holy Communion, together with related questions of ministry and priesthood, continues to be one of the main issues dividing the churches.

Perhaps Mother Teresa's simple words, with which all Christians can agree, show that the underlying unity is more important than the obvious divisions.

'When Jesus came into the world, he loved it so much that he gave his life for it. And what did he do? He made himself the Bread of Life. He became small, fragile and defenceless for us.'

Spotlight

Dietrich Bonhoeffer, a famous 20th-century German theologian, was imprisoned during the Second World War for opposing Hitler. He was executed only a matter of days before the war ended in Europe. His last act, when he knew he was to be executed, was to celebrate Holy Communion with some fellow prisoners. He ended it with the words, 'This is the end, for me the beginning of life.'

Two or seven sacraments?

Almost all Churches observe the two great sacraments of baptism and Holy Communion. These are called *Dominical Sacraments* because they originate directly from commands of Jesus

('Dominical' means 'of the Lord'). All Christians agree that these two are supreme. But the Roman Catholic and Orthodox Churches (and some Anglicans) use the word 'sacrament' to refer to five other ceremonies, in addition to baptism and Holy Communion. The catechism of the Catholic Church explains these very clearly.

▶ Confirmation

In Western churches this is a service of commissioning and full church membership, involving laying on of hands with prayer, always by a bishop in Anglican churches. This marks a conscious decision by candidates to follow the Christian way. An important feature is prayer for the strength of the Holy Spirit in the candidates' lives.

Confirmation brings an increase and deepening of baptismal grace:

- ▶ it unites the individual more firmly to Christ
- ▶ it increases the gifts of the Holy Spirit in the Christian
- ▶ it renders the bond with the Church more perfect
- ▶ it imparts a special strength of the Holy Spirit to spread and defend the faith by word and action as true witnesses of Christ, to confess the name of Christ boldly, and never to be ashamed of the Cross (CCC).

Many Anglicans would agree with this exposition. In the Eastern Orthodox Churches, confirmation is usually administered by a priest, not a bishop, immediately after baptism. This means that even infants are confirmed as well as baptized. They are also given their first Holy Communion on the same occasion. The service which includes these three sacraments is called *Chrismation*.

▶ Marriage

Christians view marriage (or matrimony) as more than a contract or exchange of promises. It is a vocation and calling, requiring God's grace. The consent by which the spouses mutually give and receive one another is sealed by God himself … Authentic married love is caught up into divine love. Thus the marriage bond has been established by God himself. By its very nature it is ordered to the good of the couple, as well as to the generation and education of children … The sacrament of matrimony signifies the union of Christ and the Church. It gives spouses the grace to love each other with the love with which Christ has loved his Church (CCC).

▶ Ordination

All Christians are called to serve – to exercise 'a ministry'.

> 'Christ – high priest and unique mediator, has made of the Church a kingdom, priests for his God and Father. The whole community of believers is, as such, priestly' (CCC).

But many churches 'set aside' some men – and increasingly women too – to exercise leadership, to teach the faith and to administer the sacraments. In Catholic theology, an ordained priesthood has a vital place, especially in relation to the sacraments. Through the ordained ministry, especially that of bishops and priests, the presence of Christ as head of the Church is made visible in the midst of the community of believers.

> 'This priesthood is ministerial. That office … which the Lord committed to the pastors of his people, is in the strict sense of the term a service' (CCC).

▶ Absolution or reconciliation

Absolution involves receiving assurance that God will forgive all who come to him in prayerful humility, with penitence and faith. No sin is too bad for God's mercy and forgiveness. Reconciliation involves confession, and this sacrament is sometimes called *penance*, *conversion*, *confession* or *forgiveness*. Lutherans have a tradition of absolution as a third Dominical Sacrament (based on John 20:23), though this is sometimes seen as an extension of baptism. We may offer the prayer of repentance in solitude, within congregational worship, or in the presence of a priest. It is the last-named that is regarded as sacramental.

> 'The movement of return to God, called conversion and repentance, entails sorrow for and abhorrence of sins committed, and the firm purpose of sinning no more in the future. Conversion touches the past and the future, and is nourished by hope in God's mercy' (CCC).

▶ Anointing of the sick

Anointing the sick with oil in the context of prayer and thanksgiving conveys assurance of God's love and ability to heal. This is based on the New Testament letter of James (5:14–15). Over the centuries the practice came to be associated with dying and it is sometimes called *extreme unction* or the *last rites*. But health, wholeness and healing have been emphasized since the Second Vatican Council (1962–5).

> 'The Anointing of the Sick is not a sacrament for those only who are at the point of death. Hence, as soon as any one of the faithful begins to be in danger of death from sickness or old age, the fitting time for him to receive this sacrament has certainly already arrived' (CCC).

OTHER TRADITIONS

In contrast to the tendency to multiply sacraments, the Salvation Army and Quakers (Society of Friends) have no specific sacraments at all. Rather, Quakers see all life as sacramental. In this view, *all* good things – the natural world, laughter, food, love, life itself – speak to us of the love of God. Salvationists view every meal as a sacrament; an opportunity to remember their crucified and risen Lord.

Other signs and symbols

In addition to the sacraments, Christianity is rich in signs and symbols. The cross has become *the* symbol of Christianity. It appears on buildings, in works of art, on clothing and in advertising. It is worn by people – as jewellery or tattoos. Go up the Seoul Tower in South Korea at night and look out over the city and you will see literally hundreds of bright neon-lit crosses all over the city. The basic design is recognizable anywhere, though there are variations:

The ankh cross is an ancient Egyptian symbol for life used by Egyptian Christians

The Greek cross, common in Eastern churches, has an equal length upright and cross beam

The Tau cross is the symbol used by the Franciscan order of friars

Each Gospel has its own symbol: Matthew, a man with wings; Mark, a lion; Luke, an ox; John, an eagle. The Holy Spirit is often represented as a dove.

There are also three common visual symbols which can be observed in many churches:

▶ *chi-rho*, based on the first two letters of the Greek word for 'Christ' (*Christos*)

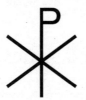

▶ IHS, a monogram for the name *Jesus* in Greek; although they look like English letters, they are in fact the Greek capital letters J (Greek uses 'I' rather than 'J'), E (an upper case 'E' in Greek looks similar to an 'H' in English) and S (these look similar in Greek and English).

▶ INRI, taken from the initial letters (in Latin) of *Iesus Nazarenus, Rex Iudaeorum*, meaning 'Jesus of Nazareth, the King of the Jews'. It reminds us that Pontius Pilate ordered this title to be placed on Jesus's cross, written in Aramaic, Latin and Greek – which were thought by those who read it to be all the languages of the world.

▶ Most famous of all is the ancient fish symbol. As some of the first disciples were fishermen, this is clearly an appropriate sign. It is suggested this was a secret sign used by Christians in the early days to identify themselves as believers. The Greek word for 'fish' is *ichthus* and each letter points to a name or title for Jesus.

I	*Iesous*	Jesus
Ch	*Christos*	Christ
Th	*Theou*	of God
U	*(H)uios*	Son
S	*Soter*	Saviour

The early form of the symbol was a very simple outline. Here it is in a modern form with the letters (in Greek) spelt out in its centre.

Key ideas

▶ Christianity is a sacramental religion. This means that certain acts and objects bear witness to spiritual truths.

▶ The two central sacraments are baptism and Holy Communion. These are called 'Dominical' sacraments, meaning 'of the Lord'.

▶ Baptism is the sacrament of Christian initiation. Baptism can be administered just once, but at any age in life – from immediately after birth to just before death.

▶ Holy Communion is based on the Last Supper which Jesus shared with his disciples.

▶ Some Churches use the word 'sacrament' for five other ceremonies: confirmation, ordination, marriage, absolution, anointing.

▶ In addition to the sacraments, Christianity is rich in other signs and symbols, e.g. the cross, the *chi-rho* and the fish.

Dig deeper

A. Davison, *Why Sacraments?* (London: SPCK, 2013).

M.E. Johnson (ed.), *Sacraments and Worship* (Louisville, KY: Westminster John Knox Press, 2012).

R. Thompson, *SCM study guide to the Sacraments* (London: SCM, 2006).

Fact check

1 Christianity is a sacramental religion. This means:
   a there are no ceremonies in Christianity
   b physical objects and actions convey spiritual truths
   c only priests can take Holy Communion
   d it is a secret religion

2 How many sacraments in Christianity are agreed upon by most Churches?
   a seven
   b eight
   c two
   d five

3 The two central sacraments in Christianity are:
   a the Old and New Testaments
   b baptism and Holy Communion
   c marriage and divorce
   d heaven and hell

4 Baptism is:
   a a daily cleansing ritual
   b the ceremony used to ordain someone
   c an initiation rite
   d a meal

5 The Last Supper, on which Holy Communion is based, took place at which Jewish festival celebrated by Jesus with his disciples?
   a Pentecost
   b Passover
   c New Year
   d Yom Kippur

6 Which of the following do *not* practise the sacrament of Holy Communion?
   a Baptists
   b Pentecostalists
   c Greek Orthodox
   d Quakers

7 Transubstantiation means:
   a bread and wine represent flesh and blood
   b bread and wine become flesh and blood
   c Jesus ate bread and drank wine
   d Jesus is present in the bread and wine of the sacrament

8 The *chi-rho* symbol stands for:
   a Christianity rules
   b church religion
   c Christos
   d charismatic

9 Which of the following are *not* included in the seven sacraments?
   a Ordination
   b Bible study
   c Confirmation
   d Anointing the sick

10 Who put forward the idea of consubstantiation?
   a John Wesley
   b Martin Luther
   c John Calvin
   d Jan Hus

Prayer and worship

In this chapter you will learn about:

▶ *different styles of prayer*
▶ *the significance of worship*
▶ *the Christian calendar.*

Christian prayer

Christians pray when they come together for worship. They also pray in private. Christian prayer is characteristically offered to God the Father, through Jesus Christ, under the leading of the Holy Spirit – it is 'Trinitarian' in form. This is no accident of history: it springs from the nature of God's revelation (see Chapter 6). That revelation reached its climax in the life, death and resurrection of Jesus Christ.

Christian prayer is offered on the basis that Jesus cleared away the 'roadblocks' between God and human beings, for on the cross he endured and overcame the alienation caused by human sin. And it is offered in recognition that what Christ did was the work of God, on behalf of the human race and the whole creation, out of love and compassion.

Christian prayer also recognizes that the Holy Spirit enables people to approach God as *Abba*, 'Father'. The Spirit guides and intercedes for humans when they do not know what to pray for, or how to pray (Romans 8:15,26). But the shape of Christian prayer is also seen in the fact that, because Christianity holds Jesus Christ and the Holy Spirit to be fully divine, prayer is addressed to:

▶ God the Father – most notably in the Lord's Prayer, the prayer which Jesus taught his first disciples, beginning 'Our Father in heaven'. It is God the Father who is most commonly addressed in prayer, through Jesus Christ, in the power of the Holy Spirit.

▶ Jesus Christ the Son – a remarkable fact, when we recall that the first disciples were Jews who believed that 'the Lord our God, the Lord is One' (Deuteronomy 6:4).

▶ The Holy Spirit – in the form of invocation, as in the ancient hymn, 'Come Holy Ghost, our souls inspire' (which has the Latin title *Veni Creator*).

THE PURPOSE OF PRAYER

Christians pray for two main reasons: to nurture, maintain and enjoy their relationship with God, and to join in God's continuing work in the world. These are deeply connected but we will look at the first of them in Chapter 9 (Christian spirituality) and so concentrate here on the second.

Christianity is deeply concerned with the world as it is. Christians are called to live in the 'here and now'. They believe that what happened 2,000 years ago affects the whole world, since God then set in motion a new order. God will eventually bring this to perfection when he makes 'all things new' (Revelation 21:5). But in the meantime Christians are called upon to work for peace and justice. They are charged with making known 'the Gospel' – the good news of God's saving work. That requires guidance and help, which is where prayer comes in.

Christian prayer seeks to 'key in' to the will and work of God, who is leading his creation towards a future of restoration, renewal and glory. *Prayer is not a matter of persuading God to do things which God might not want to do. Rather, it is a matter of aligning human action with God's purpose.* Even when (as is often the case) God's will in detail is far from clear, the desire of the praying person is to bring his or her will into conformity with God's will; to want *God's* will to be done.

The Khouds of North India have a prayer which reads: 'Lord, we don't know what is good for us. You know what it is. For it we pray. Amen'. It is a prayer of confidence in God, an honest prayer which rests in God's perfect, loving will.

Jesus Christ taught his followers to pray to the Father, 'May your will be done on earth as it is in heaven' (Matthew 6:10). This rests on the belief that the very best that could happen 'on earth' at any time is that God's will should be done. Furthermore, the Holy Spirit is always at work, guiding those who genuinely want the will of God to be done. The confidence that God is active in the world (and will one day make all things new) spurs the believer on to pray and work to make this world a better and a fairer place. This is in anticipation of the future consummation of God's kingdom. So prayer is best thought of as an active response to the will of the God of history.

In the Bible, Abraham and Moses prayed, so did Naomi and Hannah, David and Elijah, Jonah and Daniel, Elizabeth and Mary. Jesus prayed. His disciples asked him to teach them, and he did. He emphasized privacy, trust, honesty, brevity and forgiveness.

Most churches regularly use the Lord's Prayer. If any part is harder than the rest, it must be the words about forgiveness. Jesus developed this great theme in parable and instruction – and by example.

'Prayer is not escape from reality, as some may believe, but the pursuit of the real.'

G. Guiver, *Company of Voices* (SPCK, 1988), p. 5.

ASPECTS OF CHRISTIAN PRAYER

There are various kinds of prayer in the Christian tradition.

▶ Adoration and praise

The wonder of God's being and character evokes adoration. God is beyond human understanding; but he has revealed himself to humanity, supremely in Jesus Christ. God is seen as the One before whom heart and mind must bow, because in God is all perfection and beauty. Prayer may be expressed in words; but sometimes it goes beyond words into an attitude of silent and wordless devotion. A great medieval theologian, Thomas Aquinas, when at prayer in front of a crucifix, heard a voice saying, 'You have written well of me. What reward would you like to have?' He replied, 'No reward, but you yourself, Lord.'

▶ Thanksgiving

This is closely related to adoration. When Christians reflect on everything which enriches their lives, giving thanks to God for specific blessings is a natural response. But it does not stop there, for the whole work of God, past and present, occasions thanksgiving. A fine example of a prayer of thanksgiving can be found in the 1662 *Book of Common Prayer*:

> 'Almighty God, Father of all mercies, we thine unworthy servants do give thee most humble and hearty thanks for all thy goodness and loving-kindness to us and to all men. We bless thee for our creation, preservation, and all the blessings of this life; but above all for thine inestimable love in the redemption of the world by our Lord Jesus Christ; for the means of grace, and for the hope of glory' (from 'A General Thanksgiving' prayer).

▶ Confession

This begins with an awareness that nobody is without sin in God's sight. In addition to 'sinfulness' (a shared failure to love God wholeheartedly and our neighbour as ourselves) there are particular sins of thought, word and deed to be acknowledged and repented of, if God's forgiveness is to be received and a fresh start made.

Confessing particular known sins is important and can be therapeutic. However, in the course of Christian worship (i.e. worship in a Christian congregation), the prayer of confession must necessarily be general in character. The brief and beautiful 'Jesus Prayer' from the Eastern Orthodox tradition is used by many Christians: 'Lord Jesus Christ, Son of God, have mercy on me, a sinner.'

Many people find it helpful to share with another human being, in strict confidence, those things which are burdening their conscience. Some Christian traditions (such as the Roman Catholic and the Orthodox) commend the practice of personal confession to God in the presence of a priest. Some believers find that they come to an assurance of divine forgiveness more readily when they hear a declaration of that forgiveness from an authorized representative of the Church. In other traditions, having a 'soul friend' is practised. It is a close, personal and confidential friendship in which the deepest concerns, failures and fears can be shared so that healing and forgiveness can follow.

▶ Intercession

This looks out at the world. It is the prayer of concern for individual people, groups of people, causes and events. Since God wants the best for the whole of creation, the intercessor prays with confidence, asking that God's perfect will may be done. Intercession is based on whatever information is available. The blessing asked for is what seems to the intercessor to be needed, but the prayer is offered essentially as a contribution (itself God-inspired) to the realization of God's will. Just why God should wish to involve people in this way through prayer is a mystery. But, encouraged by Jesus's example and teaching about prayer, Christian believers gladly accept it as a mystery of love – and as a great privilege.

▶ Petition

The Bible encourages us to make specific requests to God. There are three important considerations.

- ▶ As the Lord's Prayer shows, the prayer of asking is meant to bind us ever more closely to God in daily life. Christians come to recognize that they are entirely dependent on God for everything.

- ▶ Jesus taught his disciples to make their requests in his name: that is, to pray as he would pray. This prevents petition from becoming selfish. Petitionary prayer is always with the proviso 'Your will be done.'

▶ A loving parent might answer a child's request with 'Yes', 'No' or 'Wait'. In the same way, any one of these three words might be the answer to a particular prayer. St Paul experienced disappointment when he prayed for the removal of a 'thorn in the flesh'. But with the 'No', God reassured Paul with a promise: 'My grace is sufficient for you, for my power is made perfect in weakness' (2 Corinthians 12:7–10).

▶ Lamentation

The Psalms cover the full range of human emotions, from joy to despair. These poems include deep expressions of sorrow and sharp questions to God about God's apparent silence and inactivity (e.g. Psalms 10 and 13). In this way Christians are encouraged to be totally honest in prayer, telling God how they really feel and what they really think.

> 'This is what prayer is: the practice of opening ourselves to God, listening to our own heart, and being attentive to the pain and suffering of others.'
> D. Tomlinson, *How to be a bad Christian ... And a better human being* (Hodder & Stoughton, 2012), p. 144.

FORMS OF CHRISTIAN PRAYER

▶ Liturgical prayer

In many Christian traditions church services make use of liturgical prayer. Some individuals also make use of this in their private prayers. 'Liturgy' comes from a combination of two Greek words which mean 'public' and 'work'. It is a similar idea to the Latin *opus Dei*, meaning 'the work of God'. Both phrases refer in some way to prayer and worship. Liturgy usually refers to written, formal prayers. Such prayers go back a long way in the Christian tradition, for example the prayers of Clement of Rome written in the first century.

▶ **Extemporary prayer**

Over the centuries, thousands of written prayers have been composed for all the above modes of prayer. Some are very beautiful; some very famous. But many Christian traditions and individual Christians use *extemporary* prayer – praying in their own words rather than from a written text. In some traditions (such as the Roman Catholic, Orthodox and Anglican), written prayers are usually preferred in public worship, though in recent times intercessory prayers are often written by lay people for the occasion. In other traditions (such as Baptist and Pentecostal), extemporary prayer (sometimes very passionate) is more usual.

PLACE AND POSTURE

Many Christians find it helpful to return to a familiar place which they associate with prayer. This might be a church building; it might be a favourite chair in a particular room. Some people use visual or audio aids – music perhaps, or a cross, a candle, a picture, an icon – but essentially Christian prayer can take place anywhere at any time.

Case study: prayer and posture

There are four principle postures adopted by people who are praying: standing; sitting; kneeling; lying (prostrating). Particular traditions in Christianity may favour one of these over the others, while some use a variety. Each one carries a particular message or meaning. Standing tends to be used for praise, thanksgiving and blessing, while kneeling is more commonly used for supplication (requesting) or confession. Lying or prostrating oneself is most commonly associated with deep penance or confession.

Sitting to pray has a long history (King David sat to pray; 2 Samuel 7:18) but was the least common posture until the invention of seating (pews) in church. In the Orthodox tradition many churches still do not have seats.

In recent years there have been studies which link posture to psychology. See, for example, B. Spilka and K.L. Ladd, *The Psychology of Prayer: A Scientific Approach* (Guildford Press, 2013)

Posture can be significant – and traditions vary. Many kneel to pray, especially in church, but some denominations pray seated (e.g. the Baptists), some standing (e.g. in Eastern Orthodox churches) and some even – on occasion – lying down (*prostrating oneself*). In Charismatic and Pentecostal churches you will often see people raising their hands in prayer and people pray with eyes closed and hands open.

MEDITATION AND CONTEMPLATION

We need to mention here one final form of prayer, that of meditation and contemplation. These are dealt with in Chapter 9 (Christian spirituality) but here we need to note that as well as describing particular forms of prayer these words also indicate *attitudes* in prayer. So even if words are used, it can be in a mood of meditation and contemplation. The Quakers would be a good example of this. Much of their worship is spent in silent reflection, members only speaking when feeling prompted by God to do so.

Christian worship

As with prayer, worship is both collective and individual. Gathering together (congregating) for worship has been the Christian practice since the days of the apostles. But Christians also worship alone. Here we concentrate on the collective aspect of worship.

> 'Christian worship has integrity when it focuses on praise, welcomes transformation, tells the story, and engages in participation, all in ways that are appropriate to yet in tension with culture.'
>
> R.C. Duck, *Worship for the Whole People of God* (Westminster John Knox Press, 2013), p. 270.

Although worship is a human activity, in Christianity it is understood to be motivated, sustained and inspired by God himself. Because worship has this character, it can be seen as a kind of 'conversation' between God and the worshipping community. Through the reading of the Bible, the preaching of a sermon, the singing of psalms, canticles, songs and hymns, and in various other ways, God makes use of human words to speak to his people. He comforts and encourages them, he challenges and inspires them, and he calls them to particular acts of service.

The congregation, hearing God's message in this way, responds in creed, prayers and hymns, and with adoration, confession and thanksgiving. The prayers which are offered for the world, and for particular people and causes, are in themselves a response to God. It is a way of declaring interest in, and loving concern for, the world which God 'loved so much that he gave his only Son' for it (John 3:16).

It would be mistaken, however, to think that worship is exclusively verbal, though it sometimes seems like that. We need only to think of the *sacraments* (Chapter 7) to see how wide of the mark this is. The sacraments have at their centre materials and actions, such as water poured, bread and wine consumed. Silence can be an important feature of worship. Some Christians (notably Quakers, as already noted) make silence central to their Sunday gatherings, as they 'wait upon God'.

Many churches are concerned that the gifts distributed by God's Spirit among the worshippers should be as fully used as possible – gifts of reading and speaking; gifts of music and the visual arts; gifts of leadership and teaching. Word and action belong together.

ALL WORSHIP IS ROOTED IN ITS CULTURE

Worship among Presbyterians in Scotland will be a more sombre experience than worship in a Pentecostal church in Barbados! Many people (particularly young people, but some adults as well) feel the need to express themselves in a style of worship which may differ markedly from that of more traditional believers. 'Alternative worship' is organized in many places; use is made of music groups, audio-visual material, dance and drama. In Britain in the third millennium there is no 'typical' church service. Variations within the Church of England alone would have astonished earlier Anglicans. But the same criteria apply: wherever worshippers give thanks and praise to God, confess their sins, and seek to serve and follow Jesus Christ in the world, *there* genuine worship is found.

As with prayer, worship is 'Trinitarian' in shape. It is offered:

▶ to God the Father, who makes himself known as the Father of the family of believers

▶ through God the Son, on whose life and work the Church depends

▶ in the power of God the Holy Spirit, who inspires the worshippers, and bestows gifts on them 'for the common good' (1 Corinthians 12:7).

Prayer has blossomed and fruited in every conceivable way – from the silence of Trappist monks or the Society of Friends (or Quakers, to use their popular name) to the formal intonations of the priest; from the succinctness of the Sunday Collect (to 'collect' our thoughts) to the different freedom of the extempore worship-leader.

Spotlight

The words 'liturgy' and 'liturgical' are sometimes used when speaking about worship. They usually refer to worship which is structured and written rather than spontaneous. They come from two Greek words – one meaning 'the people' or 'public' and the other meaning 'work'. In monasteries today, the monks may talk about the *opus Dei* – Latin for 'the work of God – by which they mean their daily round of worship and prayer.

Methodists are better than most at incorporating hymns into their private devotions. Some Christians pray by the book, as in a 'Daily Office' with its mix of constants and variables; others pray spontaneously.

Worship is not confined to services in church; it involves the entire life of members of the congregation, during the week as well as on Sundays. What happens in a church service is a focus for the worship which believers offer through their everyday activities. *This point is all important.* In the Bible we find a solemn warning: if what happens outside formal worship contradicts what is said within it, then the act of worship is invalidated (Isaiah 1; Amos 5). Worship, properly understood, is the offering of the whole of our lives to God.

'Therefore, I urge you, brothers, in view of God's mercy, to offer your bodies as living sacrifices, holy and pleasing to God – this is your spiritual act of worship. Do not conform any longer to the pattern of this world, but be transformed by the renewing of your mind.' (Romans 12:1–2)

A prayer from the American Episcopal Church captures this well:

'Send us now into the world in peace,
and grant us strength and courage
to love and serve you with gladness and singleness of heart;
through Christ our Lord. Amen.'
(from *The Book of Common Prayer*, US Episcopal Church).

The Christian year

From early days Christians followed the tradition of their Jewish roots in having a calendar marked out by particular times and seasons. The main festivals celebrate or mark key events in the story of salvation, such as Christmas and Easter. Some days are set aside to remember particular characters in the Christian story, such as the martyrdom of Stephen or the conversion of Paul. This calendar, as well as marking the great moments and themes of the Christian story, creates the rhythm and changes of mood that are a helpful aid to devotion, faith and life.

▶ Advent

Advent marks the beginning of this 'liturgical' year. It begins on the fourth Sunday before Christmas Day (not the first of December as most Advent calendars do!) The title comes from a Latin word meaning 'coming'. In Advent, Christians prepare themselves for the celebration of Christ's coming at

Christmas – and for his 'Second Coming' at the end of this age, when he will judge the world. It is a time of reflection and preparation including, in some traditions, fasting. This season is longer in the Eastern Orthodox Churches than in the West (one example of a number of variations in the Christian calendar between the Eastern and Western Churches).

▶ Christmas

The anniversary of the birth of Christ is celebrated by most Christians on 25 December, though the actual date of Christ's birth in Bethlehem is unknown. Many Eastern Orthodox Christians celebrate Christmas on 7 January (Armenians on 6 January) because of the difference between the Julian and Gregorian calendars. This most popular of all festivals replaced an older, pagan mid-winter festival. Christmas was for a long time overshadowed by Easter as the Church's main festival.

▶ Epiphany

The word is Greek in origin and means 'manifestation'. The date of this festival is 6 January. The Western Church recalls and celebrates the visit of the Magi (wise men) to the infant Jesus. Matthew's Gospel (2:1–12) tells us that they presented gifts: gold, frankincense and myrrh. This story is taken to represent the coming *to* Christ of the Gentile (non-Jewish) world, and the coming *of* Christ for all humanity. The Eastern Orthodox Churches focus on the baptism of Jesus at this time, and baptismal water is blessed.

▶ Lent

This is the period of 40 days immediately preceding Easter. The name probably has an Anglo-Saxon origin. It comes from a word meaning 'Spring', which refers to the lengthening days. Christians reflect on the 40 days which Jesus spent in the wilderness after his baptism. Lent is a solemn time, traditionally marked by fasting, when Christians consider the disciplines of their faith. Lent starts on **Ash Wednesday**, the day after **Shrove Tuesday** (from the old English verb 'shrive' – to obtain absolution for sins by confessing and doing penance). The latter is also known as 'Pancake Day', from the old custom of using up all the items of food which were forbidden in Lent. Lent is in fact 46 days – reduced to 40 because Sunday is always a 'mini Easter' and never a fasting day.

▶ Holy Week

At the end of Lent, a week is set aside for focusing on the approaching death of Christ and its meaning for the salvation of the world. In this week occurs **Maundy Thursday**, when the institution of Holy Communion is commemorated. 'Maundy' comes from the Latin phrase *mandatum novum* (new commandment) and refers to John 13 when Jesus washed his disciples' feet and added, 'A new commandment I give you … As I have loved you, so you must love one another.' **Good Friday** follows Maundy Thursday. This is the most solemn day of all, when Christians reflect on the cost of their redemption. All the prayers and devotions concentrate on the crucifixion of Jesus.

▶ Easter

This is *the* major festival of the Christian year, when Christians celebrate the resurrection of Jesus Christ from the dead after his crucifixion and burial. Every Sunday is a festival occasion because it is a 'little Easter' – the weekly celebration of the resurrection of Jesus Christ 'on the first day of the week'. On Easter Sunday, many churches include a joyful liturgical response:

> Alleluia! Christ is risen.
> He is risen indeed. Alleluia!

▶ Ascension Day

This celebrates the ascension of Jesus into heaven, where he 'sits at the right hand of the Father' and prays for the world. Central to this is the idea that Jesus took his, and everyone's, humanity into heaven. This festival marks the end of Jesus's post-resurrection appearances, which lasted for 40 days. For this reason it is celebrated 40 days after Easter Sunday, and falls on a Thursday.

► Pentecost

The name of this festival is taken directly from Judaism. The account of the bestowal of the Holy Spirit on the early church is given at the beginning of the Acts of the Apostles. Each year at Pentecost, 50 days after Easter, the Church recalls this event. Christians pray that, by his Holy Spirit, God will guide and strengthen the Church for its work and witness in the world. As with some other Christian festivals and dates, Pentecost has its roots in the Jewish tradition. Pentecost is the name given to a Jewish celebration of the first-fruits of the corn harvest, 50 days after the Passover. An alternative name for the Christian festival is *Whitsun*.

► Trinity Sunday

The theme of this day (one week after Pentecost) sums up all the observances in the Church's calendar from Advent to Pentecost. On Trinity Sunday, the Church is reminded of God's eternal nature – that he is Father, Son and Holy Spirit; three persons in one God.

► Trinity Sunday to Advent

During this period, sometimes referred to as 'Ordinary Time', many aspects of Christian life and witness are brought to the Church's attention. All these are based, in one way or another, on the life, death and resurrection of Jesus Christ and his continuing presence in the world.

► Saints' days

Throughout the year, particular saints are commemorated usually on what is believed to be the date of their birth or death. Some of these saints are New Testament figures but over the years others have been added, and even in the modern period the Roman Catholic Church continues to recognize individuals as saints; for example Pope John Paul II was canonized as a saint in 2014.

🔑 Key ideas

▶ Christian prayer is usually offered to God the Father through Jesus Christ, under the leading of the Holy Spirit.

▶ Prayer is not magic; it means seeking to align our wills with God's will.

▶ Prayer has many aspects – praise and adoration, thanksgiving, confession, petition, lament …

▶ Prayer can use the carefully crafted words of other people, making them our own as we say them; or prayer can be spontaneous and extemporary.

▶ Worship varies in mood, from deep solemnity to exuberant joy.

▶ The Christian year expresses this wide spectrum of emotions, such as the penitence of Ash Wednesday, the grief of Good Friday and the joy of Easter Sunday.

⛏ Dig deeper

P.F. Bradshaw, *The Search for the Origins of Christian Worship: Sources and methods for the study of early liturgy*, 2nd edn (London: SPCK, 2002).

J.F. White, *Introduction to Christian Worship*, 3rd edn (Nashville, TN: Abingdon, 2000).

R. Williams, *The Dwelling of the Light: Praying with icons of Christ* (Norwich: Canterbury, 2003).

Fact check

1 Christian prayer is 'Trinitarian'. This means:
   a every prayer is said three times
   b it is offered to God the Father, through Jesus Christ, under the leading of the Holy Spirit
   c it only works if there are at least three people present
   d prayer is offered three times a day

2 Advent is a time of:
   a feasting and celebration
   b preparation for Easter
   c a form of prayer
   d preparation for Christmas

3 Lent:
   a is a period of fasting and reflection
   b lasts for four days before Easter
   c is another name for Pentecost
   d is the period of forty days after Easter

4 Christians:
   a always kneel to pray
   b only stand to pray
   c adopt a variety of postures to pray
   d always pray sitting down

5 Trinity Sunday is:
   a the third Sunday after Easter
   b the Sunday after Pentecost
   c the third Sunday before Christmas
   d the beginning of Lent

6 Christian worship:
   a only takes place in church
   b is always a collective experience
   c can be an individual and/or a corporate experience
   d has to be formal and liturgical

7 Christian worship is:
  a the same all over the world
  b shaped by the culture in which it takes place
  c unchanged from the beginning of Christianity
  d always in English

8 Intercession:
  a is the prayer of concern for individual people, groups of people, causes and events
  b is another word for the Lord's Prayer
  c is a prayer said by a priest
  d means confession

9 Christian prayer is primarily about:
  a persuading God to give us things
  b aligning human action with God's purpose
  c changing God's mind
  d confession

10 Epiphany:
  a means 'manifestation'
  b tells the story of the shepherds' visit to the infant Jesus
  c is one part of the Easter celebrations of the Church
  d is another word for Christmas

Christian
spirituality

In this chapter you will learn about:

▶ *understandings of spirituality*
▶ *the development of Christian spirituality*
▶ *some contemporary developments.*

Spiritual or religious?

Spirituality has become an increasingly popular concept today, but the use of the word has changed over time and it can be somewhat vague and ill-defined! Let's consider some examples of this.

▶ It has become commonplace today for people, particularly in the West, to say 'I am not religious but I am spiritual'. Lying behind this is a belief that the two things are somehow opposed to each other: that a person is *either* religious *or* spiritual.

▶ The words 'religion' and 'religious' have become increasingly associated with the outward expression of faith – institutions, religious practice, the 'mechanics' of faith – while 'spiritual' is seen as the inward or motivational aspect of belief.

▶ Following on from this, spirituality is often seen as intensely personal and private whereas religion has to do with the collective and the public.

▶ It is often suggested that spirituality has to do with experience rather than theology or thinking. It is more about feelings and senses than thought.

▶ It is popular today to look at religion as something negative – a cause of war, oppression and fanaticism. Spirituality on the other hand is seen as positive, life-affirming and benign.

▶ Spirituality is also used today in a way which is unrelated to religion. It is often seen as distinct from the material. In this sense even those who would describe themselves as atheists or agnostics may well describe themselves as spiritual.

Added to all this there is a common misconception that Christianity is a religion with no spirituality! As we shall see in this chapter, this is very wide of the mark and Christianity has a long and rich tradition of spirituality. This chapter focuses on what spirituality has meant in the Christian faith and looks at some of the significant individuals and movements it has embraced.

Christian spirituality

Definitions can sometimes be helpful but often they run the risk of being artificial and constraining. Instead of coming up with a tidy definition it is more helpful to consider what lies at the heart of Christian spirituality, rather than trying to pin down its limits. At its heart Christian spirituality is based on Christian theology. As we have already seen, Christians believe:

▶ God is the creator and sustainer of all life

▶ God chooses to be revealed through the physical, material world, chiefly in human form in Jesus

▶ God seeks to save the world from sin and lost-ness, and calls humans into a new relationship of mutual love.

These together form the basis for Christian spirituality. The transformation of individuals and the whole world into 'the kingdom of God' is brought about through the nurturing of that relationship between God and human beings. Christian spirituality describes how this comes about. It embraces the thinking, praying, self-understanding, worshipping, humanity and practice of both the individual and the community of believers. Christian spirituality is about humans being 'in tune' with God.

> 'One afternoon I found myself chatting with a dozen or so students in a bar, none of whom had any religious affiliation, but most of whom had an interest in spirituality. As the discussion progressed, I asked them what they thought about Christian spirituality. 'Christian spirituality?' one of them mused. 'I don't think I've ever thought of putting those two words together.'
>
> D. Tomlinson, *Re-enchanting Christianity* (Canterbury Press, 2008), pp. 85–6.

The word itself – spirituality – comes from the Latin *spiritus*, but two other words, one from the Old Testament and the other from the New, carry a similar collection of meanings. *Ruah* in Hebrew and *pneuma* in Greek can be translated as 'breath', 'life' or 'soul' and are sometimes rendered as 'spirit'. They all convey the sense of an animating or motivating force in life.

In its early days Christianity was heavily influenced by Greek philosophical ideas, particularly those of Plato. He saw the world as a series of 'dualisms' – mind and body; idea and actual; body and soul. There are some echoes of this in Christian spiritual traditions. But Christianity also had a very strong Jewish heritage. Jewish thought is more pragmatic and 'concrete', less speculative or theoretical. The Jews did not develop a philosophical tradition in quite the same way as the Greeks. They talked instead about 'wisdom'. This wisdom tradition can be seen in some of the books of the Old Testament such as Proverbs, the Psalms or Job, which are meditations or reflections on God, life and human experience. Wisdom was practical guidance for living. It pondered the mystery of day-to-day life and how God was present in everything. It was based on a rather grand-sounding principle: *epistemological humility*. In simpler terms this means humans don't know everything! Only by being in tune with God can the mystery of life be experienced or lived fully.

Here we can see some of the foundations on which Christian spirituality is based. To know God goes beyond intellectual activity alone. To know oneself, or one's neighbour, to understand the earth, nature and life itself demand more than just academic answers. **Meditation** and **contemplation** in both the Jewish and Christian traditions take humans beyond 'head knowledge' into something richer. In meditation and contemplation the reasoning processes are stilled; the person praying gives attention to God through an act of love and self-offering. This attitude has been described as 'simple attention' and 'one-pointedness'. A parallel may be seen in the wonderment of a child when confronted by something new, lovely and fascinating. The child is completely absorbed, captivated, filled with delight. Contemplation, rooted in adoration, has something of this character.

Christian mystics down the centuries have done their best to write about it, but have freely admitted that it defies adequate description.

> 'So if you are to stand and not fall, never give up your firm intention: beat away at this cloud of unknowing between you and God with that sharp dart of longing love' (from *The Cloud of Unknowing*, an anonymous 14th-century mystical work).

'[Christian spirituality] is not mainly about experiences so much as experience. Experience is a matter of experiences and conceptual interpretation which are always interacting.'
R. Thompson and G. Williams, *Christian Spirituality* (SCM, 2008), p. 122.

CHRISTIAN SPIRITUALITY: SOME SNAPSHOTS IN TIME

The problem for anyone trying to give examples of Christian spirituality is the sheer volume of material: for every writer or movement chosen there are dozens which have to be rejected! Fortunately there are many books available which go into much more detail (see the end of the chapter for some suggestions), so here we confine ourselves to a series of snapshots.

▶ The New Testament and Patristic periods

The years after the crucifixion (probably *c*.AD 33) saw the writing of the New Testament (see Chapter 4). During this period many who had followed Jesus during his public ministry were still alive. The *Patristic* period (named after the early church 'fathers') is the term used to refer to the period after those first followers of Jesus had died. It acknowledges the huge amount of work done by early theologians in thinking through this new faith. Between them, the writers of the New Testament and the early church leaders produced a considerable volume of writing in the form of letters, liturgies, theological discourses, reflections and teaching manuals. These early writers rarely, if ever, use the term 'spirituality'. But from their work we can learn something of their understanding or practice.

Take the **Gospel according to John,** for example. It is sometimes described as a 'more spiritual' Gospel than the others, though this is misleading (and probably wrong!) What is often meant by this is that the writer of the fourth Gospel seems to 'play around' with historical events. He recasts them in new ways to create new insights into the life of Jesus. While John's Gospel can be read through as a fairly straightforward narrative, on closer inspection it becomes apparent that it has been constructed very thoughtfully. It contains patterns of ideas. It has interwoven themes and ideas. It tells stories familiar from the other Gospels but in a new way. It is as if the author is struggling to say something which is ultimately beyond time and human language. It is more a meditation on the Jesus 'event' than a historical narrative, though it does have deep roots in history.

Another example from the early church does not appear in the New Testament. *The Shepherd of Hermas* was probably written sometime in the second century. It was not universally popular among Christians – some thought it was heretical, while others saw it as inspired and inspirational. It contains a series of visions received by a former slave, 'Hermas', who was possibly the brother of the leader of the church in Rome at the time. These are followed by parables and 'mandates' giving instruction about Christian living.

It gives us some insight into the spirituality of the early church as well as the issues which dominated at the time. There are five visions, which are meditations on the state of the church. Even in those early days it was seen by some leading Christians to be weak and failing in its witness. (Turn to the first three chapters of the book of Revelation, the last book in the Bible, for clear examples of this.) The church is represented in the first vision as an old woman, weakened and tired by the sins of the church. As the church repents and reforms in each subsequent vision the woman becomes younger, until in the final one she is a young and beautiful bride. The imagery owes much to similar ideas contained in the New Testament: the idea of the church as 'the Bride of Christ' and Jesus as 'the Good Shepherd' are two obvious examples. *The Shepherd* gives us an insight into the 'spiritual exercises' of some in the early church.

▶ **After Constantine**

The Emperor Constantine's conversion early in the fourth century marked a watershed for Christianity. From being an underground, often persecuted minority faith, it became the single legalized faith of the Roman Empire. In spite of one of Constantine's successors, Julian (Emperor AD 361–363), trying to reinstate the old pagan religions of Rome, the foundations of Christianity as a world faith were laid by this change. It came at a price, however, and this change provides an important backdrop to the spirituality of the church in the years that followed. It became much easier to be a Christian in that the danger of persecution, even death, was removed. But being easier made it lose focus. The church became aligned with the state. It grew rich and powerful. And some feared it had lost sight of the radical simplicity of its founder.

This may account for the beginnings of **monasticism** which can be traced to this time. Some Christians retreated into lonely places to escape what they saw as the distractions of prosperous, indulgent city life. They sought to live a solitary life of prayer and contemplation (*hermits* or *eremitic* monks – *eremos* means 'desert or uninhabited place'). Others chose to live together in small settlements outside the mainstream towns and villages (cenobites). 'Cenobitic' comes from the Greek words *koinos* ('common or shared') and *bios* ('life'). Down the years, monks, nuns and friars have played a considerable role in Christian spirituality. Christians did not invent monasticism. The Jewish Essenes lived in communities very much like monasteries (the Qumran community may be an example of this) so the idea was not new.

Anthony of Egypt lived to an remarkable old age (from AD 251–356). He is sometimes referred to as 'the father of all monks' because of his role in the history of monasticism. There were others before him, but his biography by Athanasius spread the word of his life of holiness and devotion to God. It helped popularize the idea of monasticism. Anthony was born before Constantine issued the Edict of Milan (AD 313) which removed all penalties for following the Christian faith, in effect legalizing Christianity. He therefore witnessed enormous changes in the fortunes of Christianity during his own lifetime.

At roughly the same time as Anthony, another Christian, **Pachomius** (AD 292–348), likewise decided to retreat into the desert and become a hermit. His holiness and wisdom became well-known and people went out into the desert to seek his guidance and advice. Though he lived alone, other hermits settled nearby. In time they decided to form a community and Pachomius devised a set of rules to govern their community. He is therefore considered to be the founder of cenobitic monasticism.

Others followed. St Augustine, a little later than Anthony and Pachomius, wrote a 'rule of life' for a monastic community. Interestingly, his early experiments in a community life dedicated to prayer and reflection included his brother, his mother and his son! Perhaps the most famous – certainly the most enduring – is **Benedict of Nursia** (*c.*AD 480–543) who lived in central Italy. His Benedictine Rule is still in use today in monasteries around the world. As a result of the work of these pioneers, monasteries became centres of prayer, contemplation and learning.

Spotlight

A hunter in the desert saw Abba Anthony enjoying himself with the brethren and was shocked. Wanting to show him that it was necessary sometimes to meet the needs of the brethren the old man said to him, 'Put an arrow in your bow and shoot it.' So he did. The old man said, 'Shoot another', and he did so. Then the old man said, 'Shoot yet again', and the hunter replied, 'If I bend my bow so much I will break it.' Then the old man said 'It is the same with the work of God. If we stretch the brethren beyond measure they will soon break. Sometimes it is necessary to come down and meet their needs.' When he heard these words the hunter was pierced by compunction and, greatly edified by the old man, he went away. As for the brethren they went home strengthened.

© Fr Pius Sammut, Order of Discalced Carmelites

▶ **Medieval examples**

The medieval period is considered by some to be a golden age of Christian spirituality. **Francis of Assisi**'s spirituality was driven by a desire to preach a gospel of simplicity and oneness with nature. He saw the Church as having acquired such wealth and status that it had become cluttered and blind. Along with his close friend **Clare**, who founded a community of nuns (the 'Poor Clares'), Francis sought ways to make the gospel speak more clearly to ordinary people. He emphasized that the gospel demanded practical love in action above all else. A well-known saying, often attributed to him, is 'Preach the Gospel at all times. Use words if necessary.' Franciscan spirituality has enjoyed something of a revival in recent years, in part at least because of its appeal to an environmentalist agenda.

Spotlight

It is possible we can attribute to St Francis the invention of the crib scene popular at Christmas. The story goes that he re-created a 'living' image of the birth of Jesus in the stable using a real stable, people and animals near Greccio (Italy) to tell the story of the birth of Jesus.

Probably the best-known female mystic of this period is **Julian of Norwich** (1342–1417). Mother Julian (a woman who took her name from St Julian's church, where she had her cell) was an *anchorite* – a person who lived a solitary life, but close to people rather than out in the wilderness. Many lived in walled-in enclosures built into the walls of a church and were known for their piety, visions and wisdom. Perhaps Julian's most famous vision was the walnut. Seeing such a small, fragile object, she reflected on how vulnerable the world seemed. But it came to her in a vision that all is secure because 'everything is held in being by the love of God'. Her visions (which she called 'shewings') inspired some of the poetry of the 20th-century poet T.S. Eliot. In his poem 'Little Gidding V', in 'Four Quartets', he quotes one of Julian's most famous lines:

> 'And all shall be well and
> All manner of thing shall be well'

▶ The Reformation and after

The Protestant reformers are not generally known for their mystical writing, though it would be wrong to think they had no spirituality. **Martin Luther** (1483–1546) was, after all, an Augustinian monk. He spent much of his time engaged in theological dispute, but he did take time to write a book on prayer for his barber! *A Simple Way to Pray* recommends using the Bible, read slowly and meditatively, to inform devotional prayer.

Three giants of spirituality in the Catholic tradition from this period are **Ignatius Loyola** (*c.*1491–1556) who founded the Jesuit order (the Society of Jesus), **John of the Cross** (1542–91), a member of the Carmelite Order, and **Teresa of Avila** (1515–82). Ignatius's 'spiritual exercises' encourage imaginatively entering into biblical stories or scenes using the senses to bring them to life. John of the Cross wrote eloquently about some of the struggles the believer often encounters with faith. His 'Dark night of the soul' is a reflective poem on the journey of faith – which is not all 'sweetness and light', but involves mental, emotional and spiritual battles. Teresa's mystical journey is described in her *The Interior Castle* in which she visits in her imagination seven mansions, each one a little nearer to God. At the heart of her writing is the paradox that the spiritual journey is elegantly simple and profoundly difficult – both at the same time.

Born about 80 years after the death of Luther, **George Fox** (1624–91) followed in the reformers' footsteps in rejecting a lot of what the established Church taught and stood for. He believed in the idea that the 'divine spark' of God resided in everyone. There was no need for any intermediary – a priest or a minister – to lead people to God. The route was open to all. Fox founded the Quaker movement (The Society of Friends), which has no priests or ministers, no liturgy and no sacraments. Based on that belief of the 'divine spark' in everyone, the Quakers are renowned for their pacifism.

▶ Spirituality in the 18th and 19th centuries

'Holiness' is a key concept in Christianity. It is not about some kind of moral superiority ('holier than thou') but about being set apart for a special purpose. God is thought to be holy, but contained in that idea is the notion of purity, which is where morality comes in. Christians seek to be holy – to be pure; free from sin – as representatives (and representations) of God to the world. These ideas had been around a long time but the 18th and 19th centuries saw the development of a new emphasis on this called **Pietism**. Pietism lay behind the Puritan movement and was also strongly present in Lutheranism. It called for high moral standards in private and public life.

A Protestant movement called the Moravians originated in what today is called the Czech Republic. They too were deeply pietistic. And they were very influential in the conversion of **John Wesley** (1703–91). Wesley's spirituality was of a deeply practical kind, driving his social and political life. He sought to put into practice all the injunctions he found in the New Testament: to visit the sick, care for the orphan and widow and minster to the prisoners in their cells. The last letter he wrote before his death was to the MP William Wilberforce (1759–1833), in which he urged Wilberforce to 'Go on in the name of God and in the power of his might' to abolish 'that execrable villainy' which was slavery. Wesley organized his life very methodically (hence 'Methodism' – which started out as a nickname poking fun at him and his followers) in order to have the maximum amount of time for these activities. And it was all driven by his lengthy times of prayer and Bible study. He was joined in all this by his brother Charles, the great hymn writer. Methodist spirituality was shaped by prayer, Bible study – and singing.

▶ The modern era

Christian spirituality today is to some extent about the rediscovery of many of the classics mentioned above. One we have not looked at is the recent revival of interest in all things **Celtic**. This has gone beyond the religious. Interest in Celtic art, Celtic music and Celtic dance has spawned a whole industry, though it has to be said that some of this is of somewhat doubtful authenticity! Nonetheless, there are great riches in Celtic prayer and art to resource the modern Christian's spiritual quest. Religious communities such as the **Iona Community** and the **Northumbria Community** draw their inspiration from some of the great Celtic saints.

> 'The challenge to Christian spirituality is to show how its vision of God may contribute powerfully to the desire to find communion with others, express compassion for others and transform the world.'
>
> P. Sheldrake, *Spirituality and Theology* (Darton, Longman and Todd, 1998), p. 202.

PILGRIMAGE

One last aspect of spirituality to mention is **pilgrimage**. The idea of 'sacred journeys' is probably almost as old as humanity itself. And it is present in most of the world's great religions. A pilgrimage can be long or short, but it is always an intentional journey. The physical act of walking is linked to meditation and reflection. The point of the journey is to encounter God both on the journey and at the destination. Christian pilgrimage may have started with Helen, the mother of the Roman Emperor Constantine, as she sought to discover the sacred sites relating to Jesus. Over the course of Christian history a number of pilgrim routes developed. Jerusalem and Rome were popular destinations for early pilgrims. Later, Santiago de Compostela in north-west Spain and Canterbury in England attracted thousands of pilgrims in the Middle Ages. More recently, Lourdes in France has become a major pilgrim destination.

Spotlight

In 1986, 2,500 pilgrims completed the 500-mile trek from St Jean Pied de Port in France to Santiago in Spain – the most popular route for the *Camino de Santiago*. Figures for 2014 record 240,000 doing the journey – almost a hundred times as many. These are not all Christians, and not all are walking it as a pilgrimage. But it does demonstrate something of the spiritual quest which, contrary to secularization predictions, seems alive and well in the 21st century.

Key ideas

▶ Christianity has a long and rich tradition of spirituality.

▶ Christian spirituality is about the transformation of individuals and the whole world into 'the kingdom of God' brought about through the nurturing of the relationship between God and human beings.

▶ Spirituality and religion are not opposites or in competition.

▶ The word 'spirituality' comes from the Latin *spiritus* which conveys the sense of an animating or motivating force in life.

▶ *Ruah* in Hebrew and *pneuma* in Greek can be translated as 'breath', 'life' or 'soul' and are sometimes rendered as 'spirit'.

Dig deeper

A.G. Holder (ed.) *The Blackwell Companion to Christian Spirituality* (Oxford: Blackwell, 2005).

E. Howells and P. Tyler, *Sources of Transformation: Revitalizing Christian spirituality* (London: Continuum, 2010).

P. Sheldrake, *A Brief History of Spirituality* (Malden, MS; Oxford: Blackwell, 2007).

Fact check

1 Christian spirituality is:
   a reserved for monks, nuns and especially holy people
   b a modern invention
   c an ancient, and continuing, practice within the Christian tradition
   d another word for meditation

2 The 'Father of Christian monasticism' is commonly thought to be
   a St John
   b St Paul
   c Constantine
   d St Anthony of Egypt

3 Christian spirituality is based on the belief that:
   a only really holy people can be Christians
   b to know God goes beyond intellectual activity alone
   c God is impressed by long prayers
   d Christians need to memorize the whole Bible

4 'Holiness' means:
   a a kind of moral superiority
   b 'holier than thou'
   c set apart for a special purpose
   d perfection

5 Cenobitic monks differ from eremitic monks because:
   a they follow a different rule
   b they live in community rather than alone
   c they wear different habits (robes)
   d they follow the Celtic rather than the Roman tradition

6 Julian of Norwich was:
   a Bishop of Norwich
   b an anchorite
   c the founder of English monasticism
   d a Benedictine monk

7 The Iona Community and the Northumbria Community are examples of:
   a Roman monasticism
   b the Orthodox tradition
   c Benedictine monasticism
   d Celtic spirituality

8 St Francis of Assisi's spirituality was driven by a desire to:
   a preach a gospel of simplicity and oneness with nature
   b increase the church's wealth and status
   c build more churches
   d save endangered species

9 Which of these *least* captures what pilgrimage is primarily about?
   a A sacred journey
   b A form of meditation
   c A journey of discovery
   d A sign of spiritual superiority

10 Pietism called for:
   a long prayer meetings
   b lots of charitable giving
   c high moral standards in private and public life
   d a lot of hymn singing

Part 3:

The Christian Church

Saints, martyrs, sins and virtues

In this chapter you will learn about:

▶ *martyrs – ancient and modern*
▶ *the significance of Mary and other saints*
▶ *deadly sins and glorious virtues.*

In his book *Why Religions Matter*, John Bowker talks about the paradox of religions. On the one hand they can be forces for good – inspiring, creative, benevolent. On the other hand they can provoke fear, sectarianism and even violence. In the early days of Christianity the new faith was seen as a threat to both traditional Judaism and the Roman establishment. Before his terrible death by crucifixion, Jesus warned his followers that some of them would die in his service. His grim prophecy was grimly fulfilled.

But persecution was not confined to those early days of the Church. Even after Christianity became a 'legal' religion, thousands of men, women and children down the centuries have given their lives because of their allegiance to Jesus Christ. It continues to the present day. According to the US Centre for the Study of Global Christianity, 100,000 Christians died in 2014 because of their faith. Such people have been honoured by the Christian church as saints and martyrs. They are held up as examples of courage and faithfulness in the face of great trial. And, of course, adherents of other faiths have shared in this carnage and suffered for their beliefs.

Martyrs

The Greek word for 'martyr' simply means 'witness'; it soon came to be associated with 'witness unto death'. The first recorded Christian martyr was Stephen, a deacon of the church in Jerusalem. A Jew who was well-versed in the Scriptures (meaning at that time the Hebrew scriptures or, as Christians came to call it, the Old Testament), Stephen reflected on the significance of Jesus. He came to realize that by fulfilling the old prophecies, Jesus had made redundant some of the key institutions of the Jewish nation. Stephen's outspoken views were seen as an attack upon the Law and the Temple and he was stoned to death.

As Stephen died he saw Jesus, 'the Son of Man', standing to receive him into heaven (Acts 7:56). Like his Master, Stephen prayed that God would forgive his executioners. Shortly after this, James, the brother of the apostle John and an important leader in the Jerusalem church, was beheaded by King Herod. The blood had started to flow. It was that blood which became, as Tertullian (*c.*AD 160–220) put it, 'the seed of the Church'.

In AD 64 there was a great fire which destroyed large parts of the city of Rome. The Roman Emperor Nero (AD 37–68) falsely accused Christians of starting the fires. It was the perfect excuse to execute hundreds of these despised Christians. Many wild rumours circulated about this new sect. For example, the Christians were accused of cannibalism, because they ate the body of Christ! They were sometimes called atheists, because they did not believe in the Roman gods. And while they honoured the Emperor (Romans 13), Jesus – not the Emperor – was their Lord. All this was very convenient for a leader looking for a scapegoat. Paul and Peter were almost certainly martyred under Nero in the mid-60s. Many other believers died too, some as human torches.

After that, several Roman emperors persecuted Christians, who – with captives, slaves and other despised minorities – provided sport for the masses in arenas in various cities throughout the Roman Empire. There are several passages in the New Testament which illustrate how the early church leaders encouraged Christians to cope with persecution. They were exhorted to live humble, simple lives – for love and integrity were their only weapons. In the long term, such weapons proved to be extremely powerful and a growing number came to embrace Christianity, including – as we've already seen – the Roman Emperor Constantine (d. AD 337).

A problem arose concerning the desire for martyrdom. Some members of the Church went looking for martyrdom. They coveted 'the martyr's crown', believing it would speed up their arrival in heaven. This attitude was always opposed by the Church at large. Martyrdom might be inflicted; it was not to be sought.

> 'Dear friends, do not be surprised at the painful trial you
> are suffering, as though something strange were happening
> to you. But rejoice that you participate in the sufferings
> of Christ, so that you may be overjoyed when his glory is
> revealed' (1 Peter 4:12, 13).

Around AD 156 an elderly bishop, Polycarp of Smyrna, was placed in a Roman arena. He was challenged to deny Jesus Christ and embrace the pagan gods. He declared, 'For 86 years I have been his servant and he has never done me any wrong. How then can I blaspheme my King who saved me?' He was burned to death.

The public veneration of Christian martyrs has been practised since the second century; Bishop Polycarp is the first clear example of such veneration. The practice developed in local communities, usually around the martyr's tomb. It was based on the long-standing Jewish practice of venerating the memory of patriarchs, prophets and martyrs by building monuments over the places where their bones lay. An additional factor was the belief that Christian martyrs were in heaven, and therefore able to pray for those who invoked their help.

The veneration of such martyrs soon involved 'holy relics'. The bones of Polycarp, for example, were considered 'more precious than jewels of great price'. Tombs contained bones; and bones were visible – and portable. The cult of any individual could be moved from one place to another. Sometimes (later in the Christian story, after it had been legalized as a faith) they were carried into battle to give added power to the cause.

The relics of a saint were regarded as a source of healing and an agent which gave protection to the church which possessed them. Bones, commerce, superstition and local prestige made a powerful, and sometimes corrupting, combination. But reverence for saints and martyrs was often positive. No doubt many believers were encouraged in their discipleship of Christ by pondering the deeds of those who had gone before. But concern about malpractice emerged early on. Their popularity led to some fraudulent entrepreneurs 'peddling' fakes to make a living. In the fourth century, Augustine of Hippo stressed the immense difference between devotion directed to martyrs and worship offered to God. He wrote, 'We build temples to our martyrs, not like temples for the gods, but as tombs of mortal men, whose spirits live with God.'

One famous martyr, St Lawrence, was said to have been put to death in AD 258 during the reign of the Emperor Valerian. He was asked to present the riches of the church to a Roman official – and he called forward the poor, the sick, the orphans and the widows. 'These poor persons are the treasure of the church', he said. The official was so angry he ordered Lawrence to be roasted alive on a grid-iron. The story goes that Lawrence's dying words were 'Turn me over! I'm done on that side'! This may illustrate how many stories were 'embroidered' over time but there is no doubting the gruesome reality of martyrdom which lies behind them – or the courage of the martyrs.

Items other than bones were – and are – venerated. Perhaps the most famous in today's world is the Turin Shroud. This was believed to be the cloth which covered the dead body of Jesus and carries an imprint of a face. Was it the actual cloth? Is it the face of Christ? Almost certainly not in both cases, but it remains an intriguing and controversial enigma. Shrines continue to attract thousands, e.g. the shrine of St James in Santiago de Compostella, north-west Spain or Lourdes in south-west France. Britain has its share of martyrs and saints. Tombs are found in many British cathedrals. The most famous English martyr is St Thomas Becket – murdered in Canterbury Cathedral in 1170.

LATER MARTYRS: SOME EXAMPLES

Sadly, not all persecution came from outside the Church and not all Christians were martyred by those outside the faith. The 16th century saw an enormous upheaval in Europe – religious, social and political. Medieval unity, already cracking, was split apart and the Church was divided. Controversy was often bitter and it produced martyrs on both sides. Among Protestants who died were Thomas Cranmer and William Tyndale, both of whom helped to shape the English language. Many devout Catholics were equally courageous during those turbulent years. These included people like Edmund Campion and Margaret Clitherow.

▶ Thomas Cranmer (1489–1556)

Cranmer was a quiet, scholarly man and a liturgical genius who wrote the *Book of Common Prayer* (slightly amended in its final version in 1662). He was elevated to Archbishop of Canterbury by Henry VIII and lived during three turbulent reigns. He piloted the Reformation throughout the reign of the young Edward VI but was denounced as a heretic under the Catholic Queen Mary. Cranmer hesitated but eventually signed a recantation – an action which did not save him. As he was burning at the stake, he thrust the hand that had signed the recantation into the flames so that it might be the first part of his body to be burned.

▶ William Tyndale (1494–1536)

Tyndale was appalled at the ignorance of many clergy and set himself the task of making the Bible available to ordinary people. The English Bible had been banned since 1408, but Tyndale translated Hebrew (Old Testament) and Greek (New Testament) texts into English. Though banned, his translation had enormous influence upon the King James or 'Authorized' Version (1611), which became the standard English Bible for more than 300 years.

He completed the New Testament and substantial sections of the Old Testament before he was betrayed and arrested near Brussels in 1535. English church leaders feared his Protestant ideas and a year later he was strangled and burned at the stake. Tyndale died with a prayer on his lips: 'Lord, open the King of England's eyes.' His prayer was answered. In 1538, Henry VIII – for reasons rather different from Tyndale's – ordered that an English Bible should be placed in every parish church.

▶ Edmund Campion (1540–81)

Campion was a Catholic priest (a Jesuit) who worked hard in Protestant Britain to sustain the faith of his fellow Catholics. He was betrayed, tortured and condemned to death. When sentence was declared he sang the *Te Deum* ('We praise thee, O God'). Edmund was visited in his cell by the man who betrayed him. His own life was in danger and he needed

Father Edmund's help. Campion wrote a letter of introduction to a nobleman in Germany. His betrayer escaped; Edmund Campion was dragged through the streets to Tyburn where he was hanged and quartered.

▶ Margaret Clitherow (1556–86)

Margaret, a butcher's wife, was described by her contemporaries as good-looking, witty, merry and caring. She was a devout Catholic who lived in the ancient city of York. Accused of harbouring priests, she was brought to trial. Margaret refused to defend herself in court because in this way she could save her children from being forced to testify against her. She was crushed to death under immense weights. Her hand – a holy relic – is held in the Bar Convent just outside the city walls of York. Edmund Campion and Margaret Clitherow were canonized by the Roman Catholic Church in 1960.

Saints

It was natural that stories of heroic deeds, courageous deaths and godly lives should be treasured and passed on. Indeed, this process had already begun in the New Testament (Hebrews 11, 12). From this grew a desire to honour such men and women with official recognition – rather as we award medals today. In this wish we find the seeds of 'canonization' by which certain individuals are honoured with the official title 'Saint'.

The choice of that particular word was confusing, for it already had a different, though related, meaning. Several of the New Testament letters are addressed to 'the saints', a term which means 'dedicated to God for holy living'. It is a common New Testament term for all believers, much as we use the word 'Christian' today. To pick out a few particularly distinguished believers as 'saints' led to ambiguity.

The popular gospel song 'O when the saints go marching in' gives the word its biblical meaning. 'I wanna be in that number', runs the lyric. This is not a desire to be a special 'super Christian'; rather it expresses a devout wish to be included in the festival of heaven with all of God's people.

One commentator put it this way: 'the Church canonizes a few believers; the Bible canonizes all'.

The New Testament understanding is caught in the Christian festival entitled All Saints' Day (1 November). In the modern Church this is often taken as a celebration of all Christian lives – well-known and unknown, ancient and modern. This great festival enshrines another important emphasis – the communion of Saints. This belief unites all believers – past, present and future – in the family of God.

MARY, THE MOTHER OF JESUS

A special place is accorded to Mary, the Mother of Jesus, by all Christians but especially by Roman Catholics. Great devotion has been offered to her, countless statues made in her honour and thousands of paintings perpetuate her memory. The Annunciation, the occasion when the angel Gabriel announced to Mary that she would bear a son (Luke 1:26–38), is a scene depicted on countless canvases, some of them very famous.

At some periods in history (and in some places today) her prayers have been thought to be so effective that she has been called the 'lawyer of sinners'. Other titles given to Mary over the centuries are 'Mother of God', 'God-bearer' (*Theotokos*), 'Queen of Heaven', 'Mother of Humanity', 'Mother of Angels', even 'Co-redeemer' with Christ. It should be added that popular titles and devotion sometimes go further than official teaching, requiring this correction:

> 'This very special devotion [to Mary] … differs essentially from the adoration which is given to the incarnate Word and equally to the Father and the Holy Spirit' (CCC).

Other beliefs that have developed over the centuries are the Immaculate Conception of Mary (not to be confused with the virginal conception of Jesus – more commonly known as the Virgin Birth), her perpetual virginity and her Assumption (body and soul) into heaven. The last named was not officially promulgated until 1950, by Pope Pius XII. A papal Bull (official statement) from the Vatican in 1854 defined 'Immaculate Conception' as the belief that 'From the first moment of her conception the Blessed Virgin Mary was ... kept free from all stain of original sin'.

These are official doctrines within the Roman Catholic Church, but many Protestants object on three grounds. First, they argue that there is no historical evidence for these views. Second, they contend that these beliefs do a disservice to Mary, who is special enough without these false elaborations (as they regard them). Third, Protestants are concerned that these doctrines draw attention away from Jesus, who is the only and unique Saviour. All Christians agree that what is truly inspiring about Mary is:

▶ her humility and reluctance to believe that she could be honoured by the visit of an angel and the birth of such a special child

▶ her obedience and willingness to serve God (Luke 1:38)

▶ her grasp of God's priorities – his 'bias to the poor'. In the Magnificat (Luke 1:46), Mary declares, 'he has scattered those who are proud ... but has lifted up the humble'

▶ her loyalty to Jesus, seen not only at the wedding in Cana (John 2:5) but in her presence at his death. We learn that to be chosen by God brings sorrow and pain, as well as joy and privilege.

The *Oxford Dictionary of Saints* gives this balanced assessment:

> 'In both East and West Mary is accounted pre-eminent among all the saints. The unique privilege of being the mother of one who was, according to Christian belief, both God and Man is at the heart of the special honour paid to Mary, described by Aquinas as 'hyperdulia', i.e. a veneration which exceeds that paid to other saints, but is at the same time infinitely below the adoration (*latria*) due to God alone, which it would be blasphemous to attribute to any creature.'

PRAYING AND THE SAINTS
The Christian centuries have seen many faithful lives and heroic deaths; it is challenging and inspiring for modern Christians to reflect upon these. For this reason, the Christian calendar

commemorates individual saints on particular days. The first disciples of Jesus are given special honour, but many others are included too.

Some ancient saints have a dubious background. St Olave was not a godly woman but a fierce Norse king! St George, patron saint of England (also of Istanbul and the Italian cavalry!), fares slightly better. George, probably a soldier, almost certainly died as a martyr around AD 303. But little else is known of him and the story of the dragon is a late arrival on the scene. Alas, St Valentine's route to fame is also shrouded in uncertainty.

One controversial question is whether Christians should pray through – and even to – the saints. Some Christians do, feeling their near presence. They point out that it is natural to pray with living Christians so why not ask saints of old, who lived holy lives, who died in the faith of Christ, and who are in heaven? Others believe that there is a danger in praying through, or to, the saints, who were sinners like us. In their view, this obscures the uniqueness of Jesus, who prays for everyone (Romans 8:34; Hebrews 7:25) and through whom – and to whom – Christians pray.

MODERN SAINTS

The practice of canonization – the declaration by the Pope that the Church shall recognize an individual as an official saint – continues within the Roman Catholic Church. The process for declaring 'saints' also operates within the Eastern Orthodox Churches but it is a less formal procedure. In the Roman Catholic Church the process is often long and strict criteria are applied by the Vatican. Canonization is preceded by 'beatification', the means by which a person receives the title 'Blessed'. The Pope permits the person to be venerated, though not all who are honoured in this way go on to be canonized.

Mother Teresa of Calcutta was beatified in 2003 by Pope John Paul II and canonized by Pope Francis in 2016. Some opposed her beatification when letters in which she expressed the doubts she experienced about her faith surfaced in 2007. Her defenders argued that these letters instead proved the genuineness of her faith, which was tested so rigorously. They argued that she continued to follow Christ in a way which inspired millions despite being plunged into 'the dark night of the soul' – experienced by many true saints throughout the centuries.

> 'For many people the saints serve as direct intercessors between them and God but it is arguable that, even for those without strong religious beliefs, they form part of an unconscious cultural tradition that is deeply embedded in the collective psyche.'
>
> G. Morgan, *Saints* (Pocket Essentials, 2008), p. 9.

There are a number of modern examples. The Polish Roman Catholic Franciscan priest Maximilian Kolbe was arrested by the Nazis during the Second World War. In the infamous concentration camp of Auschwitz, his dignity and faith sustained many of his fellow sufferers. After an attempted escape, several prisoners were condemned to death by starvation. One victim, a sergeant called Francis Gajowniczek, was very distressed. He had a wife and children, so Maximilian volunteered to change places. The guards agreed to this grisly act of barter. The married man was spared; the rest were locked away in Cell 18 without food. Two weeks later all were dead except four men. Only Maximilian was fully conscious, and on 14 August 1941 he was given phenol poison. He was 47. On 14 August 1982 Maximilian was declared an official saint by the Polish Pope John Paul II. This was a moving occasion, attended by Francis Gajowniczek, the man whom Father Kolbe had saved.

Particular political regimes in the modern era have been persecutors of Christianity. Nazi Germany and the Soviet Union in the 20th century are notable examples, along with China. Relatively few of the martyrs under those regimes, or the rest of the estimated 70 million, have been formally canonized.

A notable death from another continent was that of the Roman Catholic Archbishop Oscar Romero of El Salvador. He sided with the poor and denounced the abuses of a state which was locked in a struggle against Marxist guerrillas. As he celebrated Mass in March 1980, he was shot through the heart.

A few years before this, in Uganda, the Anglican Archbishop Janani Luwum had been assassinated for speaking out against the atrocities perpetrated by Idi Amin in the 1970s. Uganda has a distinguished place in the history of martyrdom. In 1885 a tribal leader named Mwanga waged war against Christianity. One day, 19 men (all under 25 years old) were asked if they wished to remain Christians. Following their reply, 'Until death', they were wrapped in reed mats and burned alive. More Ugandan deaths were to follow – both Roman Catholic and Protestant. In the 20th century, Stephen Neill, a well-travelled Anglican scholar-bishop, found their memorial site outside Kampala to be the most moving place on earth. The bishop of the diocese of Uganda commented to him, 'I think the Baganda [the local people] would be ready to die for Christ today; it is living for him that they find difficult'. These Ugandan martyrs were formally canonized in 1964.

Pope John Paul II, the first-ever Polish pope, became Archbishop of Krakow when most in Eastern Europe lived under Soviet authority. His outspoken championing of political freedom gained him enormous popularity among Christians and beyond. He was beatified in 2011 and canonized in 2014.

Whatever their views on the formal canonization of saints, in all churches the memory of martyrs and other distinguished believers is kept alive, as a challenge and inspiration. Indeed, some Christians are 'canonized' unofficially by the world at large. Dr Martin Luther King, Jr (a Baptist pastor) is one example. Some churches occasionally authorize new liturgical calendars, with additional names to be remembered on particular days. The west front of Westminster Abbey, London, carries a memorial, in stone carvings, to 40 modern martyrs.

Spotlight

The practice of 'canonization' continues within the Roman Catholic Church. After research into the prospective saint's life and a period of 'beatification', the Pope declares that the individual shall be recognized as an official saint. The 20th-century Pope John Paul II created more saints than any other pope before him.

Sins and virtues

'Holiness' is what makes a saint. So when we use the word 'saint' in its biblical sense we see that holiness should characterize every Christian. Holiness means 'set apart for God'. It involves avoidance of sin, victory over temptation and the cultivation of Christian virtues.

SEVEN DEADLY SINS?

The centuries have seen the development of the popular notion of seven deadly sins, sometimes referred to as 'cardinal' sins: greed, envy, gluttony, sloth, anger, lust, pride. The Bible does not limit the number of sins to seven, but it certainly speaks of sin's 'deadliness'. 'For the wages of sin is death, but the gift of God is eternal life' (Romans 6:23). Sin is serious. At root, it is hostility or indifference towards God, his truth and his standards, which results in alienation. It is so serious that Jesus uses the imagery of being enslaved to it: locked into it and unable to break free from it (John 8:34). This is only broken by the death of Christ. Following this release from sin, the Spirit of Christ begins the work of 'sanctification', helping a person towards wholeness – even though progress is not always straightforward.

The Cathedral of Notre Dame in Paris displayed the following pithy sentence: 'Sin is a refusal to grow bigger'. This captures another important truth. Sin lowers horizons and moral and spiritual ambitions. Sin is about withholding or rationing love and acting out of self-interest. Sin is settling for second best and being small-minded. Interestingly, many sins are debasements of perfectly good and wholesome desires. Gluttony is a corruption of delight in good food: sloth an indulgent form of rest and sleep; greed is letting a desire for enough (of anything) getting out of hand. Ultimately, these things seriously diminish us as human beings.

Spotlight

'The only way to get rid of temptation is to yield to it ... I can resist everything except temptation.' So said Oscar Wilde. Does this represent defeatism or a challenge?

Salvation involves being set free to be fully human. Jesus Christ points to a world in need; and he calls his followers to love and serve it in his name and with his strength. 'The glory of God is a human being fully alive' (Irenaeus: c.AD 130–200).

The New Testament call to repentance is linked to a sense of guilt – and feeling guilty is often thought to be unhealthy. On the other hand, the modern concept of restorative justice is built on the notion that acknowledging guilt is the first step to rebuilding good relationships and a new life. Vague, unfocused feelings of guilt are indeed unhealthy and unhelpful, but guilt is an important emotion with a practical purpose. People who live entirely without it are called 'psychopaths'.

Christianity is not really interested in sin; it is far more interested in salvation and liberation. This is expressed cogently by Dr Giles Fraser:

> 'St Paul runs sin and death together. We are saved from sin/death, because sin is a form of death. Real sin – rather than the watered-down, overly-sexualized version we too often employ as a substitute – is cold, and hollow, and meaningless. Hence it is death. Furthermore, real sin is not a terribly religious thing. One does not have to be a believer to feel threatened by the deathly chill of human self-absorption.'

SEVEN GODLY VIRTUES?

Case study

'Virtue' in Greek carried the idea of excellence. To be virtuous was to use all your skill, power, energy, bravery to achieve something worthwhile. It meant working to your full potential. Over time it acquired the meaning of moral excellence with which we are familiar today.

As a term it has enjoyed a revival of interest in the field of ethics. So it is debated by philosophers – both Christian and non-Christian. Virtue ethics argues that good moral behaviour is not about following a set of moral 'rules' or making moral choices based on outcomes. Good moral choices depend on the moral character or quality of the individual making those choices.

For centuries, in the Christian West, good character was that based on Christian discipleship. It was assumed that a 'good person' was a 'good Christian'. The New Testament is full of teaching about good character based on Christ-like qualities (e.g. Ephesians 5:1–2 or Philippians 2:1–11).

In today's more pluralist society, virtue has come back into prominence along with the idea of the common good. Both ideas have a long history going back to ancient Greek and Indian cultures. Their re-emergence seems to be in part a reaction against the individualism of contemporary Western society which is blamed for a rise in a selfish, self-seeking culture.

Consider what 'virtue' means today. How might one behave virtuously? To what extent does there have to be a common understanding of what is virtuous? Does it all sound strange – or plain boring?

Long before Christianity, Aristotle and Plato described four 'virtues': temperance, wisdom, justice and courage. Early Christians picked up on these and added to them three more drawn from St Paul's first letter to the Corinthians. In it he speaks of three marks of holiness – of sanctity or 'sainthood': faith, hope and love. Added together this made for a kind of 'balance' of seven virtues to counter the seven deadly sins. St Paul's three virtues are often referred to as 'theological' or 'cardinal' virtues and the passage which contains them – 1 Corinthians 13 – is often read at wedding services.

▶ **Faith**

In one sense, faith is universal because all human beings base their lives on assumptions which cannot be proved with mathematical certainty. Every human being lives by probability, so no one can opt out of believing. This applies to the 'big' questions: questions about God and whether life has purpose and ultimate meaning. Christians believe that God exists. Atheists believe that God does not exist. Agnostics believe that we do not have enough evidence to decide either way. The indifferent person believes that it does not matter anyway.

Total certainty – absolute proof – is out of the question, though most people can give some reasons for their beliefs.

Faith is important in other areas of life too. It applies to convictions and commitments, e.g. 'I believe in abortion on demand' or 'I believe the rights of the unborn child are supreme'. And it applies to relationships: 'I trust him' is the highest form of praise. Christians are called 'believers' not because they alone live by faith, but because they live by faith in Jesus Christ. Faith is not a substitute for reason but it can be firmly based on reason. Christians argue that they have good reasons for believing in Jesus. Arising from those reasons and that belief come active faith, commitment and obedient action.

Of course, some Christians have doubts. Many would argue that these can have a positive outcome: a helpful parallel can be drawn from personal relationships. If we doubt a friend's loyalty, we put our reasons for doubting our friend alongside our experience of his or her faithfulness. Christians do the same in their relationship with God. They consider afresh God's love and faithfulness; they reflect again upon the significance of Jesus. Then they put their doubts within this framework.

Relating the story of his conversion, former US president Barack Obama said: 'The questions I had didn't magically disappear. The sceptical bent of my mind didn't suddenly vanish. But kneeling beneath that cross on the South Side [of Chicago], I felt I heard God's Spirit beckoning me.'

Faith has a passive element: 'Let go and let God.' This is caught in a popular prayer of Reinhold Niebuhr: 'God grant me the serenity to accept the things I cannot change, the courage to change the things that I can, and the wisdom to know the difference.' But as that prayer shows, faith has an active side too: it involves obedient action. Dr John Vincent captures this: 'Our word "believe" does not get the force of the Greek word. It really means give yourself over to, risk your life on.'

▶ Hope

Christian hope is captured by Mother Julian's great affirmation, 'all shall be well and all shall be well and all manner of thing shall be well'. Christian hope means facing the future with confidence. In ordinary speech, the word 'hope' can be a weak concept. 'I hope I will win a fortune on the national lottery' is a sentence running through many minds, although they are fairly sure that they will not. Christian hope has a much more confident quality. Hope enables believers to face the unknown future in quiet confidence that 'all things work together for good for those who love God' (Romans 8:28). The Christian hope of life in heaven is rooted in history, and focused on Jesus Christ. It is as strong as the evidence for Jesus and his resurrection: readers must evaluate this for themselves.

> 'Too often, the gauge used to judge the genuineness of a person's faith is their belief: do they believe a, b and c? Do they measure up to what is deemed orthodox faith? But Jesus had a different approach. He was less concerned with a person's beliefs (their orthodoxy) than with their behaviour (their orthopraxis).'
>
> D. Tomlinson, *How to be a bad Christian ... And a better human being* (Hodder & Stoughton, 2012), p. 25.

Christian hope is joyful. Christians are not always optimistic about this world, where realism sometimes leads to gloom and sadness – even desperation. There are good reasons for tears (James 4:9) considering the state of the world and the capacity of humanity to create havoc. But, overall, the New Testament is a joyful book. Saints are often thought of as other-worldly, solemn figures, associated with pain and death. But people who live close to God are often joyful and serene, with wide concerns. The biblical scholar and Anglican priest J.B. Phillips translated the word 'hope' in his New Testament as 'this happy certainty'.

▶ Love

Ancient Greeks had several different words which are translated by the one word 'love' in English: *philia* (deep friendship), *storge* (family affection), *eros* (erotic love – celebrated in the Song of Songs in the Old Testament). But the most frequent word for love in the Greek New Testament is *agape*. This refers to self-giving, sacrificial, practical love. Jesus himself showed deep compassion to those in need and especially to people who experienced rejection. He demonstrated that love must sometimes be heroic: he died on the cross. He showed that love must often be small-scale and domestic: he washed the disciples' feet. The New Testament insists that love is practical and creative, and that it includes forgiveness.

> 'Love is patient, love is kind. It does not envy, it does not boast, it is not proud. It is not rude, it is not self-seeking, it is not easily angered, it keeps no record of wrongs. Love does not delight in evil but rejoices with the truth. It always protects, always trusts, always hopes, always perseveres.'
> (1 Corinthians 13:4–7)

> 'Therefore, as God's chosen people, holy and dearly loved, clothe yourselves with compassion, kindness, humility, gentleness and patience. Bear with each other and forgive whatever grievances you may have against one another. Forgive as the Lord forgave you. And over all these virtues put on love, which binds them all together in perfect unity.'
> (Colossians 3:12–14)

'He who would do good to another, must do so in minute particulars.'
William Blake, English poet

Christian love (*agape*) is Christianity's greatest gift to the world. Tony Bridge, when Dean of Guildford Cathedral, posed the question, 'Why value love at all?' He went on to say that after 2,000 years of Christianity, this question sounds idiotic. It is taken for granted that love is a wonderful quality, even if we do not often live up to its high demands. But he then made an important contrast. 'Other civilizations have assumed no such thing. Courage, stoic endurance, the search for wisdom, intellectual integrity, strength, detachment – these are the virtues normally worshipped by mankind and preached by his many religions. And love is a contradiction of many of them.'

Ultimately – and rightly – outsiders judge Christianity by its fruit. Does it 'deliver the goods'? How many bitter people have been softened by its influence? How many nervous people have been given courage? How many selfish people have been so touched by the love of Christ that they too have been inspired to loving service? How evident in the life of Christian believers are 'the fruit of the Spirit – love, joy, peace, patience, kindness, goodness, faithfulness, gentleness and self-control' (Galatians 5:22). This is the key test which faces Christians in every generation.

> '[The] qualities and character which Jesus and his first followers insist on as the vital signs of healthy Christian life don't come about automatically. You have to develop them.'
> T. Wright, *Virtue Reborn* (SPCK, 2010), p. 25.

Key ideas

▶ The word 'martyr' comes from the Greek word meaning 'witness'.

▶ The first Christian martyr was Stephen; Peter and Paul also died for their faith.

▶ In the New Testament, the word 'saints' refers to all believers – as in the song 'O when the saints go marching in'. Over time, the word 'saint' took on a narrower meaning applied to Christians who lived especially heroic or holy lives.

▶ 'Canonization' is the process by which the Roman Catholic Church declares someone to be an official saint. This practice continues today in the Roman Catholic and Orthodox Churches.

▶ Mary, the Mother of Jesus, has a special place of honour in the Church.

▶ The three greatest Christian virtues are faith, hope and love (1 Corinthians 13).

Dig deeper

D.H. Farmer, *The Oxford Dictionary of Saints*, 5th edn (Oxford: Oxford University Press, 2003).

S. Hauerwas, *Learning to Speak Christian* (London: SCM Press, 2011).

N.T. Wright, *Virtue Reborn* (London: SPCK, 2010).

Fact check

1 The Greek word for 'martyr' comes from a word which means:
   a guilty
   b dead
   c witness
   d faithful

2 'Saint' refers to:
   a people who are perfect
   b those who died for being Christians
   c a common New Testament term for all believers
   d especially brave Christians

3 The first recorded Christian martyr was:
   a Paul
   b Peter
   c Mary
   d Stephen

4 Some persecuted Christians sought 'the martyr's crown' because:
   a the pain of persecution was too much
   b they thought it would give them a special place in heaven
   c they had a death wish
   d they wanted to prove they were better than other Christians

5 Relics were:
   a thought of as lucky charms by the early Church
   b regarded as a source of healing and an agent which gave protection to the church which possessed them
   c worshipped as manifestations of God in the church which possessed them
   d kept as proof that a martyr had been persecuted

6 'Canonization' refers to:
   a the formation of the Bible
   b the recognition of sainthood
   c the first leaders of the early Church
   d the legalizing of Christianity as a faith under Constantine

7 Which of the following is *not* one of the seven deadly sins, sometimes referred to as cardinal sins?

   a Greed

   b Impatience

   c Gluttony

   d Sloth

8 According to 1 Corinthians 13, the greatest Christian virtue is:

   a faith

   b love

   c patience

   d hope

9 To counter the seven deadly sins, seven virtues were celebrated. Which of the following is *not* counted as one of them?

   a Temperance

   b Wisdom

   c Justice

   d Honesty

10 Which Greek word for love features in 1 Corinthians 13?

   a *philia*

   b *storge*

   c *eros*

   d *agape*

One Church, many churches

In this chapter you will learn about:

▶ *statistics for the largest movement in history*

▶ *the world's many churches*

▶ *a shifting centre of gravity.*

The largest movement in history

The Church of Jesus Christ is the largest movement in all history. Modern-day disciples of Jesus are to be found on every continent, and about one-third of the world's population would call themselves Christian.

The Christian Church is like a great mountain. If you stand looking at it, and even if you are on it, you cannot see all sides at the same time. The view from one vantage point may be very different from another. The aim of this chapter is to walk round and up the mountain to gain a fuller impression of the whole.

If it is One Church, one mountain, why are there so many different churches? All Christians, whatever their race or status, are united 'in Christ' – in his love, grace and forgiveness. So there can only be One Church, one body of Christians, spread through all generations and throughout the world (for which the Greek word is *katholikos*), even if they 'gather' at different times in different places. (The Greek word *ecclesia*, from which we get 'ecclesiastical', means 'to gather' or 'gathering'.) Hence the phrase in the Nicene Creed – an important ancient summary of belief – 'We believe in one holy, catholic and apostolic Church'.

> 'A basic characteristic of the church is that it is a community. This community has two aspects: First, it is a community with God – whenever people come together in the name of Jesus, Jesus promises to be present and have fellowship with them. Second, it is a community with one another. The church is not a place where individuals meet with God on their own, but a place where people meet with God together as a fellowship.'
>
> H. Hegstad, *The Real Church: An Ecclesiology of the Visible* (James Clarke & Co., 2013), p. 97.

But this Church consists, and always has consisted, of people with different histories and cultures, living in different places. When local believers gather together, they are the church there; not the same body as a group meeting in another place halfway across the world. So the language about 'One Church but many churches' makes sense. It already occurs in the New Testament, where phrases like 'the churches of Asia', 'the churches of Galatia' or 'the churches of the Gentiles' are used.

The differences are not only of place. Differences in modes of worship, beliefs and ethical requirements are found between different denominations. Such differences were apparent even in the first few decades covered by the New Testament writings: for example, differences between the Jewish Christians and Gentile Christians (Acts 6:1) and between the apostles Peter and Paul (Galatians 2:11).

As the centuries wore on, Christianity spread through all the nations of the known world and its detailed beliefs and practices were hammered out. Different opinions and claims about authenticity and authority caused some groups of Christians to separate from others. At times they even fought and persecuted each other. One encouraging feature of the 20th century was that Christians with a different history and tradition recognized each other again. They came together in discussion, leading, in some cases, to visible reunion.

Spotlight

Walk round any city or town and you will find many churches built quite close together. They illustrate some of the sad divisions there have been down the years within the Christian community.

A man was marooned on a desert island. When he was rescued after many years, he had built himself an entire village from the trees on the island, including a house, a shop, a village hall, even a gym – and two churches. When his rescuers asked why he had built two churches, he pointed to one and said, 'That is the one I don't go to.'

But great Christian 'blocs' remain and in this chapter we shall outline the main distinctive features of:

▷ the Roman Catholic Church, with over 1 billion members (including some 6 million Catholic Christians who do not owe allegiance to Rome)

- the various Orthodox Churches, with some 220 million members

- Protestant Churches, estimated at around 277 million members

- Anglican Churches, with 83 million members worldwide

- Independent Churches, with some 438 million members

Across these various denominational groups are spread the Christians who belong to different Pentecostal or Charismatic churches or groups. In addition there are about 35 million members of groups that claim to be Christian but which are outside mainstream Christianity (such as Jehovah's Witnesses, Mormons, Christian Scientists, Unitarians, Spiritualists and British Israelites), sometimes referred to as 'marginals'.

All the above together make up some 2,200 million church members, or 33 per cent of the world's total population. (Muslims make up about 24 per cent, Hindus 13 per cent, Buddhists 6 per cent and Jews 0.2 per cent.)

'Statistics', said Dr Who, 'allow you to be wrong with authority'! Statistics are notoriously difficult to get right and can sometimes hide as much as they reveal. They don't always tell accurate stories of decline or growth but they may give a 'feel' for how things stand. They are 'snapshots' in time. Keep that in mind as you read the statistics in this section.

More statistical accounting of a precise nature takes place each year among the Christian world of denominations and agencies than for any other global movement. However, it is important to note the exact definitions of all categories thus enumerated. Almost every church has more members than regular worshippers, though some have more attenders than members! Indeed, this last point draws attention to an important trend which seems to be developing in the West – that church attendance is more fluid, and increasing numbers seem less inclined to 'join' a church even if they go there often.

Many who do not formally belong profess publicly to believe in Jesus Christ, and many of these regard themselves as 'belonging' to the Church in a loose sense. Britain illustrates this. Regular church attendance (about 7 per cent) is lower than in many other countries, but in the 2011 population census 59 per cent said they were Christian. Sample surveys reveal that about 60 per cent claim to believe in God and some 40 per cent say that they pray regularly. Many of these people regard themselves as 'belonging' to a church or denomination, even though they seldom attend.

Statisticians attempt to distinguish 'cultural Christians' from 'committed Christians'. The former are defined in the preceding paragraph; the latter are defined by varying degrees of attendance, profession of faith, giving of money, and so on. The scene is by no means static. As the world population increases rapidly, so does the number of church members.

Spotlight

'A third of the world's population are Christians'; 'A third of the world's population are Christian'. What is the difference in meaning between these two sentences? (The same question can be asked of the statements, 'A quarter of the world's population are Muslims'; 'A quarter of the world's population are Muslim' – and most other faiths!)

Here are some estimates of what appears to be happening around the world:

▶ The Church worldwide is currently growing by some 80,000 members every day.

▶ In India around 10 per cent of 'untouchables' (the lowest caste in India) are Christians.

▶ There are over 7,000 churches (mainly Presbyterian) in Seoul, the capital of South Korea.

▶ Church membership in Africa is believed to be growing by around 34,000 a day.

▶ The number of churches is increasing all the time. For example, in 2010 there were some 340 denominations in Britain, compared with 275 in 2006.

- There are far more than this in the USA (over 5,000).

- The World Council of Churches (WCC) has 345 member denominations from around the world which account for over half a billion Christians.

- Worldwide there are some 39,000 distinct denominations, though many of them are relatively small.

Though these different churches all share mainstream Christian beliefs, they each have particular characteristics which mark them out as distinct. We turn now to look at some of these.

> 'The irony is that, except for the Middle East (where Christianity was born) and Europe and America (to whose civilization it gave birth), Christianity is expanding everywhere today.'
> D. Meyer, *Witness Essentials* (InterVarsity Press, 2012), pp. 32–3.

The Churches

THE ROMAN CATHOLIC CHURCH

Christianity started its life in a province of the Roman Empire. The two greatest Christian leaders, Peter and Paul, were executed in Rome under the Emperor Nero, probably in AD 64 and 65. There is a strong tradition that Peter asked to be crucified upside down, because he felt unworthy to die exactly like his Lord. A church (believers, not a building) was founded early in Rome, through the witness to their faith of 'ordinary' believers whose names are not recorded. There were other great cities in the empire, in particular Jerusalem, Alexandria, Antioch and Constantinople, where churches were also established. They could not accept that the teachings and practices of Rome should be definitive for the whole of Christendom, nor that Rome had authority over them.

As a result of the Great Schism of 1054 (see below), the Eastern Church became known as 'Orthodox' while the Western Church took to itself the name 'Catholic'. The Catholic Church remained more or less unified for five more centuries under the leadership of Rome. The Western Church was not always united even before the Reformation. There were substantial groups in the West which remained separate from Rome, e.g. the early Celtic churches (responsible for evangelizing Ireland, Scotland, Wales and much of northern and south-west England, together with Flanders and north Germany). But broadly speaking the Church of Rome led the church in the west. Those Celtic churches remained distinct until the seventh century, when they were absorbed by the greater power of Rome.

The Bishop of Rome came to be called 'Pope' (from Latin *Papa*, 'Father'). The Church which remained faithful to his supremacy through all the changes of the Reformation period is now known as the Roman Catholic Church. It has spread from Europe to most parts of the globe and is the largest of the Christian Churches. The main characteristic of the Roman Catholic Church is *central authority*. The Pope is seen as the direct successor to St Peter, and the papal system keeps a strong hold over new ideas and threatened changes. Authority flows down from the Pope through cardinals and bishops to parish priests. Some modern Catholics, especially those in the USA and Europe, are prepared to question papal authority and even to ignore it, for example, in matters of contraception.

The teaching of the Roman Catholic Church since the Reformation has been largely focused in three Councils: the Council of Trent (1545–63), the First Vatican Council (1869–70) and the Second Vatican Council (1962–5). These councils have debated and promulgated Catholic teaching relating to all matters of faith.

Roman Catholics today live with the heritage of the Second Vatican Council, which instituted considerable changes in the hitherto rigid structures and practices of that Church. Most obvious was the shift from Latin to national languages for the Mass. At the same time, Catholics were given strong encouragement to read the Scriptures. This influential Council led to a greater openness within the Catholic Church.

To be a Roman Catholic is to be conscious of belonging to a Church of immense size and global spread, which claims to be the nearest to the sort of Church that Christ wants. It is also to be part of a long tradition of colourful worship and deep spirituality. Worship styles vary despite the rigid outward structures. The Roman Catholic Church has often been able to tolerate and live with local customs, religions and beliefs to such a degree that some other Christians accuse it of compromise.

The **monastic movement** has always played a significant role in Roman Catholicism. At their best, monasteries have been powerhouses of prayer, worship and evangelization, and centres for experimental change. Because the vast majority of parish priests are required to be celibate, the distinction between monks and parish priests is not so obvious as in the Eastern Churches.

Whether clergy should be celibate (i.e. unmarried) is keenly debated within the Roman Catholic Church today. Some of its members believe that papal insistence on this is one cause of an alarming fall in vocations to the priesthood. At the same time, many priests are not allowed to exercise their priesthood because they have married after ordination. One estimate puts this figure as high as one-fifth of the total number of priests worldwide. (Note: There are some married Roman Catholic priests but they are the exception, e.g. some married Anglican priests who left the Church of England because of the ordination of women to the priesthood and were later ordained as priests in the Roman Catholic Church.)

From time to time, decrees ('Bulls' or 'Encyclicals') are issued by the Pope on specific matters – most famously in recent years on sexual morality. Decrees of the First Vatican Council were the cause of a breakaway church by those Roman Catholics who could not accept what they saw as the novelty of *papal infallibility*. Today they constitute small groups known as 'Old Catholics'. They are found mainly in the Netherlands, Germany and Austria, and are in communion with Anglican churches.

▶ Four recent popes

When **Pope John XXIII** (in office 1958–63) was elected by the College of Cardinals, it was assumed that, at 76, he would be a 'caretaker pope'. From an Italian peasant family, he was a warm and popular figure. Pope John XXIII convened the Second Vatican Council, which ran from 1962–5 and 'opened the windows' to allow the Holy Spirit to blow through the Church. Among the results were the replacement of the Latin Mass with vernacular services, warmer relationships with other Churches and strong encouragement to read the Scriptures.

Pope John Paul II (1978–2005) was the first non-Italian pope for over 400 years. The first-ever Polish pope, he had personal experience of the suffering Church, having lived under Nazi and Communist regimes. A fine linguist and poet, Pope John Paul II was popular and charismatic. He travelled much more widely than his predecessors – kissing the soil when he landed in a new country. He encouraged good inter-faith relationships, but was very conservative and would not yield on contraception, nor on celibacy for priests. Some Christians from other Churches believe this stance on contraception to be profoundly wrong and, in a world decimated by AIDS and poverty, extremely damaging. Pope John Paul was shot and seriously injured in 1981 but recovered from this assassination attempt. (He later met and forgave his attacker.) As a result of popular acclaim at his funeral in 2005, his papal successor agreed to 'fast-track' John Paul II towards canonization.

John Paul II's successor, **Pope Benedict XVI** (2005–13) was an academic theologian who called on the nations of Europe to turn back from secularization to Christian values. Less charismatic than his predecessor, he appeared to be gentle and calm. In his preaching he emphasized 'friendship with Jesus Christ'. Like Pope John Paul II, he was conservative in outlook and theology. Critics claim that the cause of good inter-church relationships was damaged when, in 2007, the Vatican referred to the Roman Catholic Church as the one true Church of Christ – while acknowledging that salvation can be found within other Churches. In 2008 he was warmly received during an official visit to the USA where he apologized for child abuse by priests. In a church procession on Christmas Eve 2009, Pope Benedict was attacked and pulled to the ground, but not seriously injured. In 2010, in Malta, the Pope was deeply moved when he met seven men who had been sexually abused by priests while growing up in an orphanage. He expressed shame and sorrow over their suffering. Benedict took the unusual decision to retire as pope in 2013 because of ill-health and old age. He is the first pope in the modern era to have done this.

Jorge Mario Bergoglio was elected pope in 2013 following the retirement of Benedict XVI, becoming **Pope Francis (2013–)**. An Argentinian by birth, he is the first Jesuit to become pope. He has quickly become known as a humble and down-to-earth figure, choosing to live a simple life in so far as he can. For example, he chose not to move into the papal apartments in the Apostolic Palace, but to live in a simple flat in a building next door. Although he is conservative on a number of issues, he has shown evidence of moving towards a more conciliatory position on issues such as homosexuality and divorce.

THE ORTHODOX CHURCHES

As we have already seen, the church began its life in the Roman Empire. Some 300 years after the start of Christianity, that empire was beginning to show signs of weakening. Early in the fifth century its western half, centred on Rome, collapsed. The eastern empire continued for another thousand years, and in this half were the four key cities of Jerusalem, Alexandria, Antioch and Constantinople (modern-day Istanbul). Along with Rome they had formed the five major centres of Christianity for several centuries. But they didn't always see eye to eye.

The Eastern churches had a different approach to theology, to worship and to authority from that of Rome. For example, they tended to operate through councils which decided on key issues. Rome was different. Modelled more on the imperial system it took a more hierarchical approach, with key decisions being taken by the Pope and his advisors. Rome saw itself as 'first among equals' and argued that it was the leading church of the empire.

In 1054 these churches fell out: the four in the east declared Rome to be *anathema* (a formal statement of excommunication) – and Rome did the same to the four in the east. It is known as the Great Schism (Note: There was another event called the Great Schism, sometimes referred to as the Western Schism or the Papal Schism. This happened between 1378 and 1417 within the Roman Catholic Church.) The schism of 1054 gave rise to the Western church centred on Rome (later called the Roman Catholic Church) and the 'Orthodox' churches in the east.

The Orthodox Churches have preserved ancient structures and forms very tenaciously throughout the centuries. They survive as the Churches of Eastern Europe: the Greek, Balkan and Russian 'Orthodox Churches'. These Churches maintain they have kept the apostolic faith most faithfully, while alleging that Catholics and Protestants have diverged from it – by adding what is new or non-genuine, or subtracting what is original and authentic.

To go into an Eastern Orthodox church is like stepping back a thousand years or more; neither the furnishings nor the ritual seem to have changed at all. Often the building itself is centuries old and crumbling, with clouds of incense surrounding the worshippers (who stand rather than sit – often there are no seats). Religious paintings (icons) are placed around the church. They are surrounded by candles, with people bowing in reverence in front of them and kissing them. Behind an elaborate screen (the *iconostasis*), priests and deacons move about in glorious vestments, engaged in ancient ceremony. And a small choir, often at the western end, sings persistent chants in Greek or Old Church Slavonic.

To be a faithful Orthodox Christian you should attend the liturgy, pray to God, Jesus, Mary and the saints, and heed your parish priest. The parish priest is usually a married man of local origin. He is likely to remain in his village all his life – much like his flock. In general, learning belongs not to the parish clergy but to the monasteries, where celibacy, poverty and total obedience to superiors are required. All bishops come from the monasteries, although there is a long tradition of lay theologians – highly educated lay people who are teachers and writers. A number of Orthodox congregations – often small, but usually growing – have established themselves in Britain and the USA.

Similar to the above churches are the ancient groups of Christians known as Oriental Orthodox, found in Egypt, Ethiopia, Syria, Iraq, Iran, southern India and Armenia. These Churches felt obliged to leave the mainstream in the fourth and fifth centuries. They did so because they could not agree with various definitions of the faith hammered out by the majority at great councils of the Church, such as Nicaea (AD 325), Constantinople (AD 381) and Chalcedon (AD 451). The Eastern and Western Churches alike tended to regard these other groups as 'heretical', and for this reason they have lived in isolation from other Christians. The term 'heretical' originally meant 'separate, different, cut-off', but came to mean 'having wrong beliefs'. To be an Oriental Orthodox Christian is to be like the Eastern Orthodox in many ways, but to be even more tenacious in holding to inherited traditions. This tenacity comes from the fact that they feel challenged by other Christians, or by Muslims who form the majority in most of these countries.

▶ **The Russian Orthodox Church**

The Orthodox Church of Russia experienced great hostility as a result of the Russian Revolution in 1917. It was followed by 70 years of Communist (officially atheistic) rule – and most churches throughout Eastern Europe suffered a similar fate. Religion was strictly controlled. Many active believers were persecuted and imprisoned; large numbers were martyred.

The Orthodox churches survived by making an uneasy truce with the ruling powers. If they were willing to keep out of politics, to concentrate on the devotional life and curtail evangelism, they were allowed to function. Of course, this policy was controversial and some members (such as Alexander Solzhenitsyn, the Nobel Prize winning author) encouraged the church leadership to be more courageous.

With the demise of the Soviet Union in 1991, doors opened up to travellers, and the Orthodox Church faced what it sees as a new threat – missionaries from some Protestant and Pentecostal churches, as well as from some Western sects and cults, are gaining a following, especially among younger people.

▶ Further East

The churches of India, China and Japan tend not to be Orthodox, but more are closely aligned with the Western churches since they were founded largely through missions from the West during the past few centuries.

The Philippines is the only Asian country which is predominantly Christian (Roman Catholic), though the situation throughout Asia is fluid and many churches are growing. South Korea has the largest single church in the world: the Yoido Full Gospel Church in Seoul, with a membership of some 900,000. India and Japan have minority churches. About 7 per cent of the population in India are Christians and about 4 per cent in Japan. The majority of these are Catholics in communion with Rome.

While South Korea boasts the largest congregation in the world, reports from North Korea speak of tens of thousands of Christian believers enduring torture and starvation in labour camps.

China has an interesting – and highly significant – story to tell. In spite of religious practice being tightly controlled by the government, some researchers suggest that 10,000 Chinese become Christians every day. A US magazine, the *National Catholic Reporter*, has estimated that by 2150 the number of Christians in China will have doubled to 200 million – the largest concentration of Christians in any one country. This is largely the result of 'fearless grass roots evangelists'. There are, however, still examples of the Church facing difficulties. The Chinese House Church Alliance was asked to close down its churches, schools and orphanages as recently as 2007 and some persecution of unregistered Christians continues.

India is the world's largest democracy. It also has a long history of religious tolerance. Mainly Hindu, it has a sizeable Muslim minority and is home to many other faiths. Christians make up about 7 per cent of the population. In recent years there have been notable attacks on Christians, mainly by Hindu nationalists, leading to the government calling for a return to 'the welcoming of all faiths in India', a tradition in India said to be as old as India itself.

PROTESTANT CHURCHES: THE REFORMATION

In the 16th century there was turmoil in Europe. The Reformation – a movement for reform within the medieval Catholic Church – was the inspiration and ultimate cause of most Churches other than Orthodox or Catholic. The Reformation resulted partly from the rediscovery of the ancient languages of Hebrew and Greek, which meant that the Scriptures could be read in the original. For the previous 12 centuries, the Latin tradition had totally dominated the West. A second cause of the Reformation was the growing nationalism in various European countries; this led to a desire for freedom from the influence and power of Rome. A further cause was reaction to the abuses which developed in the Catholic Church during the latter decades of the Middle Ages.

The Reformation could have resulted in reforms in teaching and practice *within* the Catholic Church had it not met total resistance from the central authority in Rome. All attempts at reconciliation failed and new church groupings emerged. Each of these protested at the claims and power of Rome, hence 'Protestant' Churches. (The term was first used at the Diet of Speyer in 1529.) These Churches emphasized different elements in the practices and beliefs of the Church before it was corrupted (as they saw it) by Rome. Because of this, and since they emerged in different countries at a time when nationalism was so strong, they fell into four main groups:

▶ Lutheran

▶ Reformed (or Presbyterian)

▶ Baptist

▶ Anglican.

In later centuries they were joined by two other 'breakaway' Churches: Methodist (18th century) and Pentecostal (20th century). All these churches placed great emphasis on the Bible as the controlling authority for belief and practice. They wished to make the Scriptures readily available and easy to read. And they wanted to simplify worship, so that important elements would stand out and not be overwhelmed by trivial or misleading ceremonies, or by ornate music. They emphasized the importance of preaching alongside, or above, the administration of the sacraments. Many churches in the 16th century (including the Church of England) substituted the authority of the local monarch for that of the Pope in Rome.

▶ Lutheran Churches

The Lutheran Churches (now estimated at about 64 million members) were at first dominant in northern Germany and Scandinavia. They are now also found in Africa, America, Asia and many countries in Europe. Martin Luther (1483–1546) in northern Germany was the principal protagonist of the Reformation. Many of the features listed in the previous paragraph owe their force to his preaching and writing. The Lutheran tradition allows old customs to stay, as long as they are not deemed to be contrary to New Testament teaching. So in many Lutheran churches, customs, vestments and furnishings are still maintained – as well as an episcopal ministry (bishops) – from the old days of the united Western Catholic Church.

The teachings of the Lutheran churches are historically summed up in the *Augsburg Confession* (1530). This is a moderate statement of the universal Christian faith with an emphasis on the grace of God, which is to be responded to by faith. It is faith which is seen as the 'justifying' or saving factor, not good works: these must follow as a thanksgiving for God's grace. Lutherans practise a faith which has strong roots in the home, with family prayers.

In church, Lutherans worship with quiet dignity: hymns, Bible reading, preaching and the sacraments are the most important elements. The clergy are well-trained in theology and there is a comprehensiveness which allows quite varied practices to exist. In the 20th century, monasticism was revived within the

Lutheran Church, but the numbers remain small. Lutherans have made a distinguished contribution to the ecumenical movement, i.e. the moving together of Churches to talk, to co-operate, and even to unite (Chapter 14).

▶ Presbyterian Churches

As Lutheran Churches were banding together against Rome, John Calvin (1509–64) was teaching similar doctrines in Geneva. But he was more radical in breaking with past customs in organization and liturgy. With great rigour, he regarded the Bible as the sole authority in all matters of faith and practice. This led him to reject the ministry of bishops and all forms of decoration in churches, as well as most music and ceremony.

These Churches, founded by John Calvin and his followers (called Calvinist, Reformed or Presbyterian), have a membership of some 49 million worldwide and are the dominant form of Christianity in Scotland, the Netherlands and Switzerland. They are well-represented in most countries in Europe, America and Africa. Calvinism is usually an austere form of Christianity with dignified, simple worship and deep spirituality. Its members have made a strong contribution to Christian missions worldwide and to honesty, fairness and hard work in public life.

The ecumenical movement of recent decades has led to some Churches in the above two major Protestant traditions coming together locally. This has resulted in United Lutheran and Reformed Churches in many parts of the world. So, to the 64 million Lutherans and the 49 million Reformed Christians, we must add about 26 million in these united Churches.

▶ Baptist Churches

The Lutheran and Presbyterian Church groupings were not the only ones to emerge from the Reformation. Some felt that true Christian discipleship had been largely displaced by nominal Christianity. Virtually everyone was baptized in infancy and these new churches rebelled against this (Chapter 7). They came to be called Baptists because they insisted on the practice of plunging believers under the water (total immersion), not just pouring water over the forehead of infants. Baptists now number around 58 million and are particularly strong in the southern states of the USA.

William Carey is often credited with starting the modern Protestant missionary movement when he sailed from England to India in 1793. He was a Baptist cobbler with little formal education. Carey had a brilliant mind and during his lifetime he translated the Bible (whole or in part) into 25 languages and dialects. These emphases – love for the Bible and enthusiasm for evangelism – characterize modern Baptists. So does William Carey's challenging motto: 'Expect great things from God; attempt great things for God.'

▶ **Anglicanism**

In England, the Reformation took a different path from the rest of Europe. The English Church was greatly influenced by both Luther and Calvin but did not join either of those two Church groupings. So the Church of England maintained a position which was Luther-like in its conservative attitude to tradition and Calvin-like in its doctrine. Some Anglicans dislike being called 'Protestant', arguing that they are both Catholic and Reformed. Anglicanism's basis was defined in the *Thirty-Nine Articles* (1563 Latin; 1571 English) and the English *Book of Common Prayer* (finalized in 1662 but based on the work of Archbishop Thomas Cranmer a century earlier).

The British (and other European) churches expanded widely to other parts of the globe during the 17th, 18th and 19th centuries. This expansion arose from:

▶ the colonizing process which resulted in the British Empire (although some missionaries found it necessary to oppose some policies of the colonizers)

▶ missionary zeal which wanted to take the gospel to new areas.

One result is a great worldwide network of churches called the *Anglican Communion*, which numbers some 83 million members. Most of today's Anglicans live in Africa. Anglican Churches are sometimes called Episcopal or Episcopalian (from the Greek word *episkopos*, meaning 'bishop' or 'overseer').

Anglicans are distinguished by having created a fellowship which allows for considerable doctrinal and liturgical differences, within a recognizable organizational unity.

Anglican 'provinces' are autonomous, but still look to the Church of England as the founding Church and to the Archbishop of Canterbury as 'first bishop among equals'. Every ten years or so, Anglican bishops from around the globe gather for the Lambeth Conference, hosted by the Archbishop of Canterbury. The first conference was held in 1867.

The ordination of women to the priesthood was debated and accepted in many Anglican Churches in the final decades of the 20th century (for example, the Church of England ordained its first women priests in 1994). This initiative, welcomed by the majority of members, nevertheless caused controversy and division, which persisted into the 21st century as the question of female bishops was debated.

There are three broad, sometimes overlapping, streams within Anglicanism: Catholic, Liberal and Evangelical.

▶ Anglo-Catholics (or 'Catholic Anglicans') are 'high church' in worship. They stress the mystery and awesomeness of God, using colourful vestments and incense (hence the affectionate nickname 'smells and bells' for high church worship).

▶ Liberal theology lays stress upon questioning the tradition and requiring the Faith to respond (sometimes radically; hence 'radical theology') to changes in culture and outlook in the world outside the Church.

▶ Evangelicals (not to be confused with fundamentalists) stress the importance of the Bible and the need for conversion and commitment. In recent years, evangelicals have become strong within the Church of England. Their worship tends to be 'low church' in style with minimal ceremony, in an attempt to make church services accessible to outsiders. In recent years evangelicals have been relatively effective in attracting young people, a task with which most European churches struggle.

It is important to stress that the boundaries between these three approaches are not rigid. The Charismatic Renewal Movement has influenced all three streams, especially the evangelical. As a result, the 'feel' of Anglican worship today is much more relaxed than hitherto, with bands and music groups featuring alongside pipe organs and choirs.

The 19th-century Oxford Movement resulted in the foundation of Anglican monasteries and convents. Some continue to flourish and do distinguished pioneering work (e.g. Helen House, the first children's hospice, was founded by Sister Frances Dominica). However, many of these religious communities struggle to survive, with few younger members joining.

Other types of Christian community have been established (such as Lee Abbey in Devon; Scargill House in Yorkshire). Taizé (France) and Iona (Scotland) are flourishing communities which attract many Anglicans – though these communities are essentially ecumenical. They involve many lay people (often young) who commit themselves to communal life for a year or so; few stay in these communities for life.

▶ **Methodist Churches**

The Church of England was not always comprehensive and open. When a reform movement began in the 18th century, led by two Anglican priests, the established Church resisted it. John and Charles Wesley and their followers were nicknamed 'Methodists' because of their orderly (methodical) approach to life and faith. So a new church grouping was created which took that name with pride.

Today there are Methodist churches around the world with 23 million members. Methodists have developed strong lay leadership and a travelling ministry. They are distinguished by the prominent place given in worship to hymn singing. Many of the fine hymns written by Charles Wesley are sung wherever English is used in worship, regardless of denomination.

▶ **Salvation Army and Quakers**

Some smaller groups have made an impact beyond their size. For example, the Salvation Army, with 2.4 million members, is renowned for a combination of outdoor evangelism, brass bands and social action among the homeless and others in desperate need. It has a highly effective (and confidential) ministry in tracing missing persons and offering the possibility of reunion with their families.

'The Army' was started by William Booth, a Methodist living in Victorian London, in an attempt to bring the gospel to the thousands living in poverty following the Industrial Revolution. The Salvation Army, with its musical, practical and evangelistic concerns, has spread to other countries and is especially strong in the USA. Salvationists (together with some other Christians) have taken a clear stand against what they perceive as the damaging effects of alcohol.

The Quakers (more correctly, the Religious Society of Friends), founded by George Fox (1624–91) have no ordained ministers. Silence is central to their tradition, as they 'wait upon God' in their Sunday meetings. Anyone may speak, under the prompting of the Spirit. Quakers have a distinguished record of pacifism and heroic war service in non-combatant roles – usually para-medical. In this they are like the Christian Brethren (formerly known as the Plymouth Brethren), a group of autonomous churches with no ordained ministers. Quakers number 400,000 (16,000 in Britain) and the Brethren 3.4 million (71,000 in Britain).

PENTECOSTAL CHURCHES

Pentecostalists take their name from Acts 2, where God's Spirit came in power on Peter and the other disciples on the feast of Pentecost. God's Spirit enabled the disciples to go out with zeal to spread the gospel, and gave them miraculous powers to 'speak in tongues' and to heal the sick. Pentecostal Christians believe that such powers are still available today, through the Holy Spirit. Pentecostal Churches were established early in the 20th century and are growing fast throughout the world. Their worship is informal, exuberant and partly unplanned, because of their belief in the immediacy of the gifts of the Spirit. The word 'charismatic' is often used for this expression of Christianity, but charismatic worship of an exuberant kind is often found in the older 'mainstream' Churches too (Chapter 13).

Older independent Churches, for example, Seventh Day Adventists, Moravians, Mennonites and Nazerenes, have long been an important part of the Christian landscape.

Spotlight

An example of the early spread of the gospel: the Church of St Thomas, at Palayur in Kerala, India, is said to have been founded by St Thomas, one of Jesus's disciples, in AD 52. The original small wooden church was replaced by a stone building, but some believe the wooden altar is the original.

INDEPENDENT CHURCHES

Independent Churches (indigenous or locally founded churches) are springing up around the world. Some African and Asian churches have arisen partly in adverse reaction to the Western elements which inevitably became associated with the missionary work of previous centuries. They are strong numerically but diverse in character. Often they are Pentecostal in emphasis but some stress the practices (and sometimes also the teachings and culture) of their countries before the missionaries arrived. Throughout the world, Independent, Pentecostal and Charismatic churches are growing faster than any other tradition. Taken together, they number about 438 million, although their independent character makes them difficult to enumerate.

NEW CHURCHES

The 1960s and 1970s saw the beginnings of a number of new independent churches throughout the world. Unlike the denominations we have looked at earlier in this chapter, these did not come about primarily because of doctrinal disagreements. Two drivers led to their development:

▶ the charismatic movement

▶ a response to the decline of the mainstream churches.

The charismatic movement highlights the place of the Holy Spirit in Christian faith. In particular it emphasizes the experience known as 'baptism in the Spirit'. The day of Pentecost (recorded in

Acts) witnessed such phenomena as speaking in tongues, prophecy and miraculous healing. Those in the charismatic movement believe these experiences are not confined to the history of early Christianity but should be present in the Church today. This movement affected many mainstream churches but some felt the need to break out of what they saw as the constraints of the old denominations and started new independent churches.

Coupled with this charismatic experience, many in the mainstream churches felt the Church had lost touch with the contemporary world. They saw a need to present the Christian faith in a wholly new way, dispensing with old forms, buildings and structures. These new churches discarded many attributes of established churches and adopted very contemporary cultural forms of worship (e.g. modern music; 'concert style' worship; café church; 'messy church'), often meeting in sports halls, theatres or concert venues.

They took a functional approach to church structure and leadership and discarded or disguised any denominational allegiance. They described themselves rather as 'non-denominational' or 'in the tradition of' and chose names such as 'Vineyard Churches', 'New Frontiers Churches' or 'Calvary Chapels'. They aimed to be 'seeker friendly'. They modelled the whole church experience on activities more familiar to those outside the Church from everyday life, such as sports events, music concerts and entertainment.

A shifting centre of gravity

'In 1900, it is estimated that 70 per cent of all Christians were to be found in Europe ... whereas now, as we have seen, Christians are much more evenly distributed around the globe, and, if present church growth and population trends continue, by 2025 Africa and Latin America will be vying with one another to claim the most Christians, having about a quarter each of the world's Christian population.'

S.C.H. Kim and K. Kim, *Christianity as a World Religion* (Continuum, 2008), p. 223.

Sociologists speak about the 'European exception'. As churchgoing in Europe declines, there is fast expansion elsewhere, especially in Africa, Latin America and Asia – including, perhaps surprisingly, China. Christianity started in the Middle East and was found very early in north Africa (see Acts 8:27). But throughout most of Christianity's history Europe has taken the lead, dominating both its thinking and its expansion, although the USA took over this leadership role during the 20th century.

The 18th, 19th and early 20th centuries saw a remarkable burst of missionary zeal. European nations such as Britain, Spain, Portugal and Germany as well as the USA sent missionaries to the four corners of the earth. As a result, the Christian Church has been planted in every continent and in almost every country. Christianity has shown itself capable of adapting to all cultures. In some societies there are customs and cultures which Christianity has challenged. But in every place, aspects of local custom and culture have been preserved and built on as vehicles for Christian teaching and worship. Today, it is the relatively young churches which are flourishing. So the Christian Church worldwide is growing and the Christian faith continues to spread. Meanwhile, the Church's centre of gravity has shifted:

▶ *from* Europe and (to a lesser extent) the USA

▶ *to* Africa, Asia and Latin America.

Population trends in these continents mean that the Church in the 21st century is increasingly young, energetic, non-white and Pentecostal/Charismatic. Sociologists speak of the notable shift to Pentecostalism and the growth of the church in the global South'. In the coming decades this is likely to be hugely significant, not only for the World Church, but for the world in general. The 21st century is likely to see a culture shift, as the younger churches in the developing world become more influential, shape the future and send missionaries and mission-partners to other continents, including Europe.

What conclusions can be drawn from these statistical 'snapshots'?

▶ About 7 per cent of the population in Britain today attends church on Sundays. Of these:

  ▷ about 1.7 per cent attend a Church of England service

  ▷ about 1.9 per cent attend a Roman Catholic church

▶ Most of the remaining 3.0 per cent attend a range of Protestant churches: Baptist, Methodist, Presbyterian or United Reformed, Pentecostal, Salvation Army, Quaker, Independent or 'New Church'.

There are strong regional variations in church attendance: less than 1 per cent in some parts of some cities; about 10 per cent in Scotland and perhaps 25 per cent in Northern Ireland.

In 2005 there were 48,328 churches in the UK, of which 37,846 were in England.

Four or five new congregations are founded in Britain each week because 'church planting' is a policy adopted by most mainstream and independent churches. These new congregations often meet in schools and community halls, even pubs. However, about six churches close each week.

On 23 December 2007 the media announced that for the first time in 500 years there are more Roman Catholic than Anglican worshippers – partly as a result of Polish immigrants. The Church of England's Statistical Department pointed out that these figures relate to Sunday worship only – a large number of services and activities are also held on weekdays.

Other world faiths are found in Britain, mainly as a result of immigration in the 1950s and subsequently, especially since the mid-1990s. Numbers are not huge but are increasing: adherents of all other faiths taken together amount to about 8 per cent of the British population, of which the majority are Muslims.

In the USA, estimates suggest that about 22 per cent of Americans attend religious services in any given week, although some put this figure as high as 40 per cent. (Interestingly there is evidence that church attendance in the USA is *over*-stated and in Britain it is *under*-stated: fewer people actually attend church in the USA than say they do, and more actually attend in the UK than say they do!)

In Italy and the Republic of Ireland, attendance is still substantial (though probably declining) while in the Philippines there are nearly 2 million baptisms a year.

If current trends continue, by 2050 the world will have 3 billion Christians, and only about 20 per cent of them will be non-Hispanic whites.

Key ideas

▶ The worldwide Church is made up of a network of local churches, which belong to different 'denominations'.

▶ The largest Church is the Roman Catholic Church, with over a billion members.

▶ In Eastern Europe, the Orthodox Church is numerically strong, totalling some 220 million.

▶ During the 16th-century Reformation in Europe, the unity of the mediaeval Catholic Church was broken.

▶ As a result of the Reformation, several Protestant (from 'protest') Churches were formed.

▶ The centre of gravity for Christians is shifting from Europe to Africa, the Americas and Asia (especially China).

▶ In today's world, a typical Christian is not elderly, prosperous and white – but young, non-white, poor, energetic and Pentecostal.

Dig deeper

V.H.H. Green, *A New History of Christianity* (New York: Continuum, 2007).

A.E. McGrath, *Christianity: An introduction*, 3rd edn (Oxford: Blackwell Publishing, 2015).

D. Meyer, *Witness Essentials* (Downers Grove, IL: InterVarsity Press, 2012).

Fact check

1 The Great Schism, when the Eastern and Western Churches separated, happened around:

   a AD 325

   b 1066

   c 1549

   d 1054

2 *Katholikos* ('catholic') means

   a Roman

   b worldwide

   c holy

   d Orthodox

3 William Booth founded which one of the following?

   a The Methodist Church

   b The Salvation Army

   c The Quakers

   d Anglicanism

4 What percentage of the world's population can be described as Christian?

   a about 33 per cent

   b about 25 per cent

   c about 10 per cent

   d about 50 per cent

5 Christianity began life in:

   a Asia

   b Africa

   c Israel/Palestine

   d Europe

6 In which of the following is church attendance not increasing?

   a Latin America

   b Asia

   c Europe

   d China

7 The largest single church in the world, Yoido Full Gospel Church, is in which city?

    a San Francisco

    b Tokyo

    c Seoul

    d London

8 The largest church denomination worldwide is:

    a Russian Orthodox

    b Anglican

    c Roman Catholic

    d Quaker

9 In today's world, a typical Christian is:

    a elderly, prosperous and white

    b European, female and Protestant

    c American, male and Baptist

    d young, non-white, poor, energetic and Pentecostal

10 The Augsburg Confession (1530) is:

    a part of the Roman Catholic liturgy

    b a summary of the teachings of the Lutheran Churches

    c a document challenging political interference in the Church

    d a theological treatise by John Calvin

Holy places, art and architecture

In this chapter you will learn about:

▶ *buildings – ancient and modern*
▶ *art in western history*
▶ *Christian sites and holy places.*

Places of worship: the earliest days

Jesus's ministry took place mainly in the open air. Neither his little group of followers, nor the crowds who flocked to hear him, required a building or needed any visual magnificence. From time to time this has also been true for later Christians, and a meeting for worship in the open air – perhaps beside a lake – is often a treasured memory. But this does not mean that Jesus rejected all holy places and buildings, or their splendid decoration. Indeed, after his resurrection his first disciples met daily in the Temple precincts.

Jesus's ministry rested on the Jewish religion. He and his first followers had been brought up in this, and they remained practising members. The Gospels underline the importance of the synagogue for Jesus and his contemporaries. Judaism was, and is, intensely corporate. Private or group devotions were viewed against the background of the worship and obedience offered by all Jewish people. In Jesus's day that included the sacrifices offered daily according to the Law of Moses in the Temple at Jerusalem. This had been newly restored and lavishly decorated by King Herod 'the Great' (a tyrant whose brilliant building feats, sometimes in the desert, were breath-taking – but best remembered for killing baby boys in the attempt to remove a rival for his throne).

Some Jewish sects were strongly opposed to the Temple and its priesthood. That was not because of the building or its liturgy as such, but because Jerusalem had become tainted in their eyes by too much co-operation with the Roman occupying forces. This represented, for these groups, compromise with pagans who worshipped many gods.

Christianity quickly separated from its Jewish roots. The early believers soon realized that Jesus's life, death and resurrection had made both Temple and animal sacrifices redundant. The early Christians came to see that on the cross, Jesus had become the Great High Priest, who had offered the one perfect sacrifice for sin – his own life.

At first, Christian worship took place in people's homes or in the open air. That did not last long. Any movement which passes into a second and third generation tends to become an institution. This happened to the Church. As it increased in numbers and spread through different countries and cultures, it developed an organization with identifiable 'places'.

The best-known early places are the *catacombs* (burial chambers) on the outskirts of Rome, where people could meet underground for worship and to commemorate their dead. This invisible meeting place was ideal, for the Church was intermittently persecuted for its first 300 years. As soon as specific places became identified with Christianity, art was employed to beautify and to instruct. The catacomb paintings are the earliest known form of Christian art. They often show Jesus as:

▶ the Good Shepherd

▶ the King who promises salvation

▶ the giver of the Communion meal.

Some of the more wealthy Christians were buried after the Roman manner in ornately carved stone coffins. These carvings show Jesus and his disciples with Christian symbols instead of the gods of Greek and Roman mythologies.

Not all Christian worship had to be secretive, even during the first 300 years. The earliest known Christian church is a house adapted soon after AD 200, in Dura Europos, Syria. Two rooms were turned into a baptistery and decorated with wall paintings. A similar house church, from two centuries later, has been found in Britain at Lullingstone in Kent.

> 'In Christ, God has hallowed the material world we inhabit and made it the home of his divinity.'
> J. Inge, *A Christian Theology of Place* (Ashgate, 2003), p. 57.

CHRISTIANS BEGIN TO BUILD

When the Emperor Constantine converted to Christianity, Christianity was first 'permitted' and then, almost immediately, adopted as the official religion of the Roman Empire early in the fourth century. When this happened Christians began to build in earnest. Two kinds of building emerged: those used by local congregations as meeting places for worship; grander buildings marking key events in the Christian story. Some fourth-, fifth- and sixth-century buildings still exist, including the Church of the Holy Sepulchre (Jerusalem), the Church of the Nativity (Bethlehem) and the Church of the Holy Wisdom (Istanbul).

So church buildings were not only allowed; they were required. But because there had been no specific form of church building before, the first churches drew inspiration from three different types of building familiar to many early Christians in the Roman Empire. These were:

▶ the mausoleum

▶ the meeting hall or basilica

▶ the synagogue.

As soon as the public building of churches was possible, a longing to locate the sites of central events in Jesus's ministry made itself felt. The most holy place in all Christendom is the Church of the Holy Sepulchre in Jerusalem. This vast building stands over the place where Jesus was crucified – and where his tomb was located, according to fourth-century Christians (a claim which has been supported by recent archaeology). Around the remains of the rock tomb of Jesus, there still stands a huge octagonal shape built by the Emperor Constantine in the fourth century. He also built a basilica over the site of the Nativity in Bethlehem. The great church now standing there, over the cave celebrated as Jesus's birthplace, dates from the next century. (Caves were, and are, used as stables.)

Mausoleums were round or octagonal in shape. This enabled people to gather round a tomb for commemorations and worship (an obvious 'coming out into the open' of the catacomb tradition). The basilica was a rectangular pillared hall where hundreds, or even thousands, could gather to listen to speeches or witness ceremonies.

Synagogues were oriented towards Jerusalem. Christians picked up this idea but adapted it. Their churches were oriented towards the east, the place of the rising sun. This had a double meaning for them as they worshipped a risen Son.

These buildings could be either large or small and both have been used ever since by Christians the world over. The round shape became more common in the eastern Empire, and this is the form commonly associated with the Eastern Orthodox churches of Greece and Russia and the churches of the Middle East. The rectangular shape, with nave and aisles, became more general in the West – so much so that many Western people today think of it as the shape for a church.

Spotlight

Many churches were built on the site of former pagan religious sites. In Rudston in Yorkshire, England, All Saints' Anglican Church was built on a hilltop next to the tallest monolith (standing stone) in Britain – taller than those at Stonehenge. It probably marked a prehistoric holy site and early Christian missionaries 'Christianized' it by placing a cross on top and building their church nearby. The church and the stone can still be visited today.

The grandest early church still standing is the Church of the Holy Wisdom (*Hagia Sophia*) in Istanbul (formerly Constantinople). Built in the fifth century, it is decorated all over with mosaics in gold and other colours. It is huge enough to hold thousands at a time, magnificent even today after centuries as a mosque and now just as a museum. The mosaics show bishops and saints, and emperors and their courts, as God's servants clad in priestly garments. The Eastern emperors were the 'popes' of Church and State. They were contemptuous of the claims of the Bishop of Rome to this position.

The round, or centrally orientated, church was not totally confined to the East. Those which survive in Britain were built by the Order of Knights Templar as copies of the Holy Sepulchre (started in AD 326) in Jerusalem. Examples can be found in London (the Temple Church), in Northampton, Cambridge and Little Maplestead in Essex. This influence is seen in modern churches where a central tower dominates.

The most memorable churches are grand buildings in cities and towns, built under the patronage of a king, bishop or other wealthy person. But, of course, most churches were humble buildings in villages or towns. The vast majority of these were of timber, built in the same way as huts and barns. Few have survived from earlier than the 13th century. The earliest in Europe is in Greensted, Essex, dating from the 11th century. There are 20 or so *stave* (timber) churches in Norway which survive from the 12th century onwards. In the early days, stone churches were rare and reserved for wealthy patrons (royal, episcopal, cathedral, civic or monastic).

OPEN-AIR SITES

Although the Church of the Holy Sepulchre is nearby, Christians still gather for worship in their thousands in the 'garden tomb' in Jerusalem. This is not the actual site of Jesus's burial but it is a garden, not a huge building, and helps modern pilgrims to visualize – and 'feel' – the events of the first Easter morning.

The desire to visit open-air holy sites as well as buildings grew during the 20th century, partly as a result of renewed interest in Celtic Christianity. Lindisfarne, Iona, Glendalough and St David's welcome an increasing number of pilgrims, many attracted by the stories of Columba, Cuthbert, Aidan, Dewi, Kevin, Patrick and Brigid. Stone crosses from the days of the Celtic mission may be found in many places in Britain. They served as a gathering place and the characteristic Celtic decoration on the circular cross is often still visible.

Some holy places have no strong associations with the past. Since the 1960s, Taizé in the Burgundy region of France has become a place of inter-church pilgrimage for thousands of (mainly young) people from all over the world and from every Christian tradition – and none. The most famous holy place in France is the town of Lourdes. Its fame is based on the belief that the Virgin Mary appeared to St Bernadette in 1858 and that it is a place of healing. For over 100 years pilgrims have visited the town – some 5 million each year in the 21st century. Many seek healing, but the Roman Catholic Church authorities employ strict criteria before accepting a healing as a gift or sign from God. Some modern sceptics come away impressed by the joy and hope they witness. Research points to a widespread and long-term decrease in anxiety and depression following a pilgrimage.

In southern Italy in 2003, a huge church was dedicated to Padre Pio who died in 1968 and was canonized in 2002. Miracles were attributed to him, he bore the stigmata (wounds like Christ's) on his hands, and some 7 million pilgrims converge on this site each year.

Case study: reading church buildings

Old church buildings have much to tell the student of architecture. Because they have been built over many centuries and in different cultures they demonstrate architectural styles, fashions and innovations. But they can also be 'read' as documents of Christian belief and practice.

Look online at different churches (or visit if you can), for example, St Peter's in Rome, Yoido Full Gospel Church in Seoul, a Quaker meeting house, a local Methodist chapel, a local Anglican church, a Salvation Army citadel.

Four questions:

▶ How is the building laid out and what does this say about how it is used?

▶ What are the prominent objects on show in the building? What do they tell you about what is important to the people who use this building for worship?

▶ What does the architecture convey about the beliefs and practices of those who built it?

▶ What does the building tell you about the history of the worshipping community in this place?

CHURCH ARCHITECTURE AND FOCAL POINTS

Church buildings were influenced by the Christian ceremonies that took place inside them and for which they were built. The basilica, or the great octagon or circle, held the people, and the focal points for worship were:

- the altar or table for Holy Communion

- the lectern, pulpit or desk, from which the Scriptures were read and sermons preached

- the throne (*cathedra*) for the bishop.

These were placed together so that the people faced them. The fourth essential focal point was the font for baptisms. Originally a great basin of water, this was sometimes placed in a separate building nearby. In later church buildings it is usually found at the back, near the entrance – to symbolize that it is through baptism that people come into membership of the Church.

The mosaics which covered most of these early churches usually had a gleaming gold background and depicted prophets, saints, bishops and Christian emperors. Presiding in the centre was Mary holding the infant Jesus, or Jesus reigning in majesty. In the early period, Christ was not depicted as suffering on the cross. The emphasis was on his humble friendship, or his power and glory as resurrected Lord.

DECORATION

Art of various kinds has adorned church buildings for centuries, notably stained glass and wall paintings. Such art was designed to beautify – and to instruct. A wide range of visual arts was employed. Carvings in stone became a feature of Christian decoration from the beginning. These often depicted scenes from the Bible and the lives of saints. Carvings in wood were also made but fewer have survived, since wood is more vulnerable than stone. Work in textiles (including embroidery), gold, silver and jewellery was also commissioned by the Christian Church. The clothes worn by the ministers – and the carpets, draperies and other furnishings – should be, it was felt, the finest possible. Altar frontals, episcopal and priestly vestments, and the vessels for use in the celebration of the Eucharist became very fine – at least the equal of any to be seen in the palaces of kings and emperors.

Monasteries became centres for the production of books, many of them beautifully scripted and illustrated; the *Lindisfarne Gospels* is an outstanding example. These were made on Holy

Island (Lindisfarne) in Northumbria around 700, 'in honour of St Cuthbert'. In 950, a priest called Aldred wrote an Anglo-Saxon translation between the lines of the Latin text.

From the early days in the catacombs, Christians expressed their faith through paintings. In the East this took a unique form – the icon – which has recently become more widely known, admired and copied in the West and worldwide. An icon is a stylized painting on wood of a Christian subject, usually Christ or a saint. Icons are painted according to strict rules which are devotional as well as artistic. The resulting icon (which means 'image') is regarded not just as a picture to inform the mind or excite the emotions: in some ways it is seen as an embodiment of what it depicts. So it can be revered and gazed upon in prayer, for it was created in prayer. There is no more powerful assertion of the place of art in Christian worship than the tradition of making and using icons.

THE CROSS

In medieval Europe the Church was, at first, the only patron of the arts. This means that almost all the early examples of painting, carving and work in stained and painted glass are of Christian subjects. And many great paintings from medieval and Renaissance times are of biblical or church events or people.

In the late Middle Ages, the earlier dislike of portraying Christ's crucifixion in agony had vanished. Instead, there was a concentration on the human suffering that he, as God's Son, underwent to bring salvation to the world. There were frequent representations of episodes from Christ's final days: the whipping, the crowning with a wreath of thorns, the jeering crowds. The nailed body on the cross was no longer robed in majesty but almost naked, in pain, with wounds and blood in evidence. In this tradition there is a strong appeal to the emotions. Perhaps the most famous early example is *The Crucifixion* by Grünewald, painted in 1515–16. A representation of the death of Jesus in a painting or a sculpture is called a *pietà*. Michelangelo's sculpted version (1498) can be seen in St Peter's, Rome.

THE PURPOSE OF ART

Art performed another important function; it helped to teach an illiterate population the basic elements of the Christian faith. This is why scenes of Christ's birth, life, suffering and resurrection were so frequent, together with Old Testament figures, saints and bishops. The finest display of original stained glass *in situ* is probably in Chartres Cathedral in France. In Britain, York Minster has more than a third of the nation's surviving medieval glass. Wall paintings are much more vulnerable and few remain, although there are some notable examples. In Britain the small parish churches of Pickering in Yorkshire and Chaldon in Surrey retain impressive examples. In Denmark some 600 examples remain, notably in Aarhus Cathedral. Their survival results from the fact that the Protestant reformers ordered their removal and many were simply painted over with lime-wash. Paradoxically this preserved rather than obliterated them!

'[Art] belongs to the soul of the church and ... a church that neglects it is in danger of losing its soul.'
J.W. de Gruchy, *Christianity, Art and Transformation* (Cambridge University Press, 2001), p. 254.

The medieval age produced the most splendid churches in the Romanesque (round arch) and Gothic (pointed arch) styles. It produced and furnished them in such numbers that in many parts of Europe the local church is more likely to be medieval than of any other period. Some buildings are huge. The cathedrals in Seville, Milan and York are the largest – in that order. Some are very large (most cathedrals, collegiate and abbey churches). Even the smaller ones are often the largest building in the town. And there are little country churches by the thousand all over Europe.

The Gothic style aimed at height. Most British builders went for width as well as height. But all Gothic churches aimed to dominate the town with tall towers and spires, pointing to heaven. This was an inescapable sign of the ultimate Power to whom all must give account. The cathedral in Ulm in Germany has the highest medieval spire, at 161 metres. Britain's tallest spire is that of Salisbury Cathedral, at 123 metres. Many who have never visited Salisbury are nevertheless familiar with the cathedral through the painting by John Constable (1776–1837).

These great buildings were much more beautiful and magnificent than any other human construction seen by medieval people. The first glimpse would cause them, as it does us, to gasp in wonder and instil feelings of both lowliness and exaltation. The technical skill required was immense and sophisticated. And time was no object. Some medieval cathedrals, York Minster for example, took more than 200 years to complete.

Art beyond the church walls

Art and architecture have been first cousins from the earliest days. Christian churches have been adorned by artists and craftsmen in every possible way. And a great deal of art, also sponsored by the Church, flourished outside these buildings.

A walk around any of the great European art galleries reveals the importance of the Bible as a source of inspiration for painters and sculptors. Supreme among subjects are the annunciation to Mary by the angel Gabriel foretelling the birth of her son, the shepherds and wise men visiting the infant Christ, the Last Supper, the crucifixion and the resurrection. But we instantly think also of numerous great works of art on other biblical themes: Michelangelo's *David*; Masaccio's *The Expulsion of Adam and Eve*; Rembrandt's *Jacob Wrestling with the Angel* … . The list is endless.

In every generation there has been an attempt to make Jesus Christ contemporary. Styles of clothing, buildings and landscape often refer to the time of the artist rather than the time of Christ. In this way artists seek to capture the idea that in a profound sense those ancient events are 'happening' in the here and now. For example, in a 17th-century painting in Peru's Cuzco Cathedral, Jesus and his disciples eat guinea pig (an Andean Indian delicacy) at the Last Supper. The British artist Stanley Spencer painted many biblical scenes set in the English village of Cookham where he was born and lived for most of his life. And in the village of Dunnington just outside York in England, the stained glass window by Helen Whittaker installed in 2009 used local characters in the crowd scenes at the crucifixion.

SIMPLICITY AND DESTRUCTION

From time to time in the 2,000-year history of Christianity, there has been a reaction against prevailing artistic trends. Sometimes an attempt has been made to create Christian art and architecture which reflect the humility of Jesus Christ, rather than his glory. Occasionally, Christians have tried to do without holy places or, more often, to do without elaborate art or architecture.

In the eighth and ninth centuries, in the East, there was a movement against icons. Many were smashed or defaced. The protesters became known as *iconoclasts*, or 'image-breakers'. They argued that icons of Christ showed only his humanity. And they feared that people were tempted to worship the icons rather than God himself.

In the 12th century, a movement for greater austerity in the monastic life spread through the Benedictine houses, and the

Cistercian movement began. As well as protesting against laxity in lifestyle, Cistercians also argued for greater simplicity in the art and architecture of abbeys. Their leader, St Bernard of Clairvaux, wrote:

> 'Tell me then poor monks, what is gold doing in the holy place? For the sight of these sumptuous and amazing vanities encourages man to give rather than to pray … the poor are allowed to groan in hunger and the money they need is spent in useless luxury.'

Such accusations have often been levelled against elaborate buildings and extravagant acts. In the Reformation of the 16th century, some believers, particularly those of the Calvinist persuasion, were so antagonized by pictures and statues that they destroyed or beheaded them. But these destructive phases were intermittent and represent the extremism which occasionally strikes many religious and political traditions. This Protestant influence sometimes improved the medieval buildings. By removing a clutter of statues and altars, they allowed the simple dignity of the architecture to stand out.

The new churches built by these Reformation groups often introduced another form of church architecture. The main focus was on the pulpit rather than the altar. The seating was arranged so that as many as possible could see the preacher; galleries were often built at first-floor level. This did not mark a complete change, for the other focal points of Christian worship – the communion table, the font and the seats for the president and his assistants – were retained.

Many of these churches are very beautiful in their simplicity. Examples abound of churches erected during the 17th and 18th centuries for the Protestant denominations. Somewhat more emphasis is usually given to the holy table within Anglican buildings, such as the Wren churches built in London after the Great Fire of 1666. (Christopher Wren designed 53 churches, including St Paul's Cathedral.) In these buildings, art is still in evidence, if not through statues and vestments, then in monuments and painted patterns around biblical texts and other inscriptions.

CONTRASTS

During the Middle Ages, the Church was the dominant patron of art and architecture. Gradually, during the 16th and 17th centuries, power and wealth moved to the royal houses and the aristocracy. The kind of art and architecture favoured in their palaces and public buildings was copied also in the churches.

In southern Europe, a highly elaborate style known as Baroque produced some fantastic churches similar to theatres or opera houses. Huge canopies with angels and rays of the sun towered over the altars. Pulpits were as high as 7 metres, with so many curtains and saints and trumpet-blowing angels that the preacher could hardly be seen! The best examples of this exuberant style of decoration are to be found in Austria and southern Germany, although most countries in Europe were touched by this fashion.

There was also at that time an almost opposite enthusiasm for everything in the classical style of ancient Greece and Rome (producing the word 'Gothic' as a term of contempt for the 'barbaric' styles of the Middle Ages). So churches, as well as great houses and public buildings, were built like ancient temples: rectangular, with graceful lines and Doric, Ionic and Corinthian columns. This was the style exported by empire-builders and missionaries to the New World. So most of the older buildings in Canada and the USA are in this 'colonial' neo-classical style.

BACK TO THE FUTURE

In the 19th century, there was a reaction against simplicity: Gothic once again became popular. Not only churches, but other public buildings – and even houses – started to sprout pinnacles, traceried windows, stained glass and other features of medieval art and architecture.

The great increase in Europe's population at that time led to thousands of new churches being built. Most of them are in this medieval style, although 19th-century skills in mass manufacturing were fully employed and not much was handmade. Because of the survival of so many medieval churches in Europe, and the large number of 19th-century churches built in that style, many people still think that the only 'proper' church building is 'Gothic', i.e. one that looks 'medieval'.

In the 20th century there were many changes in fashion, in building and in decoration. Modern technology meant that new materials became readily available, such as fibreglass, concrete (in fact, invented first by the Romans), plastic, aluminium. It was a century which felt free from dominance by the past. There was much greater diversity in buildings, as people experimented with different styles and tried out new combinations.

In recent times, there has been a greater emphasis on abstract art and symbolism. This can be seen most clearly in contemporary stained glass, in textiles for church use and in paintings (and to a lesser extent in sculpture). There has also been a conscious attempt to adjust church architecture afresh to modern patterns of worship. There were disadvantages to the 19th-century enthusiasm for the building styles of the Middle Ages. In particular, church buildings were not always suitable for the styles of worship then evolving. They exercised a retrograde influence, for worship had to adjust to the building rather than the other way round. Large old buildings present real – and expensive – problems for many modern congregations.

Several contemporary churches have abandoned the basilica pattern with its eastward-facing focus, so dominant in the West for 17 centuries. Architects have experimented with the centralized plan of the Eastern tradition, with the focus nearer the centre and the congregation ranged around. One famous example is the Roman Catholic Cathedral in Liverpool. Built in the 1960s, this is affectionately known as 'the Mersey funnel'.

This freedom from tradition has been expressed in some very unusual churches, of which Gaudi's *La Sagrada Família* (Church of the Holy Family) in Barcelona is probably the best known. The first cathedral to be consecrated in the 21st century (2 September 2002) was Our Lady of the Angels in Los Angeles, which harnesses solar power.

Glory to God in the highest

In one sense Christianity has no holy places. Unlike a Muslim or a Hindu, a Christian is under no obligation to make a pilgrimage. God can be experienced with equal power and worshipped with equal validity in every place.

But it is a universal human need, which Christianity in no way denies, that people need a place, usually a building, which is set apart (which is what the word 'holy' means) for the worship of the Creator and Sustainer of the universe. These places remind them of the claims upon them of that which is greater than themselves. In building and decorating such places, Christians offer their skills, labour and most precious gifts as tokens of worship.

In recent years, interest in church buildings has grown. Many, especially cathedrals, have become extremely popular with tourists. For example, St Paul's Cathedral and Westminster Abbey in London each welcomed over 2 million visitors in 2013. In England and Wales, attendance figures of those worshipping in cathedrals on Sundays has remained fairly static since 2004, but the number attending midweek services has risen significantly. (The Church of England helpfully publishes an annual survey on its website at www.churchofengland.org)

Over many centuries such church buildings, with their architecture and artistic contents, bear witness to the immense contribution that Christianity has made to the universal human need for sacred places. They also bear witness to the billions of hours that have been devoted over the centuries, by thousands of unknown people – in planning, building, maintaining, carving, painting, weaving, etc. The exercise of these skills has produced some of the most beautiful and magnificent works of human achievement.

Why such massive endeavour? Partly because of the God-given creative drive within human beings. Partly, no doubt, to bring glory to the town or city, the clergy and the architect. But there is another motive too – a desire to glorify Almighty God, and to raise human hearts in worship, adoration and thanksgiving.

> 'So works of art can awaken faith, or at least the longing for faith. Van Gogh said he could not look at a picture by Rembrandt without believing in God. At the very least, art – in all its forms – keeps the possibilities of faith alive. Christian art makes the faith explicit.' (Richard Harries, *Art and the Beauty of God*, 1989)

Key ideas

▶ The first Christians met for worship in homes and (in Rome) in the catacombs.

▶ The earliest known Christian building was a house adapted for the purpose soon after AD 200. A similar house-church in Britain is dated around AD 400.

▶ Fine churches and cathedrals continue to be built in the 21st century.

▶ Open-air 'holy sites' are very popular with modern pilgrims.

▶ From early days, believers decorated their buildings 'to the glory of God' – with mosaics, carvings, paintings, etc.

▶ Eventually the Church became the patron of the arts, although the counter-urge for simple, plain church buildings also persisted.

▶ Early paintings of Jesus avoided his crucifixion, but from the late Middle Ages this became a common subject.

Dig deeper

R. Homan, *The Art of the Sublime: Principles of Christian art and architecture* (Aldershot: Ashgate, 2006).

P. Murray and L. Murray, *A Dictionary of Christian Art* (Oxford: Oxford University Press, 2004).

R. Taylor, *How To Read A Church: A guide to images, symbols and meanings in churches and cathedrals* (London: Rider, 2003).

Fact check

1 Early Christian church buildings owed much to existing architectural examples. Which of the following was *not* used as a model for early churches?
   a The mausoleum
   b The meeting hall or basilica
   c The Colosseum
   d The synagogue

2 The first Christians:
   a built new churches straight away
   b converted synagogues to use as churches
   c met in houses to worship
   d used Roman secular buildings as churches

3 The catacombs on the outskirts of Rome were used by early Christians as:
   a places to store the Dead Sea Scrolls
   b places to meet for worship and to commemorate their dead
   c places to continue Jewish sacrifices
   d places to avoid the plague-ridden city

4 The Church of the Holy Sepulchre in Jerusalem was believed to mark the site of:
   a the baptism of Jesus
   b the burial of Jesus
   c the ascension of Jesus
   d the birth of Jesus

5 Icons are:
   a a feature of Roman architecture
   b images used to aid prayer
   c vestments worn by priests in the Temple
   d sacred vessels used in the Mass

6 Reformation groups often introduced a form of church architecture where the main focus was on:
   a the pulpit
   b the altar
   c the pews
   d the font

7 Artistic decoration in churches performed an important function. It helped to:
   a cover up damp patches on the walls
   b frighten the congregation
   c teach an illiterate population the basic elements of the Christian faith
   d give employment to local artists

8 The Church of the Holy Wisdom (*Hagia Sophia*) is in which city?
   a Rome
   b Jerusalem
   c Paris
   d Istanbul

9 'Romanesque' refers to:
   a a style of writing
   b an architectural style
   c Italian culture
   d Roman Catholic liturgy

10 A *pietà* is:
   a an architectural feature
   b a representation of the death of Jesus
   c an icon
   d a reading desk for the Bible

Music and literature

In this chapter you will learn about:

▶ *the place of music in Christian worship and devotion*

▶ *some of the great masterpieces of Christian music*

▶ *the relationship between Christianity and literature.*

Music in worship

CONTINUITY

Jesus and his disciples ended their last supper together by singing a Psalm. From that day on, disciples of Jesus from all generations have made music in praise of God. Jesus came, he said, not to destroy the Hebrew Scriptures ('The Law and the Prophets') but to fulfil them; to bring out their full meaning. The Old Testament Law (or *Torah*) is itself rich in poetry, from the spectacular rhythms of its opening drama – the Creation story – to the song of Moses in Exodus. Among the volumes of later history, Chronicles goes into enthusiastic detail about the specialized music of the Temple. Elsewhere the prophets, impatient as they are with empty rituals and meaningless songs, themselves soar to heights of lyrical writing as they deliver the Word of God for good or ill.

The highest peaks of Israel's praises are found between the Law and the Prophets, in 'the Writings'. Job, the Song of Songs and Ecclesiastes are outstanding literary works. But the best-known, and best-loved, of all Bible poetry is the collection of Psalms. These 150 Hebrew songs in many moods were sung in the Temple and synagogues; they were adopted by Christians from the earliest days of the New Testament Church.

Those who travelled with Jesus for his three public years repeatedly heard him use these already ancient verses as inspired pointers to himself. The singing of a Psalm concluded the last meal before his death; at least two others were on his lips as he hung dying on the cross. After the resurrection they were part of his final teaching, and after Pentecost the widening circle of his followers took up the song. With few exceptions, their successors have kept such music echoing around the globe.

Slip into Evensong in an Anglican cathedral and you will hear the appointed Psalm(s) for that day. Touch down in the Western Isles of Scotland and, in tiny chapels clinging to rocky hillsides, the people will be working through their own rugged metrical forms. In the lively meetings of the less formal 'Community Church', you may clap hands to songs with phrases lifted freely from the same Bible source. And in their different forms, Psalms introduce weddings ('Praise, my soul, the King of heaven'), are sung at funerals ('The Lord's my shepherd') and accompany national remembrance ('O God, our help in ages past').

> 'One of the reasons music aids worship is that music is a more expressive medium than ordinary speech. Music enables us to express an intensity of feeling through variety in tempo, pitch, volume, melody, harmony and rhythm.'
>
> J.F. White, *Introduction to Christian Worship* (3rd edn, Abingdon Press, 2000), p. 112.

These Hebrew songs have become part of a totally international body of praise. They adapt to plainchant; Gregorian, Anglican or Taizé chanting; solemn Genevan paraphrase; exuberant hymns; and the music of flute or guitar, synthesizer or whatever is to come. In the monastic stream, notably among the Benedictines, each of the day's services has its own mood and music, with the rotation of Psalms as a fundamental element of their song.

> 'The Psalmist says, "seven times a day have I praised you". We will fulfil this sacred number of seven if we satisfy our obligations of service at Lauds, Prime, Terce, Sext, None, Vespers and Compline. Concerning the Vigils, the same Psalmist says, "At midnight I rise to give you praise." Therefore we should praise our Creator for his just judgements at these times.' (from the sixth-century Rule of St Benedict)

TRANSFORMATION

But from its earliest days Christianity had to repudiate the idea that it was simply a new sect or subdivision of Judaism. In worship as in teaching, the dying and rising again of Jesus Christ was central. His coming marked not simply a new direction, but in some ways a total contrast with what had gone before. Continuity and contrast are found in perfect balance in the New Testament Letter to the Hebrews.

The New Testament has nothing like the musical detail, or even the poetry, of the Old. What it does have, apart from encouragements to sing (Ephesians 5:19 and Colossians 3:16), is an apparently random sprinkling across its pages of some of the new songs the Christians sang (e.g. Ephesians 5; Philippians

2; 2 Timothy 2). They stand out from their prose context mainly by vocabulary and rhythmic structure. The climax of all such writing comes with the sequence of poems in the last book of the Bible (Revelation), which opens the door an inch or so to catch the sound of singing in heaven. In all these songs, the focus is different from the Old Testament Psalms. The centre of praise is now Jesus Christ the Lord: specifically the Lord once crucified, now living and reigning in the glory of the Father.

A SINGING FAITH

The pre-eminence of Jesus in the New Testament is matched exactly in one of the earliest pieces of evidence about the Church, from a writer outside its membership – even outside Judaism. 'On an appointed day', wrote Pliny the Younger to the Roman Emperor Trajan in about AD 112, the Christians 'had been accustomed to meet before daybreak, and to recite a hymn antiphonally to Christ as to a god …'.

Having gradually transferred some of the Sabbath (Saturday) traditions to the first day of the week (Sunday) in honour of Christ's resurrection, Christians went on singing this kind of hymn for the next 20 centuries. One of the finest survivors from the Church's youth (probably fourth century) is the Latin *Te Deum Laudamus*: 'We praise thee, O God, we acknowledge thee to be the Lord … Thou art the King of glory, O Christ.'

English-speakers can still enjoy the flavour of the ancient Greek and Latin hymns in the paraphrases of John Mason Neale, a Victorian pioneer in their recovery, and some more recent versions. Medieval Christendom leaned heavily on the Psalm tradition, and Miles Coverdale added 'spiritual songs' to his 16th-century translation of the Psalms. After the Reformation, it was the 'Old Version' of paraphrases by Sternhold and Hopkins which held sway in parish churches – true to the Hebrew but harsh to the ear.

'As is the case with space and symbol, music and song are often close to the heart of participants' emotional engagement in worship. Musical dimensions of liturgy may express deeply felt devotion …'

S. Burns, *Liturgy* (SCM, 2006) p. 70.

Martin Luther, the father of the European Reformation, was a keen singer, a gifted musician and a strong believer in the power of hymns (not just Psalms) in his vernacular German (not just Latin). 'Next to the word of God', he said, 'music deserves the highest praise'. Not only Germans but most English-speaking Christians still sing his tunes and themes, e.g. *Ein' feste Burg* ('A safe stronghold our God is still'), as well as much gentler music and the secular melodies he adapted for sacred purposes. John Calvin, by contrast, determined to stick to Psalms in church.

By around 1700, however, there was a new version of the Psalms by Nahum Tate and Nicholas Brady – more poetic and soon popular enough to be bound alongside the *Book of Common Prayer* (1662). This practice continued for a further hundred years.

Also around 1700, a young Southampton man named Isaac Watts (1674–1748) complained about the version of the Psalms sung in his dissenting chapel. His father challenged him to do better, and the English hymn as we know it was born. Just turned 30 years, Watts wrote with a scholar's discipline, a communicator's clarity, a preacher's passion – and sometimes a patriot's idiosyncrasy. He pioneered original hymns ('When I survey the wondrous cross') as well as transforming the Psalter – an alternative name for the Psalms.

> 'When I survey the wondrous cross
> On which the Prince of Glory died,
> My richest gain I count but loss,
> And pour contempt on all my pride.'
> (Isaac Watts)

> 'Hymns and worship songs have a way of sticking in the memory when far grander verses fade away.'
> N. Page, *And now let's move into a time of nonsense* (Authentic, 2004), p. 11–12.

A generation later, Charles Wesley (1707–88) greatly extended the range of hymnody. His hymns were enlivened by the direct freshness of his evangelistic travels on horseback, informed by his encyclopaedic memory of the Bible and constructed with amazing speed. His soaring verse still dominates most major hymn books and adorns many literary anthologies as poetry in its own right. Charles was uniquely assisted by his elder brother John, who also wrote hymns and translated others from German, as well as promoting and publishing Charles' hymns. To this day, the Methodist Church is renowned for its hymn singing.

> 'Hark! The herald angels sing
> Glory to the new-born King,
> Peace on earth, and mercy mild,
> God and sinners reconciled.'
> (Charles Wesley)

Other writers continued where the Wesleys left off. From a long list we may select John Newton (1725–1807), a converted slave-trader, and William Cowper (1731–1800), a poet of the first rank. Distinguished Victorian writers include Catherine Winkworth, Frances Ridley Havergal and (Mrs) Cecil Frances Alexander. In their hymns we hear a clearer call to worldwide mission. Meanwhile, James Montgomery and Philip Doddridge led the Free Church stream. Reginald Heber, Christina Rossetti and Robert Bridges were genuine poets whose gifts were also used in hymn-writing.

Spotlight

The word 'hymn' probably comes from the Greek *hymnos*, which was a song or poem of praise to a god. But some think it might be based on the name of the Greek god for marriage, Hymen. A *hymenaios* was a wedding song.

TO THE PRESENT DAY

The first half of the 20th century saw some falling-off in hymn writing, and the consolidation of *Hymns Ancient and Modern* (which began in 1861) as *the* archetypal English-speaking hymn book. Its nearest rival was the *English Hymnal* (1906), revised by Ralph Vaughan Williams in 1933.

Recent decades have seen a worldwide explosion of hymnody, still too close for evaluation. Three of today's most popular writers of hymns and songs are Bishop Timothy Dudley-Smith, Graham Kendrick and Christopher Idle. The Taizé and Iona communities (notably John Bell) also produce music which is sung around the world.

With increasing technology and mass communication, Christian songs and hymns have crossed confessional and national boundaries more quickly than ever. American, Afro-Caribbean and Australasian tastes may not be the same, but styles overlap and mingle in recent hymnals and songbooks. However, it is possible to move from one church to its next-door neighbour and find an entirely different pool of favourites. These are often sung with the aid of a large screen rather than a book.

SPIRITUALS

The Spiritual, whose mood and rhythms have crossed the Atlantic twice over, has proved to be an enduring art form. Its roots are in black Africa; its main development was among the slaves of the American continent. Its more genteel flowering, adopted by white North Americans and Europeans, has found ready affinities with folk-song and gospel hymns.

Oppressed peoples of many nations still find in them a vehicle for their cries to God for help in this life and the next. But it is not only the persecuted and poor who enjoy and appreciate them, and gospel choirs have never been more popular.

MUSIC VERSUS WORDS

The art of written musical notation was developing around AD 1000. The choir could now sing a tune its members had never heard, simply by reading marks on paper! For the first time, a melody could be fixed and even attached to a composer's name. The art of harmony grew and musical decoration became increasingly complex. Reformers like John Wycliffe in the 14th century sounded a warning which was repeated four centuries later by John Wesley and is still heard today. What is the point of lovely music, he asked, if it obscures the sense of the words and is produced by those who neither mean nor believe what they sing? In 1519, Erasmus expressed a trenchant criticism of ornate music that obscured the text:

> 'Modern church music is so constructed that the congregation cannot hear one distinct word. The choristers themselves do not understand what they are singing … Words nowadays mean nothing.'

At the Reformation, the emphasis changed markedly from long, intricate lines and harmonies with Latin words to simple settings in the vernacular, which had to be comprehensible to the listener. Archbishop Holgate's injunction in 1552 to the Dean and Chapter of York Minster reveals this tension:

> 'We will and command that there be none other note sung or used … saving square note plain, so that every syllable may be plainly and distinctly pronounced, and without any reports of repeating which may induce any obscureness to the hearers.'

The Council of Trent (1545–63) decreed that liturgical words should be clearly heard, and that music should avoid profane origins and associations. Both of these directives proved something of a losing battle.

In 1550, John Merbecke produced his 'noted' version of the main church services in line with Reformation ideals, and with free rhythms matching the natural flow of the words. His acclaim came much later in the revival of his work, for different reasons, nearer our own times. The work of Thomas Tallis and William Byrd, also in the 16th century, and Henry Purcell in the 17th, retains its power and attraction for many.

MAGNIFICENT MUSIC TO WONDERFUL WORDS

The decades from 1600 onwards saw a magnificent flowering of church music, notably in Italy, and the beginnings of oratorio. But it was the German Lutheran J.S. Bach (1685–1750) who emerged as possibly the greatest composer ever produced by Western culture. As an organist he was breath-taking, as a composer, prolific. He set Bible narrative to music as none before or since. His music itself – apart from the words – was designed to carry theological truths. Bach's contemporary

G.F. Handel wrote many oratorios, including *Messiah* (1741) – possibly the most popular of all religious compositions. This work retains its wide appeal, and has given rise to many choirs formed to sing it. Haydn's *The Creation* (composed in 1798) is another great work from the oratorio repertoire by a devout Christian.

Applause for popular oratorios like *Messiah* was not universal. Was it right to make the person of Jesus Christ the subject of what looked like, and was promoted as, popular entertainment?

Case study

In Chapter 6 we looked at Christian beliefs. These are expressed in the creeds as ideas – intellectual statements which capture the central tenets of the faith. Music and literature (as well as architecture, art and other forms of expression) do something else. They engage the senses, the emotions, the imagination. Down the years many Christians have written specifically Christian music and literature, but must Christians only use these? Think about the following:

▶ Is it dangerous or wrong of Christians to use secular artistic material? Why?

▶ Is it legitimate to read Christian ideas 'into' secular literature? If so, how is this justified?

▶ Is it legitimate to use secular music for Christian worship? If so, on what grounds?

Similar questions have greeted more recent shows and films. Critics argue that shows like *Jesus Christ Superstar* create an entirely new 'Jesus' and wrap him up in the pop music of its day. Others argue that musicals like *Godspell*, plays like Dennis Potter's *Son of Man* and films like *Jesus of Nazareth* contain substantial material from the Gospels. They can and do speak with a fresh voice to those outside the community of faith.

Haydn, Schubert, Verdi and Brahms are among a number of leading composers who wrote a Mass (sometimes more than one). This is a musical setting to five lyrical and significant passages from the Latin service. Among the greatest are Mozart's Requiem Mass (1791), Bach's Mass in B Minor (completed in 1738), and Beethoven's Mass in D (1825). The Passion narratives, using the words of the New Testament Gospels, have also been a fruitful source of musical inspiration. Two of the greatest examples of this form are the *St Matthew Passion* and *St John Passion* by J.S. Bach.

Spotlight

Classical music is not the only genre to be used in Christian compositions. Duke Ellington wrote three 'Sacred Concerts' late in his life – 'the most important thing I have ever done', he said – using jazz as a musical medium to accompany Christian liturgy.

Composers continued to be inspired by the Scriptures, the liturgy and Christian poetry. Still popular with choirs is Stainer's *The Crucifixion* (1887). More recent works of note include Edward Elgar's setting of Cardinal Newman's poem *The Dream of Gerontius* (1900); William Walton's *Belshazzar's Feast* (1931); Benjamin Britten's *Noye's Fludde* (1957), Leonard Bernstein's *Chichester Psalms* (1965) and David Willcocks' many carols. Many contemporary composers – such as John Rutter, John Tavener, James MacMillan, Andrew Carter, Malcolm Archer, Philip Moore, Bob Chilcott and Richard Shephard – find inspiration from Christian themes.

MUSIC IN THE LOCAL CHURCHES

The works mentioned above are essentially 'performance' works requiring great skill, talent and hard work in rehearsal. Back in the English parish church in the 19th century, music was again on the move. Thomas Hardy's novel *Under the Greenwood Tree* (1872) reflects the sadness of villagers in his father's time at losing their gallery orchestra and choir as the organ took over. Parish churches began to imitate a style more appropriate to the cathedral; this initiative was driven forward by the spirit of the Oxford Movement. Less affluent churches opted for harmoniums or even a barrel organ. The chanting of Psalms, in Coverdale's Prayer Book version, came to appear characteristically Anglican. But chanting is losing ground today, except where a strong and older musical tradition is maintained.

Today, the pendulum has swung again as the organ in its turn is replaced in many churches by music groups and bands leading the worship. In many places 'worship' is synonymous with 'music' and 'singing'. With the age of the internet, music has gone global. New music is composed and shared almost instantly around the world. Much of it is short-lived but available across cultures and time zones.

THE MUSIC INDUSTRY

The Second Vatican Council in the 1960s gave encouragement to Roman Catholic writers and composers alike. New responsorial settings of the Psalms have been one outcome. But the older monastic music continues to be popular. Gregorian chant, once confined to monasteries and 'church', has become popular among non-Christian (even non-religious) people. Bible stories, themes and words have been used in the secular music world by artists such as Bob Dylan and Van Morrison. The distinction between 'sacred' and 'secular' appears to have become somewhat blurred.

The literature of faith

The earliest English literature is almost entirely Christian in character. Over the centuries the number of writers – dramatists, poets, novelists – who worked on Christian themes reads like a list of all-time greats in English literature: from Caedmon to Shakespeare, Milton to Charles Dickens, and on to the present day.

Caedmon (seventh century) is the earliest known English Christian poet; he is credited with the earliest surviving Christian hymn in the English language. The prose of King Alfred (848–99), like much of the whole corpus of Old and Middle English, clearly comes within the same tradition of faith.

The Mystery Plays of the 13th to 16th centuries have enjoyed a new lease of life in our own day. Following the Miracle Plays, they probably took their name from the 'mysteries' or trade guilds who performed them. They vividly presented great Bible events from the Creation onwards, developing strong local styles and texts. Similar to these is the world-famous Oberammergau Passion Play. Started in the 17th century as a thanksgiving to God for deliverance from the plague, the villagers vowed to continue to perform it every ten years.

The writing of Geoffrey Chaucer (c.1342–1400), together with his near contemporary William Langland and his successors, Spenser, Shakespeare and other Elizabethans, reflect their Christian heritage. Two masters of English prose who paid for their writings with their lives were the liturgical reformer Archbishop Thomas Cranmer and the Bible translator William Tyndale. The former enabled English speakers to pray in their own tongue; the latter made it possible for them to read or hear the Scriptures in English. We have already noted Melvyn Bragg's astonishing statement that Tyndale's work is 'probably the most influential book that's ever been in the history of language – English or any other'.

'In addition to the Bible itself, Christians have used literature to express, challenge, and analyse their faith for centuries.'
J.R. Adair, *Introducing Christianity* (Routledge, 2008) p. 416.

The poet George Herbert (1593–1633) and the satirist Jonathan Swift (1667–1745) were clergymen and Samuel Johnson (1709–84) was a devout layman. John Donne, appointed Dean of St Paul's Cathedral in 1621, is remembered for both religious and erotic poetry and for his powerful and original sermons.

'All mankind is of one author, and is one volume. When one man dies, one chapter is not torn out of the book, but translated into a better language; and every chapter must be so translated ... No man is an island, entire of itself. Every man is a piece of the continent, a part of the main. If a clod be washed away by the sea, Europe is the less, as well as if a promontory were, as well as if a manor of thy friends or of thine own were. Any man's death diminishes me, because I am involved with mankind. And therefore never send to know for whom the bell tolls; it tolls for thee.' (John Donne, *Devotions upon Emergent Occasions*)

Two other Johns, Milton (1608–74) and Bunyan (1628–88), the scholar-statesman and the tinker-preacher, both stand in the Puritan tradition. Each produced several works of enduring worth and one masterpiece; in order, *Paradise Lost* and *The Pilgrim's Progress*. Both created unforgettable images in verse and prose respectively, one from his study, the other largely from a prison cell. Each used his powerful imagination to illuminate eternal truth and practical living, from the enticement of temptation in the garden of Eden to the trials and triumphs of Christian pilgrims in this world's Vanity Fair.

Among the more committed, but less predictable authors was William Blake (1757–1827), visionary poet, painter and engraver. His poem 'Jerusalem' has become a popular and rousing hymn. Blake is one of those who would be surprised to find their prophetic verses adopted and domesticated in this way.

TO THE PRESENT DAY

Many 19th-century poets explored questions of religious faith and doubt, including Samuel Taylor Coleridge, William Wordsworth, Robert Browning, Alfred, Lord Tennyson and Matthew Arnold. Among 20th-century Christian poets we note T.S. Eliot (a key figure in the transformation of poetry), Gerard Manley Hopkins (d. 1889, but undiscovered until the 20th century), Jack Clemo, Norman Nicholson, R.S. Thomas and W.H. Auden. David Adam and others have popularized a revived Celtic culture. The river wanders, varies in pace and depth, but never runs dry.

> 'Twenty years ago, I was driving up the M1 to Sheffield on All Souls' night. It was the year after my mother died and the *Messiah* was playing full blast on the car radio. And just for a moment, I had the certainty of resurrection. Maybe that's what great art does. Maybe art – music, writing, whatever – is a kind of resurrection, a redemption of the past … or, maybe, that's all just part of the illusion.' (Margaret Drabble, novelist)

Spotlight

J.R.R. Tolkein said that *The Lord of the Rings* trilogy was 'fundamentally religious and Catholic' (he was a Roman Catholic). He believed this happened unconsciously when he wrote the first draft, but when he came to revise it he consciously sought to incorporate Christian truths in his mythical tales.

The desire to explore and explain the Christian faith has prompted apologetics (the defence of the faith), novels, poetry, essays and drama from 20th-century believers such as Dorothy L. Sayers, C.S. Lewis, G.K. Chesterton, J.R.R. Tolkien and Charles Williams. Three Catholic writers – Anthony Burgess, Graham Greene and Evelyn Waugh – were powerful novelists whose religious background and troubled faith strongly influenced their work. Novels and plays by Christians and unbelievers continue to explore great themes such as the existence and nature of God, suffering, meaning and purpose. Among modern writers the Pulitzer Prize-winning novelist Marilynne Robinson has received widespread critical acclaim for her explicitly Christian novels set in an small American town called Gilead.

In this brief note we have concentrated on English literature, but the Christian legacy is to be found in many languages. Christian writers find inspiration in a short passage originally written in Greek: a passage which reminds us of the power of words – and the significance of 'the Word made flesh'.

> 'In the beginning was the Word, and the Word was with God, and the Word was God ... In him was life, and the life was the light of men. The light shines in the darkness, and the darkness has not overcome it ... And the Word became flesh and dwelt among us, full of grace and truth.' (John 1:1,4–5,14; RSV)

Jonathan Miller, for example, who comes from a secular Jewish background, has said that Christian imagery constantly reinforces his sense of human tragedy.

> 'The tragedy of being human, and the idea of the Incarnation is one of the great imaginative inventions of

the moral imagination. I would find it very hard to think forcefully and properly without in fact being stocked with such images.'

To a Christian, such a positive affirmation of Christian imagery should not be as surprising as at first glance it might appear. For Christian truths are not just beliefs which a select body of believers happen to hold. They are the reality in which the whole universe is grounded.

Key ideas

▶ Jesus and his disciples said and sang the same psalms from the Jewish Scriptures (the Old Testament) that Christians still sing today.

▶ Martin Luther (1483–1546), Isaac Watts (1674–1748) and Charles Wesley (1707–88) are key names in the history of hymn writing.

▶ Victorian hymn writers included many women – perhaps the best known is (Mrs) Cecil Frances Alexander.

▶ Spirituals such as 'Swing Low, Sweet Chariot' have become a popular vehicle for worship – and for England rugby fans!

▶ Many of the greatest composers wrote church music.

▶ Much of the earliest English literature was Christian in content.

▶ Melvyn Bragg made the remarkable claim that William Tyndale's Bible translation is 'probably the most influential book that's ever been in the history of language – English or any other'.

Dig deeper

J. Begbie, *Music, Modernity and God* (Oxford: Oxford University Press, 2015).

A. Gant, *O Sing Unto the Lord: A history of church music* (London: Profile, 2015).

A. Hass, D. Jasper and E. Jay (eds), *The Oxford Handbook of English Literature and Theology* (Oxford: Oxford University Press, 2007).

Fact check

1 Psalms are:
   a a set of rules governing worship
   b a collection of wise sayings
   c a collection of poems, meditations and prayers
   d Greek hymns

2 According to the Gospel narratives, Jesus and his disciples ended their last supper together by:
   a reciting a Hebrew prayer
   b shaking hands
   c weeping
   d singing a Psalm

3 The New Testament contains:
   a no Christian hymns
   b a lot of new Christian hymns
   c a lot of Old Testament hymns
   d some examples of early Christian hymns

4 Martin Luther:
   a was a keen singer and gifted musician
   b thought music was 'of the devil'
   c had no interest in music
   d thought music was a dangerous distraction

5 John Wycliffe (and John Wesley) argued that:
   a the most important thing was the high quality of the music
   b only professional musicians should be involved in church music
   c lovely music had no point if it obscured the sense of the words
   d it didn't matter if music was produced by those who neither meant nor believed what they sang

6 William Tyndale is famous as:
   a a hymn writer
   b a composer
   c a translator
   d a singer

7 Who wrote *The Pilgrim's Progress?*
   a John Wesley
   b John Milton
   c John Tavener
   d John Bunyan

8 The Mystery Plays of the 13th to 16th centuries:
   a were complex medieval 'whodunnits'
   b vividly presented great Bible events from the Creation to Revelation
   c were performed in Latin so were not understood by the people
   d are so called because we only know of them from other sources and have no copies of them

9 Of what work did Melvyn Bragg say '[It is] probably the most influential book that's ever been [written] in the history of language – English or any other'?
   a Tyndale's translation of the Bible
   b John Donne's *Devotions upon Emergent Occasions*
   c Milton's *Paradise Lost*
   d George Herbert's *The Country Parson*

10 Who said of their three 'Sacred Concerts' that they were 'the most important thing I have ever done'?
   a Nat King Cole
   b Louis Armstrong
   c Ella Fitzgerald
   d Duke Ellington

Part 4:

The modern world

Modern challenges

In this chapter you will learn about the impact on Christianity of:

▶ *global developments in theology*
▶ *secularization and modernism*
▶ *globalization*
▶ *postmodernism.*

By 1900 Christianity was a truly worldwide faith. Through the missionary movements of the 19th century it had been planted in every continent of the world. It was closely associated with the secular governments of the leading industrial nations of the world. It led huge parts of the world in art and culture. But the dawn of the 20th century saw unimagined changes both inside the Church and in the world it inhabited. The first half of that century was dominated by two world wars. Both were essentially European wars which spread to draw in many other parts of the world – but at the heart of them the Christian nations of Europe were locked in military and political conflict. The fallout from these conflicts was far-reaching, affecting virtually all areas of life.

The world was also growing rapidly. Estimates of world population around the year of Jesus's birth are usually put at about 200 million. By 1800 the world's population passed the one billion mark, doubling by 1927 and again by 1975 to four billion. Today it is just short of seven and half billion. The world that Christianity now inhabits is vastly different from that of the early Christians.

Two movements

Of the many movements which emerged in the 20th century, two within the Church can be singled out as of particular importance. The **ecumenical movement** was anticipated by the formation of the Evangelical Alliance in 1846, when individuals from more than 50 American and British Protestant denominations agreed to pursue religious liberty and to co-operate in various evangelistic and educational endeavours. But the intended unity was selective: one aim was to unite Protestants in resistance to Catholicism.

The 20th-century ecumenical movement attempted to bring together churches with widely differing approaches to the Christian faith. In 1910, at an international missionary conference in Edinburgh led by the American Methodist John R. Mott, 1,000 delegates shared his desire for Christian unity. Structures were established in an attempt to give shape and substance to their vision. Eventually this initiative gave rise to the formation of the World Council of Churches (WCC); 351 delegates from 147 denominations and 44 countries gathered for the first General Assembly in Amsterdam in 1948. The movement was earning the right to call itself 'ecumenical' – from the Greek word *oikoumene*, meaning 'the whole inhabited earth'.

Further General Assemblies were organized every six years or so. At New Delhi in 1961 there were two important developments: the Russian Orthodox Church joined the Council and a formal confessional basis was adopted. This stated that:

> 'The World Council of Churches is a fellowship of Churches which confess the Lord Jesus Christ as God and Saviour according to the Scriptures and therefore seek to fulfil together their common calling to the glory of one God, Father, Son, and Holy Spirit.'

In the 1960s, the WCC caused controversy by its involvement in political issues. It made grants to 'freedom fighters' in national struggles, arguing that they were oppressed minorities engaged in a 'just war'. Some member churches expressed strong disagreement with the leadership of the WCC on this matter. Critics pointed out that the WCC leadership was selective in the causes it championed – appearing to be less critical of Marxist and Maoist regimes. They also argued that the WCC is not a 'super Church' but should be a servant of all the churches; it has no mandate to take sides in this way.

Conspicuous by its absence from these ecumenical endeavours has been the Roman Catholic Church. Issues such as the primacy of the Pope, the nature of the priesthood and the meaning and practice of the Eucharist have made it difficult for that Church to participate fully. However, from 1961 senior Roman Catholics have attended WCC assemblies as official observers. Under the leadership of the reforming Pope John XXIII, the Second Vatican Council (1962–65) opened the door to closer ecumenical activity. For the first time a Roman Catholic Council acknowledged that there are authentic Christians ('separated brethren') outside the Roman fold. Reflecting this new spirit, in 1968 the

Patriarch of Constantinople and the Pope mutually lifted the excommunications which had divided the Catholic and Eastern Orthodox Churches since 1054.

Several churches have entered into bilateral or multilateral talks – sometimes on specific issues (e.g. baptism, Eucharist and ministry), sometimes about the possibility of uniting. Organic unity has been achieved in some cases: for example, in 1947 several churches united to form the Church of South India (CSI). Not all attempts at formal unity between churches have succeeded. Critics of such schemes argue that variety in worship and church order is a good thing (matching different histories, theologies and personalities), provided there is an underlying unity of spirit and purpose.

The second movement to note is **liberation theology**. If Roman Catholicism was late in getting involved in the ecumenical movement, it was very much in evidence in liberation theology. Liberation theology emerged in Latin America in the 1960s led by Roman Catholic priests and churches. In 1968, at a conference of Roman Catholic bishops from Latin America held in Colombia, some members insisted that the starting point for theological reflection must be the situation of the poor. At the forefront of this movement is the belief that the God of the Bible is on the side of the downtrodden and marginalized: it has a 'bias to the poor'.

Liberation theology has three main strands to it:

▶ an agenda which reframes the gospel in political terms

▶ liberating theology itself

▶ recovering the human Jesus.

Reframing the gospel did not turn it into a political entity but argued that it was not possible to separate the material and the spiritual. There could be no legitimate preaching of the gospel ('the good news') which persuaded the poor to put up with their poverty on earth because they would be rewarded with 'riches in heaven'. 'Salvation' was about freedom from oppression as much as freedom from sin. The 'heavenly' gospel had to make an 'earthly' difference. It resulted in the church challenging oppression, exploitation and inequality.

Liberating theology gave the task of theological thinking back to the people. It meant arguing that it was not just priests and academics who should be doing theological thinking: it was the right and responsibility of every Christian. What were called 'base ecclesial communities' formed: local communities of Christians who brought together the spiritual and the social to reform society. They were led by lay people – that is, they didn't have a priest or a professional in charge.

Recovering the human Jesus was based on the idea that the 'Christ' of the church had become so elevated, so sanitized, so remote that he no longer spoke to ordinary men and women. The radical, disturbing preacher who founded the faith had been domesticated! Liberation theologians argued that to rest content with the status quo in unjust societies was to side with the oppressors against the oppressed. It was not without its critics in the early days.

Spotlight

A famous Brazilian priest, Archbishop Helder Camara, cryptically commented, 'When I give food to the poor they call me a saint. When I ask why they are poor, they call me a Communist.'

A wider significance of the advent of liberation theology in Latin America is that it gave rise to a number of other 'liberation theologies'. Poverty and oppression was not just about economics. Women had agitated for equality with men for decades. **Feminist theology** lent weight to their demands but also pushed it further. The gospel that had been preached for generations assumed 'male' was the norm. It had seen the gospel only from the male perspective. How could that be when half the global population was female? Look at the hymns and prayers of the vast majority of pre-20th century Christianity and you find the 'Christian' is assumed to be male, e.g. in the hymn 'He who would valiant be'.

And not only had the gospel assumed maleness: it assumed whiteness as well. **Black theology** emerged as the quest to 'see Jesus through black eyes' as the liberator of an oppressed people.

The influence of liberation theology remains strong and many Christians endorse its challenge to the view that the Church should concentrate only on 'spiritual matters'. They argue that Christian faith, and hence the Church, must be concerned with the *whole* of life and give a voice to *all* people because the God of the Bible is concerned with such.

These two movements give us a brief glimpse into the state of the Christian faith at the end of the 20th century – and it is slightly paradoxical. On the one hand, there was a coming together of the different strands of Christianity in the ecumenical movement. Much of the hostility which had led to denominational fragmentation had subsided. There was an increasing recognition of the need to work together and to celebrate difference rather than trying to eliminate it. On the other hand, there was evidence of a new kind of fragmentation. Christians were thinking through how the faith speaks to their particular condition or context. New and radical interpretations of Christianity were emerging.

All of this leads us into our next section. If Christianity was changing, so was the world. And religion – especially Christianity – was to face unprecedented challenges to its place in the world.

Secularization and modernism

'[Quite] suddenly in 1963 something very profound ruptured the character of the [British] nation and its people, sending organized Christianity on a downward spiral to the margins of social significance.'

C.G. Brown, *The Death of Christian Britain* (Routledge, 2009) p. 1.

The idea of **secularization** has been around for some time and there are differing opinions about when it started. Some say it was the First World War; others that it began with the socio-cultural upheaval of the 19th-century industrial revolution in Europe; some argue it began with the Darwinian revolution; some say the 18th-century 'Age of Reason' and the rise of science; others argue it began as far back as the 12th and 13th centuries with the rise of the universities. Brown's suggestion links it to the 'swinging 60s'.

Whenever secularization began it was initially a Western phenomenon. It refers to four significant shifts in the fortunes of Christianity:

- a decline in the public influence and role of Christian institutions
- a decline in the belief in God (particularly the Christian God)
- a decline in church attendance and membership
- the decline of a shared Christian heritage.

Up to the middle of the 19th century, western Europe was a largely rural economy. Most people lived in relatively small village communities, relying on local crafts and trades for their needs. The Church (even if split into different denominations) was a key institution providing for the educational, welfare and spiritual needs of the community. Modernism swept that away. The population rose rapidly. Agriculture became mechanized, local crafts became industrialized and the population moved from villages to the urban and suburban sprawls around the rapidly expanding cities. The Church's response was mixed. Some, like the Methodists, free from state legislation and control, were able to follow the populace into the cities and start new churches with welfare provision attached. Others, like the Church of England, were slowed down by bureaucracy and tradition. They struggled initially to start new churches where the people were.

Such massive social change carried with it changed attitudes and beliefs. Instead of being integral to society, religion became an option, a personal choice. No longer was faith passed on within the family. Families were disrupted and dislocated. The church as an institution became increasingly marginalized.

What we have just described is a *process*. It was a by-product of the socio-cultural, economic and political changes going on in society. But it led to something else. *Secularization* as a process gave rise to *secularism* as a policy.

Technically, **secularism** is about the separation of Church and State. But there are differing manifestations of it. The USA, for example, was established as a secular state. That is, there was an acknowledgement from the beginning that Church and State each had their discreet areas of responsibility or activity, and they should not be mixed. That is not to say the USA is not religious. The Christian Church remains strong and most would-be Presidents have to appeal to the large number of Christian voters in order to get elected!

Other states have become secular in organization and 'tone'. France is a clear example. The close connection between Church and State was dismantled in the French Revolution. Religion was seen as socially divisive by the likes of Voltaire and Montesquieu. In ways reminiscent of the Reformation in England, church property was seized and priests were made to swear oaths of loyalty to the state. Secularism continues as a policy in France. The state is strictly neutral in matters of religion, schools are not allowed to teach religion and the wearing of conspicuous religious symbols such as the hijab or a crucifix is banned. It is a policy based on the belief that religion should be confined to the personal or private world of the individual. It has no place in the public square.

China has a long history of secularism reaching back centuries. This is partly because the predominant ancient philosophy of China was Confucianism. But in more recent times the aggressive secularism of the Chinese Communist Party under Mao Zedong ('Chairman Mao') opposed religion in any form and sought to stamp it out. This is more relaxed today: as we have already seen, the huge number of Christians in China is growing. But the idea of a secular state (and society) is maintained.

Secularization and secularism have had a profound effect on the Church. Christianity's place in the modern world is very different from a century ago. However, we must be careful. Secularization and secularism do not happen in the same way everywhere – nor are they happening everywhere. It is interesting to reflect that in the countries where Christianity was culturally embedded, it appears to be in decline: in countries where it was not, it seems to be growing.

> 'It seems that the current situation, particularly in the West, is one of simultaneous religious decline, mutation and resurgence.'
>
> E. Graham, *Between a Rock and a Hard Place* (SCM, 2013) p. 3.

But Christians are not complacent; nor are socio-cultural trends static. Today many scholars talk about post-secularization. This is not suggesting secularization is over and done with. Rather it recognizes that religion cannot be corralled into a discreet part of life. 'Religion is back on the agenda' stated Callum Brown (C. Brown, *Religion and Society in Twentieth-Century Britain* (Longman, 2006), p. xv). 'Scientific' rationalism has not done away with religion and it is obvious that faith still plays an important part in the lives of many individuals and communities. Post-secularism is therefore (in part at least) about renegotiating the relationship between Church and State. It is concerned with the dialogue between the sacred and the secular which we will look at in Chapter 15.

Globalization

The word 'globalization' first appeared in the Oxford English Dictionary in 1930. Like many words it was coined for one purpose and was then used for others. Some think the idea really took off following the publication of a photograph of the earth taken by astronauts seeing the earth rise over the horizon of the moon. The small sphere appears to hang precariously in mid-air. It gave rise to talk of a 'global village' – seeing the world as contracted into a small entity. Much of what developed from that was linked to the world of economics, markets and business. Since then globalization has acquired a number of complex and disputed meanings which go further. We shall consider three aspects of its meaning here.

▶ Beyond the national

Globalization seems to have made national borders less important in some respects. For example, multi-national companies spread their operations around the globe. Their manufacturing base can be in one country, their finance department in another and their headquarters in yet another. Spreading the company around in this way maximizes resources and opportunities specific to those locations. This breaks the link between an industry and a national economy, creating globalized economies. As a result national governments are now considerably less powerful in managing their own domestic economies.

▶ Global urbanization

By the mid-19th century in Britain the number of people living in cities overtook the number living in the countryside. The 20th century saw this urbanization spread to become a worldwide phenomenon. UNESCO chose a symbolic date – Wednesday 23 May 2007 (based on population estimates) – to signify the point at which the urban population of the world overtook the rural population for the first time.

Such changes have an effect on religion. Communities change the way they function. The more or less static relationship between the church and its locality becomes much more fluid. Populations move about more and are less rooted in one place. All this has an effect on issues such as family and identity. Christianity has had to adapt to these huge changes.

▶ **Cultural uniformity**

Global markets have inevitably led to a large degree of standardization around the world. The easy access to global brands in technology, fashion, cars, cuisine and such like has changed how the world looks. Being in another country is not as 'foreign' as it used to be! The high street, the roads, the restaurants, the leisure centres all look very familiar wherever you are on the planet.

This has led to some local cultures and identities being diluted or even destroyed. It has also led to a reaction against this, with attempts to reassert or reinvigorate local cultures. The effects on religion are profound and we shall look at some of these in Chapter 16.

Spotlight

If globalization is about the world becoming 'standardized', homogenized and uniform, why is it we can't agree on how to spell the word – is it with an 's' or a 'z'!

Postmodernism

The third major socio-cultural shift we need to look at is postmodernism. It was originally a term used in the world of art and design but it has spread to embrace much more of life – politics, philosophy, culture, literature and even history. It is now a diverse and complex topic. Fortunately there are books which deal with it much more fully (see the end of the chapter). Here we will focus only on four features which have particular importance for Christianity.

Spotlight

Look:

► around your house

► in your fridge and freezer

► at your clothes

► at the car you drive (if you have one/do drive)

► at the music you listen to

► at the TV programmes you watch.

What different countries are represented by what you see? We each demonstrate in many ways the idea of a 'global village'.

► Postmodernism as a reaction

In some ways modernism was quite brutal. It swept away much from the past in its belief in 'progress'. Scientific and technological advances were happening very rapidly. At the time of writing, the oldest woman living in Britain was born before the Wright brothers made their first flight in 1903. Just look at where flying has got to today – in the span of a single lifetime! The iPhone in your pocket is significantly more powerful and sophisticated than all the computers on the space craft which took the first astronauts to the moon.

It was not just science and technology which was changing. Social conditions and attitudes were changing as well. Move people from small, intimate villages into vast, anonymous cities and they don't just change their lifestyle: they change the way they think. They change their perceptions, outlook, understandings and what they believe in.

Postmodernism seeks to describe this shift. It does not do away with modernism: indeed it overlaps with modernism and holds to many of modernism's ideas and attitudes. But it also questions them. Had some good things been discarded inadvertently? Had all progress been beneficial? Indeed, what is progress anyway? Were there casualties as well as winners? Major rethinking and re-evaluating was underway.

Religion – a casualty of the secularization mind-set dismissed as old-fashioned, primitive or unnecessary – was included in this re-evaluation. Not only was it found to have 'not gone away': it was found to have resources and attitudes which had a place in the contemporary world. Though there were differences in this 'brave new world'. As we saw in Chapter 9, organized religion began to give way to spirituality: regarded as a more personal and personalized way to access the mystical or the divine.

▷ Postmodernism and identity: who am I?

Perhaps one of the biggest changes in postmodernism relates to the idea of identity. 'Who am I?' According to postmodernism this is not the question of the amnesiac: it is the question of everyone. The fluidity of modern life, the multiple spheres we all inhabit (the place I live; the place I work; the place I worship; the 'me' in the flesh; the 'me' on the internet) create the possibility of numerous 'selfs'. Who I am depends less and less on who I am *expected* to be and more and more on who I *choose* to be. We must not overstate this but in a world which is increasingly 'privatized' – with more opportunities for secrecy even – the fluidity of identity is new territory. We will look at this again in Chapter 16.

▷ Truth and authenticity in postmodernity: it's true if it's true for me

Modernism was about democratization but not just in the political sense. It was about the democratization of knowledge and ideas. At school in the 1950s, the English essay question was 'What is Shakespeare's *Hamlet* all about?' What the pupil had to come up with was the answer – the *right* answer, the one the teacher had taught. Today the question posed is 'What do *you* think Shakespeare's *Hamlet* is all about?' (Actually, the question is probably no longer about Shakespeare – another victim of postmodernity?) Truth and authenticity are less and less judged by external agents. There are few (if any) 'right' answers any more: there are personal answers, personal truths, personal interpretations.

Such changes affect the relationship between individuals, institutions and communities. The power balance has shifted away from the institution towards the individual. We could express this in terms of a shift from 'I belong to it (the institution)' to 'it (the institution) belongs to me'. The effect on the Church is significant. Lieven Boeve, a Belgian theologian, has written that in the postmodern world 'the church is seen by many as a reservoir of take-it-or-leave-it fragments of meaning … a stock of items intended to assist in … personal religious formation …' (L. Boeve, *Interrupting Tradition* (Peeters Press, 2002), p. 57). It is not so much a question of whether the Church has a future but whether Church *itself* as an idea has a future.

Spotlight

In what ways might these be appropriate images to represent the pre-modern, modern and postmodern?

▶ pre-modern: the painted portrait in a hand-carved frame

▶ modern: the photograph in a photo album

▶ postmodern: the selfie on an iPhone.

▶ Pluralism

The fourth aspect of postmodernism we must look at is pluralism. Here is something of a paradox. In a globalized world where so many things are becoming the same – Ritzer's 1993 idea of 'the McDonaldization of Society' – pluralism is about multiplicity and diversity. But it is more than simply acknowledging difference: it is about actively and positively engaging with it. In areas such as race, ethnicity, religion and culture, pluralism is about active understanding and engagement. It is about dialogue and crossing boundaries. Underpinning it is the belief that no one philosophy, religion or viewpoint has a monopoly of truth.

For the best part of 2,000 years Christianity in the West enjoyed a primacy of position which was largely unchallenged. Contemporary pluralism has therefore had a profound impact on it. In this beleaguered situation is Christianity holding its nerve?

There are many examples of robust responses and resilience. Academics such as Alister McGrath, Tom Wright, Keith Ward and Rowan Williams take on the intellectual challenge facing contemporary Christianity. One example is the development of *Scriptural Reasoning* by David Ford, Regius Professor of Divinity at Cambridge University, England. It is a form of inter-faith dialogue based on careful and respectful listening to the 'other', not seeking to convert but to understand and value. At a popular level, in spite of falling numbers at church, the media regularly highlights that there are still many Christians active and involved in society.

Pluralism, of course, is present in many more (mundane) ways than at this intellectual level. People live side by side with people from many cultures and backgrounds, and a walk down any city high street will reveal a multiplicity of eateries from around the globe.

Key ideas

▶ By 1900 Christianity was a truly worldwide religion.

▶ The World Council of Churches (WCC), founded in 1948, sought to bring together all the mainstream denominations of Christianity.

- ▶ Liberation theology emerged in Latin America in the 1960s led by Roman Catholic priests and communities with a deep concern for the poor.

- ▶ Liberation theology gave birth to many other movements around the world, e.g. Feminist theology, Black theology, Womanist theology.

- ▶ Secularization is concerned with the declining influence of Christianity in public life.

- ▶ By the start of the 21st century the global urban population surpassed the rural population for the first time.

Dig deeper

E.L. Graham, *Between a Rock and a Hard Place: Public theology in a post-secular age* (London: SCM, 2013).

P. Jenkins, *The Next Christendom: The coming of global Christianity* (Oxford: Oxford University Press, 2003).

S. Kim and K. Kim, *Christianity as a World Religion* (London: Continuum, 2008).

C.D. Moe-Lobeda, *Healing a Broken World: Globalization and God* (Minneapolis, MN: Fortress Press, 2002).

B. Walsh and R. Middleton, *Truth is Stranger Than it Used to be: Biblical faith in a postmodern Age* (London: SPCK, 1995).

Fact check

1 The world population around the time of the birth of Jesus is estimated at about:
   a 2 billion
   b 2 million
   c 200 million
   d 20 million

2 'Ecumenical' comes from a Greek word which means:
   a Greek
   b united
   c the whole world
   d Eastern Orthodoxy

3 The ecumenical movement led to the founding of:
   a the United Nations
   b the European Union
   c NATO
   d the World Council of Churches

4 The Second Vatican Council (Vatican II) was held in:
   a 1948–55
   b 1962–65
   c 1888–90
   d 1965–68

5 Which of the following is *not* part of liberation theology's agenda?
   a Reframing the gospel
   b Recovering the human Jesus
   c Giving theology back to the people
   d Promoting Latin American political ideas

6 'Secularization' describes:
   a a decline in the public influence and role of Christian institutions
   b a state policy to close church buildings down
   c a church policy to close church buildings down
   d making the Christian faith illegal

7 Secularism is about:
  a new forms of worship
  b a church policy to close church buildings down
  c the separation of church and state
  d making Christianity illegal

8 'Globalization' first appeared in the Oxford English Dictionary in:
  a 1930
  b 1940
  c 1950
  d 1960

9 It is estimated that the world's urban population first exceeded that of the rural population:
  a by the start of the 20th century
  b by 1850
  c by the start of the 21st century
  d by 1950

10 The 'McDonaldization of Society' was coined by Ritzer in 1993:
  a as the title of a policy document by McDonald's
  b to describe the expansion of fast-food outlets
  c to describe the use of cafés for worship
  d as a feature of globalization

Church and society

In this chapter you will learn about:

▶ *Christianity and politics*
▶ *Christianity in the public square*
▶ *Christianity and contemporary society*
▶ *contemporary challenges.*

A key question

The Church's relation to society has gone through many changes since the early days. At first it was a small, often persecuted, minority group. Those early disciples developed a distinctive lifestyle based on love for God and neighbour, and witness to their risen Lord, within a suspicious and hostile society. They drew guidance from the vivid images used by Jesus; they were to be 'salt', 'light' and 'peacemakers' within their communities. They shared their goods and income and some of them may have lived some kind of 'common life'. It seems that in the early days they believed Jesus would return soon (the 'Second Coming'). He would usher in the new kingdom. So initially they did not get involved in public life. Indeed, as a discredited, illegal group they were often barred from doing so.

But as time went on and the Second Coming of Christ did not happen, they had to think through how they related to society. Several of the early letters in the New Testament give advice on how they were to live. Paul tells Titus to, 'Remind the people to be subject to rulers and authorities, to be obedient, to be ready to do whatever is good, to slander no one, to be peaceable and considerate, and always to be gentle towards everyone' (Titus 3:1–2). He tells the Christians in Rome to, 'be subject to the governing authorities' (Romans 13:1) – remarkable when you consider how oppressive or corrupt those authorities could be.

A radical change took place when the Emperor Constantine embraced the Christian faith in AD 312. No longer outlawed or marginalized, Christians had to learn how to wield secular, earthly power. Their relationship with the world around them had to be re-evaluated.

As we saw in Chapter 6, Christians believe in an afterlife. The opening verses of Revelation 21 speak of God creating 'a new heaven and a new earth' – after the old earth has passed away. Whatever is understood by this, it raises the question of how Christians should relate to this world in the light of the next world. Is effort spent making this world a better place simply wasted effort – it's going to end one day so perhaps Christians should just bide their time waiting for the end? Or should they use their time to make this a better world even if it is going to disappear one day? These viewpoints are sometimes referred to as 'world-affirming' and 'world-denying'. At times they have been seen as opposites.

One of the early Christian thinkers, who brought his powerful intellect to this question, was Augustine of Hippo (AD 354–430, not to be confused with Augustine of Canterbury who became the first Archbishop of Canterbury after leading a mission to England in 597). He lived in turbulent times. Christianity had been established as the official religion of Rome for some 40 years by the time he was born. During his lifetime the Emperor Julian the Apostate had briefly reversed this, seeking to re-impose paganism. Then Rome itself came under attack and the western Roman Empire began to disintegrate. In this context Augustine wrote his major work *The City of God*.

Augustine describes two institutions, the Church and the State. The Church is God's agent on earth, charged with teaching people how to live a good life to prepare them for heaven. The State is also an agency of God. It exists to order things peacefully and justly so that the Church can get on with its work. If these two fulfil their roles, working together in harmony, then their citizens will end up in the City of Heaven, the place where the 'saved' go. If not, the people will end up in the City of the World – the place of the lost. Augustine saw the Church and the State working together, complementing each other in God's grand design. In reality it often did not work like this. Their agendas sometimes clashed or tensions arose between their spheres of influence. Many times throughout history, each saw the other as 'trespassing' on what it regarded as its territory.

This sets the scene for what we will look at next. In what ways do Christians get involved in society? What do they do to make society better? And just how do Christianity and politics mix?

The Church and politics

Before we can look at the Church's role in politics it is worth pausing to think about what we mean by 'politics'. Broadly speaking, it has to do with the management of society (*polis* means 'city' in Greek). How does society organize itself? What structures and systems does it set in place which will deliver the greatest good to the greatest number of people? How will it manage conflict? How will it organize and prioritize resources? All this is political activity. More particularly, when we talk of politics we mean the work of government – Politics with a capital 'P'.

> *'[How] can someone care about their neighbour today without being concerned about the public policies which affect so much of their lives, either for good or ill? Love of neighbour today has an inescapable political dimension.'*
> R. Harries, *Faith in Politics?* (Darton, Longman and Todd, 2010) p. 11.

Politics operates at different levels – international, national and local – and there are appropriate levels of government for each of them. Christians are present at all three levels and are inescapably involved as active citizens of any society. *How* they are involved varies from place to place. In some countries the Church is closely allied to the government. It has a place in the constitutional running of the country and is directly involved in politics. In others it is an influential force in society but with no formal role in government. And in yet others it is illegal or such a small minority that it appears to have neither power nor influence.

INTERNATIONAL POLITICS

Many church leaders are international figures in their own right. Their opinions command respect even if they are disagreed with. In Chapter 11 we mentioned Pope John Paul II. He grew up in Poland. As a teenager his country was invaded by Nazi Germany and later became a satellite state of the Soviet Union. He attended an illegal, underground seminary to train as a priest and by 1963 had become Archbishop of Krakow. It was a difficult office to hold. He had to be careful in his opposition to a totalitarian regime not to increase the oppression endured by his fellow Christians. He was elected pope in 1978 when the Soviet Union still ruled huge swathes of Eastern Europe. As pope he stepped onto the world stage, where his voice was less easily silenced. He spoke out on social and political issues, criticizing the human rights record of the Soviet Union. Some years after he became pope, the Soviet Union was disbanded. We cannot say he was directly responsible for this but undoubtedly his outspoken criticisms played a significant part.

Desmond Tutu became the first black Anglican Archbishop of Cape Town in South Africa. When he became archbishop the white minority government of South Africa still maintained the racial segregation policy of apartheid. As with Pope John Paul II, being archbishop allowed Tutu's voice to be heard far and wide. Within five years of his appointment, apartheid was ended. Again, he did not bring this about on his own but his courageous stand was instrumental. Tutu did not stop there. Inspired by his deeply held Christian convictions he went on to assist in rebuilding post-apartheid South Africa. He took his message of truth and reconciliation to other post-conflict places. On a number of occasions he has been asked to address the United Nations.

Both of these Christian leaders rose to prominence within a domestic context but they spoke out – and continued to speak out – on international political issues.

Martin Luther King, Jr (1929–68) was pastor of Ebenezer Baptist Church in Atlanta, USA. Through personal charisma, courage, brilliant organization and moving rhetoric, he led a massive, non-violent movement in an attempt to establish equality for black citizens in the USA. The achievements of the civil rights movement were considerable, and related issues (such as positive discrimination) are still on the political agenda in the USA. Like Gandhi, upon whom he based his campaign of non-violent resistance, Dr King was assassinated. Few individuals are honoured shortly after death by the creation of an annual public holiday in their name, but in the USA the third Monday of January every year is a federal holiday marking Martin Luther King Day.

NATIONAL POLITICS
The role of the Church in national politics differs according to many factors. In many countries Christianity is recognized as

the state religion but has no role in government. In Costa Rica, for example, the Roman Catholic Church is the official state religion and the government contributes to its maintenance. The Church does not have any direct role in the government but it is strong and therefore inevitably influential in what goes on.

In Finland the Lutheran Church has a special and close relationship with the state. The state collects taxes on behalf of the Church to support it and the President of Finland has certain powers and responsibilities within the Church. But the Church is not involved in the secular government of the country.

The United Kingdom is an interesting example of a nation in which the Church does have a direct role in politics. The Anglican Church is 'established' by law. In England the monarch is the head of state and the head of the Church. In both cases the role has more symbolic significance than actual power, but senior bishops of the Church of England sit in the House of Lords and have a say in the governance of the country. In Scotland the monarch is head of state but is also charged with preserving the rights and responsibilities of the Church of Scotland, and is present in person or by a representative at the Church's annual assembly.

We also need to mention Rome. Or rather the Vatican City – which is a city within a city and a state within a state. Once it was a very powerful state with all the paraphernalia that involved. It still exists but today it is a small area around St Peter's Church and the Papal Palace with only about 850 residents. The Pope is the absolute monarch of this tiny state which appoints ambassadors. Here the Church is the government!

CONTESTED SPACE?

There are many examples of the Church speaking out on political issues at all levels of society. In some contexts it has *only* been the Church which has been able to speak out. We have already cited examples such as Pope John Paul II and Desmond Tutu. Other examples would be major moral issues such as the anti-slavery movement of the 19th century. This was led by William Wilberforce, an MP and devout Christian, and strongly supported by Quakers, John Wesley and many others.

Faith in the City was a report published in 1985 against the background of riots in inner city areas of Britain. The Archbishop of Canterbury set up a commission to investigate those events. It concluded that there were enormous problems of disaffection, deprivation and unease in inner city areas. It made uncomfortable reading for the Church itself, as it criticized the lack of resources committed to the inner cities, along with outdated attitudes and policies. In the light of these, the report made recommendations to the Church on such issues as clergy recruitment, training and deployment. It recommended setting up the Church Urban Fund (CUF) to assist churches working in inner city areas where there was significant deprivation. CUF continues to do much-needed work today.

But although the majority of its recommendations were aimed at the Church, the report made suggestions to the government as well. The response was dramatic. The loudest criticism was that the Church should keep out of politics. The right-wing press and some politicians dismissed it as 'Marxist' and the Church of England was accused of being led by 'Communist clerics'.

That view that the Church should not be involved in politics is often heard, usually when the Church speaks out against the government. A former British MP is reported to have said that, 'The Church should get back to its prime business of praising the Almighty, saving souls and considering its own diminishing position in this society'. He went on to suggest that, 'the big boys will manage the money, while the Church makes jam for the fete'.

This is contrary to Augustine's original argument in *The City of God*. Those who criticize the Church's involvement in political life seem to argue that it is the task of the *Church* to order things peacefully and justly so that the *State* can get on with its work. But if politics is about the ordering of society, the Church will and should get involved. The nature of that involvement in a post-secular world is what we need to turn to next. As Desmond Tutu put it, 'I am puzzled about which Bible people are reading when they suggest religion and politics don't mix'.

Public theology

Recent years have seen the rise of a new development called **public theology**. Christian theology held a key place in society for centuries. Secularization challenged that place and suggested that religion was on its way out. Today it is increasingly recognized that religion has not gone away and that it remains a powerful source of motivation, meaning and inspiration for millions of people. Governments have had to recognize that Christianity is still around, but the Church has also had to recognize that its place and role in society is now different.

'I understand public theology to be a collaborative exercise in theological reflection on public issues which is prompted by disruptive social experiences that call for our thoughtful and faithful response.'

W. Storrar, 'A Kairos Moment for Public Theology' in *The International Journal of Public Theology* (Brill), vol. 1 (2007), Issue 1, pp. 5–25.

In looking at public theology we must consider four questions:

▶ Audience: who does public theology address?
In part, public theology seeks to make sense of the Church's beliefs – it has an 'apologetic' task – for the world around it. *Apologetics* is not about saying sorry! An *apologia* is a reasoned defence of one's beliefs or opinions. In a world where understanding of religion seems to be declining, it is increasingly important for the Church to say what – and why – it believes. It speaks to all.

▶ Agency: who does public theology?
Just as liberation theology challenged all church members to defend and promote their faith, so does public theology. It

argues that there is a growing need for Christians to be able to demonstrate how their faith can impact positively on the world around them. It is no longer the sole task of church leaders or academics, but of every church member.

▶ Agenda: what does public theology speak about?
The Church has a prophetic role. That is not about 'predicting the future'. Prophecy in the Christian and Jewish traditions is not about the future so much as about interpreting the present. It means applying the insights of the Christian faith to the events, trends, attitudes and concerns of the wider world. It attempts to shed light on the dark places of life. In this sense, its agenda is set by the world around it.

▶ Arena: where does public theology happen?
You will find many books and journal articles on the subject of public theology which use the phrase 'theology in the public square'. This raises the issue of where theology is done. Public theology is about leaving the confines of the church or the academy and doing theology where people are. Instead of asking people to come *in* to the church, public theology takes its thinking and thoughts *out* to the public sphere – through the press or social media, for example. In some ways this is similar to evangelism – the preaching of the good news (gospel) – but there is a difference which may appear subtle. Evangelism is primarily aimed at *conversion*. It is most often aimed at individual responses to the gospel message. Public theology is more collective. It is aimed more at society as a whole. It seeks to bring the insights and wisdom of the gospel to the public domain, to society, rather than simply to the individual. The two are not and cannot be mutually exclusive; nor are they in opposition.

'Public theology, as I understand it, is not primarily and directly evangelical theology which addresses the Gospel to the world in the hope of repentance and conversion. Rather, it is theology which seeks the welfare of the city before protecting the interests of the Church, or its proper liberty to preach the Gospel and celebrate the sacraments. Accordingly, public theology often takes 'the world's agenda', or parts of it, as its own agenda, and seeks to offer distinctive and constructive *insights from the treasury of faith to help in the building of a decent society, the restraint of evil, the curbing of violence, nation-building, and reconciliation in the public arena, and so forth.'*

D.B. Forrester, 'The Scope of Public Theology' in *Studies in Christian Ethics* (Sage Journals) August 2004, vol. 17, No. 2, pp. 5–19.

Church and society

▶ Welfare

Many Christians feel they are called to make the world a better place: they are world-affirming. In fulfilling the great commandment – 'Love God with all your heart, soul, mind and strength and love your neighbour as yourself' – the impact of the Church on society has been enormous. In medieval Europe the Church founded universities and hospitals and pioneered schools. The Church has fed the hungry, housed the homeless and taken care of the elderly and sick. Throughout Europe, Protestant Christianity gave rise to the liberal democratic state. In the modern era, Christian Socialists like Archbishop William Temple helped create Britain's welfare state and many modern caring agencies have Christian origins. Here are a few more examples:

The Samaritans began as a result of the concern of an Anglican rector in London. Chad Varah became aware that a large number of people were in despair and suicidal. He invited them to ring Mansion House 9000. Within 20 years this telephone ministry of listening and befriending had grown into an international movement.

The Red Cross was founded by a Christian, Henri Dunant, as a result of the suffering he witnessed in the Austro-Sardinian War. He was a Calvinist and grew up with a strong belief in Christian social responsibility. The Red Cross started as an agency providing medical care for the wounded but went on to be instrumental in the development of the Geneva Conventions – protocols aimed at minimizing suffering and evil in time of war. Today it is renowned not only as an aid agency but also as an arbiter in conflict zones around the world. Dunant's organization became a movement and has now spread to include people of all faiths and none.

Shelter is an influential pressure group for good housing in Britain. It began on 1 December 1966 as the result of the united concern of five housing organizations, three of which contained the word 'Catholic', 'Christian' or 'Church'. Christian leaders were key figures in those early days and Shelter's first chairman, Bruce Kenrick, was a Christian minister.

Around the world the Church has been involved in working to relieve the plight of children. **The Children's Society** was founded in England in the late 19th century by Edward Rudolf, a Sunday school teacher from London, to care for children left vulnerable by poverty and homelessness. Over the years it has helped thousands of children to a better life. It continues to do so today, not only offering practical help but lobbying governments on behalf of children. **Save the Children** was founded by a remarkable young woman, Eglantyne Jebb (1876–1928). After Oxford and school teaching she suffered self-doubt. Then she had a spiritual experience which changed her life: 'I knew what I had never known before, how we need God in Christ, as well as God the Father'. As a result of this she fought for social justice on many fronts. Save the Children grew from her work for starving children in central Europe after the First World War. 'Surely,' she said, 'it is impossible for us, as normal human beings, to watch children starve to death without making an effort to save them.' Save the Children now works in more than 120 countries. **Barnado's** also has its roots in Christian faith. Thomas Barnado (1845–1905) had hoped to go to China as a missionary, but encountering poor and destitute children on the streets of London, he resolved to devote his life to helping them.

Habitat for Humanity is an American initiative which builds subsidized homes for needy families in the USA. It has also pioneered 'appropriate technology' homes in other continents and countries, for example, Tanzania.

The hospice movement was started in Britain under the inspiration of Dame Cicely Saunders. She pioneered pain control and saw the need for small, intimate units where terminally ill patients could be cared for and families and friends welcomed. Dame Cicely gladly acknowledged that without the inspiration and power of Jesus Christ in her life, she would have lacked the strength needed to establish the movement. Her vision and practical ideas caught on and hospices are now found around the world.

Amnesty International was founded by Peter Benenson, a Christian lawyer. Concerned at the plight of prisoners of conscience, he prayed in the crypt of St Martin-in-the-Fields in London's Trafalgar Square. He developed the idea of a network of people who would write to, and about, prisoners of conscience and speak on their behalf. At a practical level, the existing network of churches was important. Peter Benenson launched the movement on Trinity Sunday 1961 to emphasize 'that the power of the Holy Spirit works to bring together people of diverse origins by influencing their common conscience'.

> 'When the first 200 letters came, the guards gave me back my clothes. When the next 200 letters came, the prison Director came to see me. When the next pile of letters arrived, the Director got in touch with his superior. The letters kept arriving, and the President was informed. The letters still kept arriving, and the President called the prison and told them to let me go.'
>
> From a letter by a former prisoner of conscience, writing about the work of Amnesty International.

To these we could add work among refugees and in areas struck by famine, drought and endemic poverty. Christian organizations seek not only to help at the moment of crisis by bringing emergency aid: they also seek to influence long-term policy. The above movements are not limited to Christian believers. In most cases a wide range of views and beliefs are to be found among their activists. But it remains true that these organizations were built on Christian foundations, with Christian vision and energy.

While secular governments have taken over much of the 'social' or welfare work that the church used to do, it is still the case that Christian organizations are actively involved. And when governments cut funding from welfare projects it is often faith-based communities such as the Church which step up to meet the needs of those left vulnerable and in need.

> *Habermas argues that we live in a world in which 'a post-secular self-understanding of society as a whole, in which the vigorous continuation of religion in a continually secularizing environment must be reckoned with ...'*
> J. Habermas, 'Equal Treatment of Cultures and the Limits of Postmodern Liberalism', *The Journal of Political Philosophy*, vol. 13, No. 1, 2005, pp. 1–28.

▶ Social cohesion

We looked earlier at secularization – the idea that religion is becoming less influential in society, particularly in many Western countries. Part of the reason for this is that a lot of people see religions as divisive and dangerous. Do an internet search asking 'would the world be a safer place without religion?' and it yields a huge response; we got 208 million responses – and counting – in half a second! Most of the first few pages were of the opinion that the answer was 'yes' – the world would be better off without religion. How might Christianity respond to this?

Case study

Would the world be a safer place without religion? Here are three issues to think about.

▶ The first is to consider the simple fact that religion shows no signs of going away. The secularization theory predicted it would disappear as the world became more scientific, rational and technological. But this has proved not to be the case. Christianity (along with other religions) has proved to be extremely resilient.

▶ The second is to ask if this negative view of religion is mainly a response to media coverage of religion. In an age of instant news, 24-hour saturation coverage and multiple competing news agencies, it is the dramatic – even sensational – which receives most attention. The portrayal of religion in the media is therefore often dominated by extremist activity, scandals and bad news. There is some good, balanced reporting (the BBC still has a worldwide reputation for fairness and careful, insightful reporting). But on the whole the negative side often receives more attention.

▶ Christianity has been and still can be a positive force in society. The reality is that politicians in many places see a positive value in religions. Faith is a very powerful source of commitment to social good, honesty and generosity. It promotes many of the values which are necessary to hold society together and build the common good. As one writer has put it, in a world where it has been marginalized there is a growing case for bringing 'religion back in from the secular cold' (W. Keenan, 'Post-Secular Sociology: Effusions of Religion' in *Late Modernity in European Journal of Social Theory*, 2002 5 (2), pp. 279–90).

In reality, Christians – along with other faith communities – are often among the most committed to making society work. Faith inspires great levels of sacrificial effort in caring for the sick and vulnerable, championing the rights of the marginalized and pursuing social justice. While a minority may seize the headlines with their extremist views or actions, the vast majority of Christians are deeply committed to a 'world-affirming' view of their faith. They still have a powerful part to play in society. Indeed, in many places Christians are among the most heavily involved group of those working to make societies better.

Challenging areas: Christianity and other faiths

The final area we must look at in the contemporary world is the relationship between Christianity and other faiths.

A common view is that 'all religions are the same': they may have different names for God, or different practices and festivals, but essentially they are the same. Any careful study of the major world religions will demonstrate this is not the case. They may have *similarities* – but there are big differences as well. What they have in common is to do with their purpose.

▶ They provide a way of understanding the reality of the world around. *Religions give explanations.*

▶ They describe what it is to be fully human and truly fulfilled. *Religions give something to aspire to.*

▶ They give a framework for life. *Religions provide beliefs and practices which enable people to live fulfilled lives.*

For centuries religions tended to be located in specific geographical areas and tied to their local culture. It was only the (few) travellers and traders who encountered the religions practised in other places. As travel became more common and as nations began expanding into new territories for trade or conquest, religion became a controversial issue. For much of human history since then – and still today in some areas – religions were in competition. But as travellers became settlers, in many societies people of different faiths learned to live side by side.

Spotlight

The Council for a Parliament of the World's Religions (CPWR) is a 23-year-old non-profit organization whose mission is to cultivate harmony among the world's religious and spiritual communities and foster their engagement with the world and its guiding institutions in order to achieve a just, peaceful and sustainable world.

Christianity has adopted a number of approaches to other faiths over the years. Sometimes it has held that it is the only true religion. This **exclusivist** stance argues that Christianity alone is true and all other faiths are wrong. Those who hold such a view tend to be either **active exclusivists**, believing it is imperative that people convert from other faiths to Christianity, or **passive exclusivists**. The latter hold the view that, while there are other faiths around, Christianity is the true faith. They coexist with these other faiths, welcoming rather than seeking converts from them. Yet another view is that other religions have partial understandings of the truth but need to be **completed** by the person and work of Jesus Christ. Others take an **inclusive** view. They believe that all religions have some valuable insights but only by taking all faiths together can the complete picture be known.

In more recent times, travel, migration and the media have meant contact between religions has increased. We now live in a far more mixed and multicultural world. This has led to a more **dialogic approach**. Dialogue seeks to safeguard the uniqueness of each faith tradition while allowing rigorous and honest debate over differences of belief. It does this with mutual respect and in a constructive manner. It also maintains the right of individuals and communities to practise their faith. In the face of the secularism policies of some governments, religions increasingly co-operate with one another to defend the rights of people to hold religious beliefs.

There are many examples of this dialogic approach around the world. For example, in 2003 the National Council of Churches in Australia got together with the Australian Federation of Islamic Councils and the Executive Council of Australian Jewry to form the Australian National Dialogue of Christian, Muslims and Jews. It aims to 'provide opportunity for the national bodies of each faith to come together to build understanding and harmony in the Australian context'. Its objectives (see www.ncca.org.au) are:

▶ to be a model of how different faiths can live harmoniously together in Australia

▶ to build understanding, goodwill and a sense of community between people of different faiths

▶ to explore and learn about each other and our faith traditions

▶ to share our knowledge and insights with others

- to work together to achieve common goals in Australia
- to support each other in times of difficulty.

Spotlight

Syncretism – which is about 'mixing' together ideas and beliefs from different religions – literally means 'Cretan federation'. According to the first-century Greek historian Plutarch, the people of Crete compromised their differences in order to unite against an enemy. Much later on the word was applied to mixing together different religious beliefs.

Undoubtedly there are many pressing questions for contemporary Christianity in a world of many faiths:

- What does it mean to believe Jesus is '*the* way, *the* truth and *the* life' (John 14:6)?

- On what grounds do some Christians argue that it is the only true religion?

- What are the implications for Christianity of believing that there might be many paths to God?

- Is it possible to gain insights into *Christian* faith from other religions?

Though the context has changed, Christians continue to believe as passionately as ever that they have 'good news' to share – boldly but sensitively.

Key ideas

- Christians draw inspiration from the vivid images used by Jesus; to be 'salt', 'light' and 'peacemakers' within their communities.

- Christian leaders down the years have made positive contributions to international political issues.

- Christians continue to be involved in the social, cultural and political life of their communities in various ways.

▶ Many international, national and local humanitarian organizations have been built on Christian foundations, driven by the vision of Christians.

▶ Inter-faith dialogue seeks to safeguard the uniqueness of each faith tradition while allowing rigorous and honest debate over differences of belief.

Dig deeper

C. Baker, *The Hybrid Church in the City: Third space thinking* (Aldershot: Ashgate, 2007).

L. Bretherton, *Christianity and Contemporary Politics: The conditions and possibilities of faithful witness* (Chichester; Malden, MA: Wiley-Blackwell, 2010).

R. Harries, *Faith in Politics?* (London: Darton, Longman and Todd, 2010).

P.M. Hedges and A. Race, *Christian Approaches to Other Faiths* (London: SCM, 2008).

Fact check

1 Constantine's conversion led to Christians:
    a forming the Christian Socialist Party
    b being barred from political life
    c having to seek new ways to relate to society
    d becoming political outcasts

2 Augustine's *City of God* was:
    a a blueprint for town planners
    b a treatise on how Church and State should function
    c a map of Jerusalem
    d an argument for why the Church should run the state

3 In medieval Europe, the Church:
    a closed schools down as agents of the devil
    b opposed the establishing of universities
    c believed hospitals delayed people getting to heaven
    d founded universities and hospitals, and pioneered schools

4 'Theology in the public square' means:
    a open-air evangelism
    b theology which seeks the welfare of the city
    c abolishing the use of church buildings
    d open-air services of worship

5 The Vatican City is:
    a a small area around St Peter's Church and the Papal Palace with under 1,000 residents
    b another name for Rome
    c the trading name of the Roman Catholic Church
    d the central area of Rome with a population of around 250,000

6 Syncretism is:
    a a new political system
    b a fusing together of different religions and religious ideas
    c a form of evangelism
    d the abolition of religion

7 Inter-faith dialogue:
- **a** is a form of Christian evangelism
- **b** seeks to safeguard the uniqueness of each faith tradition while allowing rigorous and honest debate over differences of belief
- **c** means different faiths all worshipping together
- **d** is the process of finding the best in each religion and combining it in a new religion

8 Chad Varah founded:
- **a** Shelter
- **b** The Samaritans
- **c** The hospice movement
- **d** Amnesty International

9 Which of the following is *not* one of the objectives of the Australian National Dialogue of Christian, Muslims and Jews?
- **a** To be a model of how different faiths can live harmoniously together in Australia
- **b** To build understanding, goodwill and a sense of community between people of different faiths
- **c** To share our knowledge and insights with others
- **d** To promote the distinctive contribution of Australian culture to the Abrahamic faiths

10 Which church leader was directly involved in opposing the political system of apartheid in South Africa?
- **a** Archbishop Helder Camara
- **b** Pope John Paul II
- **c** Archbishop William Temple
- **d** Archbishop Desmond Tutu

Christianity and the world of science, cyberspace and the internet

In this chapter you will learn about:

▶ *science and Christianity*
▶ *the challenges of a computerized world*
▶ *new forms of church brought about by the internet*
▶ *Christianity on the web.*

Science and faith

'In the beginning God created the heavens and the earth' (Genesis 1:1). These opening words from the Bible were read to the world by the crew of Apollo 8 on Christmas Eve 1968 as their spacecraft circled the moon – the first human beings to do so.

The Vatican has its own observatory (*Specola Vaticana*) – one of the oldest astronomical institutes in the world. Several religious orders have contributed personnel to the observatory and the 19th-century Jesuit Father Angelo Secchi was the first to classify stars according to their spectra. Nevertheless, as science has grown in stature, so religion in Europe (the cradle of modern science) has become less central to many people's lives. There is a likely connection between these two facts.

The explanation for the existence of the world given in the Bible focuses on *purpose* rather than *process*. It affirms that the universe was created and is sustained by the will of a loving God. Science also gives an explanation: a different kind of explanation which excludes purpose, and focuses on *cause and effect*. It is sometimes assumed that these *why* and *how* explanations are mutually exclusive. If so – if they really are in competition – there is no real contest. It is game, set and match to science.

A recent survey taken among British teenagers revealed that a large number believe that science has disproved religion. Clearly, if they are right, then Christian believers have no credibility in the modern world. In the light of this we need to examine some significant facts.

Science is a self-limiting activity – as single-minded about what it *excludes* as what it *includes*. Science raises many fascinating issues but, by definition, it does not address some other important questions we face as human beings – about love, duty, honour and meaning, for example. Off-duty, scientists are as concerned with these non-scientific questions as anyone else. Questions such as:

▶ Does my life have any ultimate meaning and purpose?

▸ Was I dumped here by chance, or loved into existence?

▸ Where does my sense of duty – and of beauty – come from?

It is because Christianity addresses these in a 'real' way, without offering easy answers, that it convinces many – though certainly not all – scientists.

> 'Theology, like science, is a search for intelligibility but, unlike science, it also seeks the human need to discern meaning which has generated religion as a social phenomenon in all human societies.'
>
> A. Peacocke, *Paths from Science Towards God* (One World Publishing, 2001) p.15.

THE ORIGINS OF MODERN SCIENCE

In a remarkable statement, the philosopher John Macmurray asserted that 'science is the legitimate child of a great religious movement, and its genealogy goes back to Jesus'. This is not to deny other important influences: Greek, Chinese, Egyptian, Arabian mathematics, the Old Testament (with its Wisdom literature and Creation narratives). But it is to affirm the importance for the rise of science of a widespread and particular way of looking at the universe, which Christianity gave to the Western world. Others have made the same point. For example, the philosopher A.N. Whitehead and the historian Herbert Butterfield both affirmed that science is a child of Christian thought.

As already indicated, some ancient civilizations were deeply interested in mathematical and scientific questions. There were important advances. But in the event it was Christian civilization which brought scientific thought to birth. Dr Peter Hodgson, who lectured in nuclear physics at Oxford, put it this way (*Science and Belief in a Nuclear Age*, 2005):

> 'Christianity provided just those beliefs that are essential for science, and the whole moral climate that encourages its growth.'

In this view, modern science could only 'take off' when certain factors were present. An eagerness to ask questions and a willingness to doubt received wisdom were crucial. So was a wide range of accepted beliefs about the nature of the universe. Central among these were the belief that:

- the material world is good, because it is created by God

- the same physical laws apply throughout the universe

- time moves forward rather than round in circles

- there is order in the universe because God is One and God is rational and loving.

These views are expounded in the Bible. In contrast, some religions teach that matter is evil; or that we should be detached from the world; or that different gods rule different aspects of life; or that time goes round in endless cycles; or (in ancient Greek thought) that there is a given pattern to which the 'demi-urge' creator had to conform.

So it comes as no surprise to learn that the prestigious Royal Society (founded by a gathering of leading British scientists in the 17th century) is dedicated 'to the Glory of God the Creator, and the benefit of the human race'. Two centuries later the British Association for the Advancement of Science held its first meeting in York. Those who gathered at that meeting in 1831 paid tribute to the Church, 'without whose aid the Association would never have been founded'. They went on to declare that 'true religion and true science ever lead to the same great end'. The first two presidents of the Association were clergymen.

Several famous early scientists were devout Christians, some of whom wrote theological books as well as scientific works. Among many others we note: Isaac Newton (1642–1727), thought by many to be the greatest scientist of all time; Robert Boyle (1627–91), famous for Boyle's Law; Michael Faraday (1791–1867) who harnessed electro-magnetism; and Gregor Mendel (1822–84) who laid the groundwork for modern genetics while abbot of a monastery. James Young Simpson (1811–70) was the first surgeon to employ the anaesthetic properties of chloroform. When asked to name his greatest discovery, his reported reply was, 'It is not chloroform.

My greatest discovery has been to know that I am a sinner and that I could be saved by the grace of God.'

THE PRESENT DAY

Francis Collins held the highly prestigious post of head of the Human Genome Project. He is a leading scientist with an international reputation – and an active Christian. He wrote, 'In my view, there is no conflict in being a rigorous scientist and a person who believes in a God who takes a personal interest in each one of us.' This is not an isolated viewpoint. Many professional scientists believe in God and a number are convinced Christians. Christians in Science (formerly The Research Scientists' Christian Fellowship) has some 700 members in Britain; its American counterpart has about 2,000.

> 'Both theology and science are seeking to make sense of the world that they experience, and their methodologies are not totally different. In each case the search for a rational understanding is motivated by belief and a desire for truth. As such there must be a common ground for dialogue.'
> J. Weaver, *Christianity and Science* (SCM, 2010), p.16.

In Britain there is a flourishing Society for Ordained Scientists. Both Oxford and Cambridge universities have established centres to explore the interface between science and religion. Somewhat similar initiatives have been taken in the USA – at Berkeley, California and in Chicago, for example. Many believing scientists, including Professors Ian Barbour, John Lennox, Arthur Peacocke, John Polkinghorne and Russell Stannard, have written about the relationship between Christianity and science. From a very long list, we might also mention Professor 'Sam' Berry who, together with Dr Francis Collins, led the Human Genome Project for many years.

Of course, none of the above *proves* that Christianity is true. What it *does* show is that Christianity and science are not opposed. They are certainly not mutually exclusive. If two teams really are in competition, no key player can be on both sides at the same time. And because scientists are intelligent people, the significant number of scientifically literate Christians also suggests that Christianity is not just a fairy story, suitable only for those who are unable to think for themselves.

> *'Science investigates; religion interprets. Science gives man knowledge, which is power; religion gives man wisdom, which is control.'*
>
> Martin Luther King, Jr, American civil rights movement leader

THE SEEDS OF CONFLICT

In view of all this, why has the notion that science has disproved religion become so widespread? We shall consider six reasons.

First, the notion of *purpose* lies outside scientific endeavour, by definition and choice, i.e. science is a deliberately 'self-limiting' activity. So science as an enterprise excludes the concept of God. Early on, the notion that the intervention of God was necessary to explain the gaps in scientific knowledge ('God of the Gaps') was rightly seen to be false. In principle (much harder in practice) it was claimed that *everything* could be explained in terms of cause and effect. From there it was a short (but inaccurate) step to the conclusion that, because concepts like 'God' and 'purpose' are outside the scope of science, they are unimportant or non-existent or even anti-science. While many of the founders of modern science were convinced believers, some of the later popularizers of science were militant atheists or agnostics. They spread their views with missionary zeal.

A second factor was the Galileo debate. **Galileo Galilei** (1564–1642) remained a Catholic throughout his life, but his harsh treatment at the hands of church officials is well known. Galileo built on the work of Copernicus (who was a canon – a senior position – in the church) in suggesting that the earth is not at the centre of the universe, an idea which was resisted by the church leadership of his day. The Catholic Church's dispute with Galileo (who was a member of that Church) is a blot on the Church's reputation. The Vatican now supports scientific research and has its own world-famous observatory staffed by world-class scientists (see above).

At stake was scientific method itself. Observation, followed by hypothesis and experimentation, could not be contained within limits already laid down by religious authority. Although it is over 300 years ago, memories of the Galileo dispute live on because it is such a dramatic story (Bertolt Brecht, among others, wrote a play based upon it). This reinforces the popular view that religion is anti-science and that science is a threat to religion.

Spotlight

Copernicus (1473–1543) first put forward his revolutionary idea that the earth rotated around the sun in a lecture to the Pope – who approved. Copernicus was encouraged to publish his work by a Catholic bishop and a Protestant professor. None of them believed his work disproved the Bible or the existence of God.

A third factor was the controversy over **Charles Darwin**'s research. His *On the Origin of Species by Means of Natural Selection* (1859) gave a very different account of the origins of life from that given in the Bible. At a famous debate in 1861 (not with Darwin himself but with T.H. Huxley), the Bishop of Oxford suggested that it was 'either-or': *either* Darwin was right *or* the Genesis account of Creation in the Bible was right. Battle lines were drawn up.

Charles Darwin's views rocked Victorian society. Several leading Christians supported Charles Darwin – and some leading scientists argued against him. To describe the dispute as 'science versus religion' is wrong. Some Christians were unhappy with the Bishop of Oxford's debating stance (although it should be noted that careful research has shown that the bishop was, and still is, inaccurately reported; he was more subtle than is commonly supposed). They looked again at the Bible and came to the conclusion that the beautiful poetic language of Genesis is just that: beautiful poetic language, written in a pre-scientific age. This does not mean that it is unimportant; it does mean that it is not a scientific treatise.

Genesis describes and explains the human situation in a most profound way. The glory and the tragedy are both there.

It raises deep questions about our relationship with God, with Nature, and with one another. The rest of the Bible shows the solution to these vital questions being worked out in the lives of individuals and nations. Such literature is quite different from a scientific treatise on the origins of the universe – but no less important.

Charles Darwin himself was not an opponent of Christianity. It is true that he gradually lost his faith (partly through the death of his young daughter Annie). But in 1872 (13 years after *On the Origin of Species* was published) he gladly accepted honorary membership of the Anglican South American Missionary Society because he was so impressed with their work. In reply to their invitation, he wrote, 'I shall feel proud if your committee think fit to elect me an honorary member of your society.' SAMS continues to do excellent work today.

A fourth factor relates to the above. Some modern fundamentalist Christians are keen to keep the Darwinian controversy alive. They assert that evolution is a discredited theory and that the chapters on the Creation in Genesis should be read literally.

A fifth factor arises from the work of **Sigmund Freud** (1856–1939), who made an immense impact upon the way we view the world. Freud has given us a new vocabulary ('unconscious', 'ego', 'id', 'superego', 'Oedipus complex', 'Freudian slip') and a new understanding of ourselves. Freud maintained that he was making a *scientific* analysis of human behaviour – a view contested by many, including some non-Christians. He wrote about religion and asserted that a key Christian insight should be inverted. God has not made us in his image; rather, we have made God in our image – according to our deepest needs.

Carl Gustav Jung, another of the founders of modern psychology, was much more sympathetic to religion. He made the following remarkable statement: 'During the past 30 years people from all the civilized countries of the earth have consulted me … Among my patients in the second half of life – that is to say over 35 – there has not been one whose problem in the last resort was not that of finding a religious outlook on life.'

But Freud's views are firmly established in popular thought. His insights have been modified and criticized by psychologists and philosophers, but he raises significant challenges for religious believers. Together with Darwin and Marx (in their very different ways), he gave considerable impetus to a secular way of viewing the world, in which religion is marginalized or excluded.

Finally, we note the hostility or indifference towards religion of some articulate present-day exponents of science. As we have seen, many scientists are practising Christians. But some non-Christian scientists have captured the popular imagination. Richard Dawkins with *The Selfish Gene* and his best-seller *The God Delusion* is the best known. Such aggressively atheistic scientists may appear to be speaking 'on behalf of science'; in fact, they are private individuals, whose views on religion are opposed by many of their fellow scientists. Significantly, many atheists and scientists criticize belligerent 'atheistic fundamentalism'.

Perhaps the most famous of all modern scientists is the cosmologist Stephen Hawking, whose book *A Brief History of Time* leaves the door firmly open to the possibility of God, in a teasing conclusion: 'Only time (whatever that might be) will tell us.'

RESOLVING THE TENSION: 'COMPLEMENTARITY'
Reductionism refers to the process of 'reducing' complex areas of life to a simple one-level explanation. Notable among such explanations is Professor C.E.M. Joad's description of human beings (*Recovery of Belief*, 1951).

> 'Man (sic) is <u>nothing but</u>:
> FAT enough for seven bars of soap
> LIME enough to whitewash one chicken coop
> PHOSPHORUS enough to tip 2,200 matches
> IRON enough for one medium-sized nail
> MAGNESIUM enough for one dose of salts
> POTASH enough to explode one toy crane
> SUGAR enough for seven cups of tea
> SULPHUR enough to rid one dog of fleas.'

In this tongue-in-cheek description, Professor Joad (who came to embrace the Christian faith in later life), provides a classic example of reductionism, or 'nothing buttery' as it is colloquially called! His description gives a perfectly legitimate description of a human being. But to say humans are 'nothing but' these things is incomplete; other kinds and levels of description are required.

We need to add *psychological* categories, for human beings have emotions and ideas. We will wish to add *sociological* categories, for human beings function in communities. And these descriptions do not rule out the possibility of *spiritual* categories, for human beings experience love and have an instinct for worship. These various levels of description and explanation are 'complementary': each adds to the others and together they give a fuller and more accurate account.

This approach applies to everything. Music *is* vibrations in the air and ink dots on paper (even cat-gut or steel on horse hair, if we are listening to a cello). But it is not *just* these things. Ask the audience. And we are bound to ask how it is that music and art have the power to inspire and disturb us. The same approach is true when we consider the universe itself. We might describe it in terms of its origins in 'the Big Bang' some 13.7 billion years ago. But this explanation, which uses the categories of modern physics, does not rule out the possibility of explaining the universe as the creation of a God of love.

Why does the earth support life? An answer in *scientific* terms will discuss factors like the importance of carbon, the immensity of space, the size of the earth (just right to support an atmosphere) and the theory of evolution. But it is equally possible to give an explanation in *theological* terms – by maintaining that God designed the earth so that these factors apply. If this is the case, then scientists are discovering the way in which God has designed the world – 'thinking God's thoughts after him' as the early astronomer Johannes Kepler put it. Science itself can help us to see the grandeur of God.

Of course, this theological explanation may be untrue. But not *because* of the fact that Nature can be explained in scientific terms.

RESOLVING THE TENSION: FACTS AND FAITH

It is often asserted that science is about facts, and religion is about faith. Now of course all religions involve faith. But they include facts too. This is certainly true of Christianity which, like science, is based on *interpreted facts*. One fact is the Bible's account of Jesus of Nazareth which, as C.S. Lewis put it, is very difficult to explain in other than Christian terms. Another fact is the rise of the Christian movement in apparently impossible circumstances (with a shrinking number of demoralized disciples and an executed leader). And so we could go on. There are plenty of facts; and faith builds on these.

Conversely, there is plenty of *faith* in science. Scientific method can be described as observation, hypothesis and experimentation, leading to inference and theory. But it can equally well be described in terms of hunch, intuition, gamble, accident, teamwork, flashes of insight, patient slog, with plenty of faith mixed in; and numerous conversations over coffee and beer! Both sets of factors are present all the time. The great Albert Einstein asserted that 'God does not play dice'. And his statement of faith, that there is a constancy and reality about nature, is fundamental to the scientific enterprise.

Despite their hugely impressive achievements, most modern scientists have a greater humility than many of their predecessors. They do not believe that nature is a book simply waiting to be read. They acknowledge mystery and contemplate with awe the inexhaustible riches within nature which they have only begun to glimpse. The awe-inspiring universe in which we live is both beautiful and terrifying – and full of surprises. Despite astonishing progress, modern scientists realize their own practical limitations. 'Chaos theory' (an intriguing but misleading name for a vital insight) suggests that science will never be able to deliver an accurate long-term weather forecast!

Humility is linked with *wonder*. Science – this deliberately self-limiting enterprise – excludes consideration of widespread human experiences of goodness, beauty and obligation. But most scientists are driven by both fascination and wonder. They do not see the physical world as something to be tamed or subjugated, but as something infinitely wonderful in its complexity.

Christians were forced to take their own journey into humility long ago. The days when theology was 'Queen of the Sciences', and every facet of life came within an overarching system of Christian belief and explanation, have long gone. But Christians do claim to have some insights into the nature and ways of God – whom they believe to be both Creator and Redeemer – not because they are clever but because God is gracious. God is revealed in Nature and in Scripture – and supremely in Jesus Christ. But while they might glimpse the glory and recognize that God is 'full of grace and truth' (John 1:14), many questions remain. As St Paul puts it, 'now we only see in part' (1 Corinthians 13:12).

Meanwhile, new ideas surface and buzz. The suggestion of a 'multiverse' (containing parallel universes) is fascinating; the possibility of detecting intelligent life on other planets is exciting. Christianity is open to truth from every quarter and welcomes speculation and research into these, and other, intriguing possibilities. Faith involves living with questions which we cannot answer. But this is not 'blind faith'. Christians live with these questions in the light of the great answers which they believe they do possess. To the questions 'Does life have meaning?' and 'Is it all heading somewhere?' Christianity argues that Jesus Christ is God's resounding 'Yes!'

ETHICAL DILEMMAS

Science has given the world many blessings: most of us would not wish to live in a world without anaesthetics, without technology and without toothpaste! But science has raised enormous problems too. Many new discoveries are ethically neutral in themselves; others are not. Alfred Nobel (instigator of the Nobel Peace Prize) invented dynamite as a safe explosive for use in mining and quarrying. He had no thought that it would be used for destroying *people*. How new technologies are used raises ethical dilemmas.

Technologies which can keep us warm, enable us to travel vast distances quickly or tame nature, can also themselves lead to possible destruction of our planet by nuclear explosion or global warming. Science, technology and industrialization are feared and welcomed in equal measure.

Medical science in particular has presented us with numerous blessings but also with some great ethical dilemmas. We now have the ability to discern early in pregnancy whether a baby is likely to have certain grave health problems and whether it will be male or female. This means that we also therefore have the ability to decide which babies will actually be born. Towards the end of life, we can keep the human body alive by artificial (mechanical) means. But when, and why, and by whom is the machine turned off? Because we *can* do something, does it mean we *should*?

The scientist's first priority is the furtherance of knowledge. Society cannot leave the burden of decision-making resulting from their discoveries to the scientists alone. It is a task for everyone in society – a task which Christians, together with many others, take very seriously. Christians argue that the wisdom to be found in previous generations – especially in their ancient Scriptures – have a practical part to play in seeking to ensure that science enriches, and does not destroy, life on planet Earth. In particular, the biblical teaching that God has given us stewardship of our world is a vital insight. Nature is not a treasure-trove to be ransacked; it is a delicate network to be respected, cherished and left in good order for future generations.

From Gutenberg to Google (and beyond): IT, cyberspace and Christianity

Johannes Gutenberg's invention of the European printing press in the 15th century made the mass production of cheap books possible. It led to a communication and information revolution which changed the very fabric of Europe. The computer has done something similar in the modern era – but on a global scale.

'After sex, religion is one of the most popular and pervasive topics of interest online.' (L.L. Lawson and D.E. Cowan, *Religion Online* (Routledge, 2004), Introduction)

In Chapter 14 we mentioned how aviation had developed spectacularly within a generation. Compared with computers, that is quite slow! Though computers have been around for a long time, the invention of the silicon chip in 1961 revolutionized them. It paved the way for the rapid development of faster smaller computers capable of doing more and more. Bill Gates' dream of a 'computer on every desk and in every home' was not only achieved within 30 years: many people have several in their homes, in their cars and even one in their pocket!

Spotlight

It is estimated that less than 1 per cent of the world's population had access to the internet in 1995 (it was only invented in 1991). It is now around 40 per cent and rising. So, is the Common Core State Standards Initiative in the USA right to preference learning to *type* over learning to *write* for school children?

THE CHALLENGES OF A COMPUTERIZED WORLD

The term 'information technology' seems to have been first used by Leavitt and Whisler in 1958 in the *Harvard Business Review*. Since then it has become 'IT' – firmly embedded in everyday language – and has raised many issues. It can be helpful to think of those issues as rather like the deep end and the shallow end of a swimming pool! They are obviously connected – it is one pool. But as you move from one end to the other, different dynamics come into play.

At the 'shallow end' IT has brought about a revolution in communication. We can store and share vast amounts of information. From that vast quantity we can selectively retrieve information in a fraction of second. We can produce sophisticated websites accessible around the globe 24/7. We can 'talk' to huge numbers of people by sending a single message – all the time anywhere. Locally produced magazines and posters are infinitely more attractive and 'professional' than ever before because of computers. Church websites, church magazines and church noticeboards have been transformed! New music, study courses and other resources are only a click away. We talk of things 'going viral', meaning within minutes an idea or image can spread around the globe, accessed by hundreds of thousands – if not millions – of people. Social media can 'activate' people around the world and share the plight of an individual or group almost instantly.

But as we move towards the deep end of the IT 'pool' the issues start to change. They become more philosophical in nature. Look at the language of the computerized world. We talk about 'virtual reality' and 'virtual space', sometimes collectively referred to as the 'cyber spatial environment'. How are words like 'virtual', 'space' and 'reality' being used here? What do they mean?

> 'For the sacred to have substance, each generation must articulate ideas of the divine that are credible and meaningful against the backdrop of its time.'
> B.E. Brasher, *Give Me That Online Religion* (Rutgers University Press, 2004), p. 186.

Perhaps the online world of Second Life illustrates this best. Individuals can 'live' in this online world. In such a world they can create their identity, buy property, work, relate to others, marry – even pursue a religious faith of their own creation (or a 'real' one – whatever that means!). The *physicality* of being human – the body, the place I am in – is bypassed in this world. Who we are is potentially infinitely variable. But in what sense is it 'real'? We cannot simply dismiss it as 'unreal': we have to think of reality in new ways.

As we saw with science earlier in this chapter, IT creates both possibilities and problems. Perhaps the greatest of those is the 'dis-connecting' of the self and the body. Walter Mitty's daydream world takes on a new level (or a new kind?) of reality when supported by the sort of technologies we see developing. People can inhabit a world – or several – unseen by those who live around them. This can have some advantages. It can 'hide' such things as gender, age or ethnicity which may, in the physical world, hinder communication and dialogue. In this sense it can create a more level playing field, where prejudices or presuppositions can be sidestepped.

There is also a surprising connection between this virtual world and that of religion. In the past, a mystical experience was sometimes described as 'an out-of-body experience'. It meant an experience which transcended time and space. Does the ultra-modern technological world of cyberspace somehow connect with the ancient world of spirituality through a shared use of language?

But if IT can hide prejudices and presuppositions it can also hide things in more sinister ways. 'False' identities can entrap the unwary with catastrophic consequences. Radicalization of religious and political views can be fostered slowly and innocuously online. Religions once led and governed by 'elders', 'priests' and 'pastors' who were known, respected and visible in the local community can now be led by anyone, anywhere. Radical agendas or dangerous ideas can be spread rapidly and as far and wide as good ideas.

Spotlight

Person holding an iPhone: 'In my hand I have a device which – in a fraction of a second – can access virtually the whole of human knowledge. I use it for taking photographs of my lunch and sending them to friends …!'

We can also 'do community' differently. It is early days in social media in many ways but it is already apparent that we spend more time with our online communities than we do with those who are physically around us. Certainly we meet up physically with those in our social circles: social media does not replace that. But we are becoming far more selective about who we mix with. Next time you are in a waiting room, at a concert or gig, on a train, in a queue or even walking down the street – look at how many people are interacting online instead of with those around them! Life in public places is becoming more private!

Case study: iChurch

One response to the advent of IT is the development of iChurches. These are online communities of believers. They are accessible globally – you can join one 'located' anywhere in the world – and they operate 24/7. They raise some interesting and complex questions:

▶ (How) does God exist in cyberspace?

▶ Is an online religious experience the same as any other?

▶ Can you take communion (Mass) online?

▶ (How) can cyberspace be sacred space?

▶ How can we understand 'community' in cyberspace?

The world of IT presents the world with significant challenges. A world in which people spend more time online, more time with manufactured ('man-made') things, means they spend less time with the natural world and with people face to face. We cannot yet know what the consequences of this will be. Christianity faces particular challenges in this regard. At its heart is the idea of Incarnation – that 'God became flesh' in Jesus Christ. As in Judaism, the Christian doctrine of the Creation celebrates the physical, material world. How will a God who is known through the world of nature – through human experience, through the human senses – be known in the virtual reality of virtual space? As it always has during its 2,000-year history, Christianity will need to find ways to adapt.

Key ideas

▶ The explanation for the existence of the world given in the Bible focuses on *purpose* rather than *process*.

▶ It was Christian civilization which brought Western scientific thought to birth.

▶ Several famous early scientists were devout Christians, some of whom wrote theological books as well as scientific works.

- IT is not just about technology: it raises philosophical questions such as what is meant by 'virtual reality' or 'virtual space'.

- After sex, religion is one of the most popular and pervasive topics of interest online.

Dig deeper

B.E. Brasher, *Give Me That Online Religion* (New Brunswick, NJ: Rutgers University Press, 2004).

L.L. Dawson and D.E. Cowan (eds), *Religion Online: Finding faith on the internet* (Abingdon: Routledge, 2004).

J. Navarro (ed.), *Science and Faith Within Reason: Reality, creation, life and design* (Farnham: Ashgate, 2011).

F. Watts and C.C. Knight (eds), *God and the Scientist: Exploring the work of John Polkinghorne* (Farnham: Ashgate, 2012).

J.D. Weaver, *Christianity and Science* (London: SCM, 2010).

1 Galileo:
    a determined to disprove the existence of God
    b tried to prove God's existence scientifically
    c became an atheist as a result of his scientific work
    d remained a Catholic throughout his life

2 Darwin's work provoked deep debate in which:
    a all leading Christians denounced him and all leading scientists supported him
    b no leading Christians denounced him and no leading scientists supported him
    c some leading Christians supported him and some leading scientists argued against him
    d all leading scientists and all leading Christians supported him

3 The 19th-century Jesuit Father Angelo Secchi was the first to:
    a suggest the earth went around the sun
    b put forward the idea of natural selection
    c measure the universe
    d classify stars according to their spectra

4 The Vatican has its own:
    a observatory
    b space lab
    c particle accelerator
    d nuclear reactor

5 James Young Simpson (1811–70) claimed his greatest discovery was:
    a chloroform
    b his faith in God
    c Pluto
    d that God did not exist

6 'Reductionism' refers to:
  a the universe getting smaller
  b the process of reducing complex areas of life to a simple one-level explanation
  c the extinction of diverse life forms
  d the belief that God created the world in six days

7 The Royal Society in Britain is dedicated to:
  a 'the furtherance of science and the eradication of religion'
  b 'the Glory of God the Creator, and the benefit of the human race'
  c 'the Glory of the King and the advance of his empire'
  d 'the promotion of science teaching in schools'

8 Francis Collins of the Human Genome Project declared:
  a 'I think science will one day disprove God's existence'
  b 'I think science will one day prove God's existence'
  c 'In my view, there is no conflict in being a rigorous scientist and a person who believes in a God who takes a personal interest in each one of us'
  d 'I think science has nothing to do with God'

9 iChurches are:
  a non-denominational churches
  b online faith communities
  c churches you design yourself
  d churches with only one member

10 *Second Life* is:
  a life after death
  b an online virtual world
  c a secret society
  d life after conversion

17

Where now?

Twenty-one centuries of Christian discipleship

In Chapter 1, at the start of our journey, we noted that Christianity began as a tiny movement in a hostile world. We also noted that it has grown into the largest movement ever in all human history. How did it survive and flourish? This is the final question we shall address.

'Amazing grace! How sweet the sound that saved a wretch like me!' Written by John Newton, an 18th-century slave-ship captain turned vicar, this hymn has become famous around the globe. John Newton's personal experience takes us back to some words of Jesus: 'I have not come to call the righteous but sinners to repentance' (Mark 2:17.) In acknowledgement of this, church services usually start with a time of confession.

This is a reminder that from the beginning the Church has been made up of self-confessed moral failures. But Christianity is also about redemption. Christian discipleship involves a new start in life with the promise that God will forgive us and that by his Spirit Jesus Christ will guide us, strengthen us and grow within our lives the beautiful 'fruit of the Spirit': love, joy, peace, patience, kindness, generosity and faithfulness (Galatians 5:22). This is the simple but profound basis on which Christianity rests: it involves a personal relationship with God the Father, as believers seek to follow Jesus Christ the Son in the strength and love of the Holy Spirit.

In its earliest days these simple truths were the Church's only resource as it faced a hostile or indifferent world. Then came the Emperor Constantine and, in a flash (in AD 312) Christianity enjoyed imperial patronage. A mixed blessing. Great power corrupts. Great power attracts. Men and women (mainly men) far from the Spirit of Christ, and distorting the teaching of Christ, nevertheless gained power within the Church of Christ. A study of Christian history shows that the struggle between the humility of true discipleship and the pride of power has run through the centuries. This same kind of struggle is experienced in every individual Christian life. There do seem to be notable exceptions: St Francis, who walked with 'Sister

Poverty', is one such example – but if we were able to speak to him, perhaps we would find that his struggles were very fierce indeed. This is certainly what the saintly Mother Teresa of Calcutta experienced. Her deep faith and committed life were accompanied by many 'dark nights of the soul'.

This 2,000-year struggle continues today. At some times and in some places the Church has an easy ride – and often gets flabby as a result. Sometimes the opposition is almost overwhelming – as in Nero's Rome; in Nazi Germany; in Mao's China; in Stalin's Soviet Union, in today's North Korea ... In some cultures, including our own, it faces the hostility that comes with being unfashionable and out of step.

Yet in every age Jesus Christ has his witnesses. Imperfect people who convey something of the grace and love of Jesus Christ. Today's zeitgeist ('spirit of the age') is very dismissive of Christian beliefs and the Christian Church, certainly in the West. In modern Britain many young people have never entered a church building and have no contact at all with their local churches – unthinkable just a generation ago.

Nevertheless, people continue to catch the vision and decide to follow Jesus Christ. This can be the result of years of intellectual wrestling, or a sudden and deep personal experience of Christ, or a fiery sermon or reading a book ... . More often it results from the quiet witness to the faith of ordinary Christians. In his second letter to the Christians in Corinth – a seaport that was notorious for licentious living – the apostle Paul wrote that the Christians there were 'living letters'. So below are a few examples of those whose lives have been touched by Christ in more recent times. Some are famous; some are known only to a few. All are impressive.

When asked if he were a saint, **Nelson Mandela** replied, 'I'm not a saint unless you think of a saint as a sinner who keeps on trying'. In his long years as a prisoner on Robben Island he was sustained by his fellow prisoners and by his Christian faith. He wrote letters of thanks for the encouraging visits from chaplains. Nelson and other prisoners gathered regularly at the Lord's Table – even encouraging his white warder, Christo

Brand, to participate with them. They remained firm friends after his release.

Many famous sportsmen and women declare their faith by crossing themselves on the track or field of play. Notable among them is **Usain Bolt**, who is a Roman Catholic. Two of his tweets are worth noting: 'I want to thank GOD for everything he has done for me cause without him none of this wouldn't be possible'; 'Never forget the true meaning of the day' (Good Friday 2015).

During the First World War **Edith Cavell**, a senior nurse working in Belgium, was found guilty of helping Allied prisoners to escape. She was sentenced to death by firing squad. Like the pioneering nurse Florence Nightingale before her, Edith drew strength and comfort from her Christian faith. Edith carried with her Thomas à Kempis' spiritual classic *The Imitation of Christ*. On the night before her execution she received Holy Communion. Her life – and death – were a huge inspiration to her generation. She has come to public notice again during the centenary commemorations of the Great War (1914–18).

Barack Obama (US president 2009–16) has said that he's a 'Christian by choice' who prays every day. He has spoken of finding Christianity as an adult and about the inspirational role of Jesus in his life. He affirmed that, 'my public service is part of that effort to express my Christian faith'. He added: 'I came to my Christian faith later in life, and it was because the precepts of Jesus Christ spoke to me in terms of the kind of life that I would want to lead, being my brothers' and sisters' keeper, treating others as they would treat me. And I think also understanding that Jesus Christ dying for my sins spoke to the humility we all have to have as human beings – that we're sinful and we're flawed and we make mistakes, and that we achieve salvation through the grace of God. But what we can do, as flawed as we are, is still see God in other people, and do our best to help them find their own grace.'

Virginia McLaurin worked as a seamstress. She was a very ordinary black woman, apart from one notable 'achievement'. Aged almost 107, she was invited to the White House, where she famously danced for joy with President Barack Obama and the First Lady, Michelle. Asked the usual question about the secret of her long life, she concluded with the words: 'Go to church. Serve the Lord.' A video of the moving encounter was uploaded to the White House's Facebook page and immediately went viral, with nearly 9 million views in less than five hours.

The Vicar of Baghdad, **Andrew White**, was a young medical doctor when he felt called by God to become an ordained minister in the Church of England. After ordination, his ministry at Coventry Cathedral focused on reconciliation. He developed a deep desire to bring Jews, Muslims and Christians together. He visited Iraq – including the rundown Church of St George in Baghdad. Then Andrew developed multiple sclerosis.

He accepted an invitation to minister at St George's, where he helped build a large congregation – 'commuting' to Baghdad, leaving his wife and two young sons in Britain. Andrew continues to have a hugely effective, largely unseen ministry of reconciliation among political and religious leaders across the Middle East. And he raises funds for relief work. His life is fraught with danger. 'I have been beaten, held at gunpoint, left for hours in rat-infested rooms and much more besides.' Asked about her husband's ministry and lifestyle, his wife said: 'I have survived by being realistic about Andrew, his health and his work. We felt that it would be better to die by a bullet in Baghdad than by a steady deterioration in his body that can come with MS. But as it happens his MS has improved. In Baghdad he's had stem cell treatment not available in Britain, using his own stem cells, which has turned his health around ... We all have to face the life we have and accept it, and I feel so blessed to be able to do that with God's help rather than on my own.'

David Suchet, a fine stage actor, is best-known for portraying Agatha Christie's fictional detective Hercule Poirot on television. His brother, John, is also well-known as a newscaster and musicologist. Their father was Jewish, but their upbringing was not religious. In 1986, while staying in a hotel, David picked up a Bible and read Paul's letter to the Romans, which made an immense impact upon him. He underwent a conversion experience to Christianity which continues to sustain his life. Chapter 8 of Paul's great New Testament letter to the Romans ends with a ringing affirmation of God's love, when the apostle says: 'I am convinced that neither death nor life … nor anything else in all creation, will be able to separate us from the love of God that is in Christ Jesus our Lord'.

C.S. Lewis was a brilliant young lecturer in English Literature at Oxford University when he began to doubt his atheistic creed. Through reading, through his Christian colleague J.R.R. Tolkein (subsequently famous as the author of *The Lord of the Rings*) and through a religious experience (on the top of an Oxford bus!), Lewis became 'the most reluctant convert in all England'. He went on to write numerous books, including children's books (the 'Chronicles of Narnia'), science fiction, academic work and several books exploring and explaining the Christian faith.

The eminent scientist **Francis Collins** held the highly prestigious post of head of the Human Genome Project. This involved working at the cutting edge of the study of DNA, the 'code of life'. He is a leading scientist with an international reputation. Francis was brought up in a home where faith in God was not important, and he carried this easy indifference to religious questions into his adult life. When practising as a young doctor it was his patients who challenged him to think hard about questions of life and death. He was impressed by the resilience and fortitude of believers as death approached. Then one of his patients challenged him directly to think hard about life, God and meaning. So Francis started to read Christian books and this prompted him to question his secular creed. It was C.S. Lewis' famous book *Mere Christianity* that finally drew him to faith in Christ.

In the summer of 2000 Francis stood in the White House with US president Bill Clinton. They broadcast to the world an astounding fact: the script carrying all the instructions needed for building a human being had been decoded. The president said: 'Today we are learning the language in which God created life.' Francis Collins followed with these words: 'It's a happy day for the world. It is humbling for me, and awe-inspiring, to realize that we have caught the first glimpse of our own instruction book, previously known only to God.'

As a young man **Bob Holman** was Professor of Social Administration at Bath University. He then decided to put theory into practice. So in 1987 he and his wife Annette moved to a former council house in Glasgow's Easterhouse, where, with others, they established Family Action in Rogerfield and Easterhouse (FARE; www.fare-scotland.org) with the aim of improving community life. In his seventies, Bob developed cancer and also motor neurone disease. Reflecting on this in a personal letter, he wrote:

> 'Recently, in the midst of over 200 people, a tough young man picked me up, kissed me, thanked me and prayed for me. Years ago he was a violent member of a gang and went to prison. On release, he associated with FARE, became a volunteer, and is now a paid member of staff. It has been worthwhile. … I am thankful for a long life in which I have participated in a number of social activities. As a Christian, I trust and believe that death means transition to the Lord God.'

Queen Elizabeth II in her Christmas broadcasts often refers to her Christian faith. In her first broadcast in 1952 she asked the people of the Commonwealth and Empire to pray for her as she prepared to dedicate herself to their service at her coronation. In *The Servant Queen and the King She Serves*, published in 2016 to mark her 90th birthday, the Queen comments, 'I have been – and remain – very grateful to you for your prayers and to God for His steadfast love. I have indeed seen his faithfulness.' She goes on to say how much she relies on her faith to guide her in good times and bad, and adds, 'I draw strength from the message of hope in the Christian gospel.'

There are countless other witnesses. The Christian story down the years is not mainly of the famous and the powerful. It is the story of ordinary women and men from every culture and personality type who in the past – and still today – embrace the faith of the carpenter from Nazareth.

Into the future

This book began with the statement that Christianity did not appear 'ready-made' out of nowhere. The first disciples needed to make sense of what they had experienced since meeting Jesus. They sought to live in the light of that experience and to communicate it for their time and place. The Christian faith faces no less a challenge today.

All of this leaves us with some interesting questions. Over 2,000 years, what has changed and what has stayed the same? How does the faith of a Christian today compare with that of those first disciples? And what of the future? How is Christianity likely to fare in the 21st century?

Predicting the future requires caution. Many in the 19th century predicted the 20th would be a 'Christian century'. The missionary movement, the ecumenical movement and the industrial revolution seemed to suggest uninterrupted progress. Indeed, progress had emerged in the 18th century as a socio-cultural idea that many thought was unstoppable. A few years into the 20th century brought an abrupt halt, not only to progress, but to optimism and hope as well, as first Europe, then the world, was plunged into war. But for all those who predicted a 'Christian century', there were probably just as many who predicted the demise of Christianity. They too, got it wrong. As the third Christian millennium gets under way, the world continues to be unstable, fragmented and dangerous. Yet the Christian Church worldwide continues to grow.

Following the Christian Way involves much more than 'going to church' or belonging to a cultural group. When it is true to itself, Christian faith engages with real life. It brings challenge and inspiration; it gives strength and comfort in times of trouble. Harry Williams CR, an Anglican monk who was Prince Charles's tutor at Cambridge University, put it like this:

> 'Being a Christian means … being a person in whom his [Jesus'] life and character and power are manifest and energized … Christian experience is not so much a matter of imitating a leader as accepting and receiving a new quality of life – a life infinitely more profound and dynamic and meaningful than human life without Christ.'

Glossary

Abba: *Abba* ('Father') is one of the few Aramaic words found in the New Testament (Aramaic was Jesus's first language). It is an intimate family word – the nearest English equivalent is probably 'Dad' or 'Daddy'. Jesus addressed God the Father in this way; so did the first Christians. The word, and the close relationship to God which it describes, was a gift from Jesus to his disciples.

canon: a Greek word meaning 'rod' or 'rule', which came to signify a list or catalogue. In Christian usage it denotes the list of books regarded as Holy Scripture.

creed: a definition or summary of Christian belief. The earliest creeds are found in the New Testament, for example Romans 10:9 ('Jesus is Lord') and 1 Corinthians 15:3. Later creeds include the Apostles' Creed and the Nicene Creed.

eternal life: a new quality of life to be entered into, by God's grace, through faith in Jesus Christ. It starts in this world and continues beyond death – into eternity. The phrase is found frequently in John's Gospel and first letter.

evangelism: proclaiming or sharing the good news of God's love revealed in Jesus Christ. Roman Catholics tend to use the word 'evangelization'. Sometimes this means the same as evangelism; sometimes it refers to the permeation of relationships and cultures with gospel values.

the gospel: the good news of God's love revealed supremely in the life, teaching, death and resurrection of Jesus Christ. It means 'Glad tidings of great joy' (Luke 2:10). William Tyndale wrote: 'Evangelio (that we cal gospel) is a greke word, and signyfyth good, mery, glad and joyfull tidings, that maketh a mannes hert glad, and maketh hym synge, daunce and leepe for joye.'

Gospels, synoptic: the term used for the first three accounts of the life of Jesus in the New Testament. The Gospels of Matthew, Mark and Luke each have distinctive features but they share much similar material. The fourth Gospel (the Gospel according to John) takes a very different approach to the life, teaching, death and resurrection of Jesus.

high priest: a title given to Jesus in the New Testament (especially in the letter to the Hebrews), signifying the fact that he has dealt with human sin. The offering he made was the perfect sacrifice of his own life.

Holy Spirit: in the New Testament the Holy Spirit has many titles: the Spirit of God, the Spirit of Christ, the Spirit of Jesus, the Spirit of Truth, the Counsellor … Many of these titles convey the notion of the closeness (the 'immanence') of God, as opposed to the 'transcendence' of God the Father.

Incarnation: the Christian belief that in Jesus, God became a human being in order to save the world. (This is quite different from reincarnation.)

liturgy: in Greek, literally 'the work of the people'. It came to be applied to worship offered in the Temple and, later, to Christian worship, especially the Eucharist.

mission: mission is a wider concept than evangelism, though it includes this. It embraces all that God calls his Church to do in the world: care for Creation and the pursuit of justice and peace, as well as praying for the world and spreading the gospel of Jesus Christ. The Swiss theologian Emil Brunner declared that 'the Church exists by mission as a fire exists by burning'.

monotheism: belief in one God. The three great monotheistic faiths are Judaism, Islam and Christianity. Because all three look back to the patriarch Abraham, they are sometimes called 'the Abrahamic faiths'.

myth: in common usage, this is usually a 'bad' word, referring to something which is untrue: a fabricated story, perhaps even a lie. In theological language, it is usually a 'good' word, referring to something so important and profoundly true that it can only be conveyed in the form of a story.

New Age: 'The fastest growing spiritual movement in the world today' (Margaret Brierly). It is a movement without hierarchy or central organization. It stresses spirituality, which in this context means 'doing your own thing' – anything from meditation to hugging trees. 'In one sense the New Age Movement is a religion without being a religion, with its emphasis on self-realization rather than upon God.' (Graham Cray). See **postmodernism**.

polytheism: those religions which, like Hinduism, honour many gods. Some Hindus believe in One Supreme Being. It is their belief that the 'many Gods' are different manifestations of the One God.

postmodernism: 'Modernism' was the child of the Enlightenment. 'Post-modernism' is a buzzword suggesting a time of rapid transition – a new way of viewing the world. 'Post-modernity is a flux of images and fictions … truth is human, socially produced, historically developed, plural and changing' (Don Cupitt). Truth is viewed as relative, not absolute, and insights from various places may be pulled together to form a view of life – a 'pick and mix approach' (see **New Age**).

salvation: the activity of God which – supremely in Jesus Christ – brings healing, wholeness and reconciliation with God and one another.

Son of Man: the title which, in the synoptic Gospels, is used by Jesus to refer to himself. Scholars have debated its background and significance, and whether Jesus did in fact use the phrase. Its likely origins can be found in two Old Testament books. Throughout Ezekiel, God addresses the prophet as 'son of man', i.e. as a fragile human being. In Daniel 7:13–14, the phrase refers to an awesome heavenly figure.

synagogue: a Jewish meeting place for worship. Unlike worship in the Temple, synagogue worship did not (and does not) include animal sacrifice, but is based on prayers and readings from the Hebrew Scriptures. At the time of Jesus, as now, synagogues were established in every town with a Jewish community.

tabernacle: a portable sanctuary (an elaborate 'tent') in which God 'dwelt' among the Israelites in the desert. It was the forerunner of the Temple.

Temple: the first Temple was built by King Solomon (2 Chronicles 3). At the time of Jesus, the Temple in Jerusalem (built by Herod the Great) was the focus for national worship, including animal sacrifice. Herod's great Temple was destroyed by the Romans in AD 70. The Western Wall (sometimes called 'the Wailing Wall') remains from the original building and is a place for Jewish prayer and pilgrimage.

the Trinity: the Christian doctrine that there are three 'persons' in one God.

Virgin Birth: the belief that Jesus Christ had no human father, but was conceived by Mary through the power of the Holy Spirit (Matthew 1; Luke 2). More properly called 'the virginal conception'.

wish-fulfilment: the view of Sigmund Freud and others that Christians believe in God because (unconsciously) they find reassurance in the notion of a 'Father in heaven'. This criticism can be turned against itself. For example, Aldous Huxley admitted that for years he believed that the world was without ultimate meaning and moral purpose, because he wished to be free of irksome moral constraints.

Please refer to the Index for other topics.

Taking it further

Many new books on various aspects of Christianity are published every month. It is therefore difficult to compile a list of titles which will not soon be out of date. To help readers who wish to explore further, some useful websites are given below, together with the names of some established authors and their areas of expertise.

Standard texts

MacCulloch, D., *A History of Christianity* (Penguin, 2010)

McGrath, A.E., *Christianity: An Introduction* (3rd edn, Wiley-Blackwell, 2015)

McManners, J. (ed.), *Illustrated History of Christianity* (OUP, 2001)

Oxford Dictionary of the Christian Church (revised edn, OUP, 2005)

Publishers of Christian books

Ashgate
www.ashgate.com

Bible Reading Fellowship
www.brf.org.uk

Cambridge University Press
www.cambridge.org

Church House Publishing
www.chpublishing.co.uk

Columba Press
www.columba.ie

Continuum
www.continuumbooks.com

Darton, Longman & Todd
www.darton-longman-todd.co.uk

Hodder & Stoughton
www.hodderchristianbooks.co.uk

Lion-Hudson plc
www.lionhudson.com

Oxford University Press
global.oup.com

SCM-Canterbury Press Ltd
www.scmpress.co.uk

SPCK
www.spck.org.uk

York Courses
www.yorkcourses.co.uk

Other useful websites
www.anglicancommunion.org

www.caseresources.org (Catholic)

www.catholic-church.org.uk

www.christianaid.org.uk

www.christianityonline.co.uk

www.christianity.org.uk (Christian Enquiry Agency)

www.cofe.anglican.org

www.damaris.org

www.freshexpressions.org.uk

www.justchurch.info (Church Action on Poverty)

www.thegoodbookstall.org.uk

www.rejesus.co.uk

www.yorkcourses.co.uk (group study material)

Some established authors

David Adam: Celtic spirituality; prayer

Richard Bauckham: the Gospels – eyewitnesses and reliability

Stephen Cottrell: living the faith; spirituality

Grace Davie: sociology of religion

John Drane: Christianity and New Age ideas

Eamon Duffy: Church history

James Dunn: accessible scholarly works on early Christianity

David L. Edwards: history; Christian commentary on our times

David Ford: Christian theology; inter-faith relations

Paula Gooder: New Testament; devotional

Elaine Graham: secularization; post secularism

David Hay: religious experience

Joyce Huggett: prayer

Gerard Hughes (Jesuit priest): spirituality

Bob Jackson: Church growth strategy

Martin Luther King, Jr: American civil rights leader

Hans Küng: history; Christian commentary on our times

C.S. Lewis: modest-sized paperbacks on apologetics, plus the Narnia Chronicles and science fiction

Alister McGrath: scholarly and evangelical, including *The Dawkins Delusion*

Henri J.M. Nouwen (Catholic with wide appeal): spirituality

Daniel J. O'Leary: Catholic spirituality

Rob Parsons: family life

Adrian Plass: living the Christian faith – a humorous approach

John Polkinghorne: science and religion

John Pollock: Christian biographies

John Stott: scholarly evangelical

Desmond Tutu: faith in turbulent times

Keith Ward: philosophy; Christian commentary on our times

Rick Warren: strategy for leadership

Robert Warren: Church strategy; living the faith

Rowan Williams: living and understanding the faith

Lucy Winkett: Christian life and faith

N.T. (Tom) Wright: popular paperbacks and large academic works

Philip Yancy: living the faith – an evangelical perspective

Fact-check answers

CHAPTER 1
1 c
2 a, c
3 d
4 b, c
5 b
6 b, c
7 c, d
8 b
9 b
10 b

CHAPTER 2
1 b
2 c
3 b
4 c
5 b
6 d
7 c
8 c
9 c
10 d

CHAPTER 3
1 d
2 b
3 c
4 d
5 b
6 c
7 d
8 b
9 c
10 d

CHAPTER 4
1 b
2 d
3 c
4 c
5 b
6 d
7 b
8 b
9 b
10 a, c

CHAPTER 5
1 c
2 d
3 b
4 c
5 b
6 d
7 c
8 d
9 c
10 c

CHAPTER 6
1 b
2 d
3 c
4 c
5 b
6 b
7 b
8 c
9 c
10 d

CHAPTER 7	CHAPTER 9	CHAPTER 11
1 b	1 c	1 d
2 c	2 d	2 b
3 b	3 b	3 b
4 c	4 c	4 a
5 b	5 b	5 c
6 d	6 b	6 c
7 b	7 d	7 c
8 c	8 a	8 c
9 b	9 d	9 d
10 b	10 c	10 b

CHAPTER 8	CHAPTER 10	CHAPTER 12
1 b	1 c	1 c
2 d	2 c	2 c
3 a	3 d	3 b
4 c	4 b	4 b
5 b	5 b	5 b
6 c	6 b	6 a
7 b	7 b	7 c
8 a	8 b	8 d
9 b	9 d	9 b
10 a	10 d	10 b

CHAPTER 13

1 c
2 d
3 d
4 a
5 c
6 c
7 d
8 b
9 a
10 d

CHAPTER 14

1 c
2 c
3 d
4 b
5 d
6 a
7 c
8 a
9 c
10 d

CHAPTER 15

1 c
2 b
3 d
4 b
5 a
6 b
7 b
8 b
9 d
10 d

CHAPTER 16

1 d
2 c
3 d
4 a
5 b
6 b
7 b
8 c
9 b
10 b

Also by John Young

Christianity Made Simple (Hodder Flash series)

Lord, Help My Unbelief (BRF)

Booklets for group discussion courses including: *The Lord's Prayer*; *Faith, Hope and Love*; *Can we build a better world?* (www.yorkcourses.co.uk)

CD Conversations with eminent Christians, including:

▶ *Climate change and Christian faith*, featuring Nobel Prize winner Professor Sir John Houghton

▶ *Why I believe in God*, featuring Oxford philosopher professor Keith Ward

▶ *Rowan revealed*, featuring Rowan Williams, the 104th Archbishop of Canterbury

▶ *Hawking, Dawkins and GOD* and *Science and Christian faith*, featuring John Polkinghorne, former professor of mathematical physics at Cambridge University

'John Young has a great gift for communicating profound ideas simply and readably.'

Lord Habgood, former Archbishop of York

Index

doubting/doubts 44, 188
Drabble, Margaret 255

Easter 46, 150
ecumenical movement 264–6
Edwards, David 110–11
Edwards, Jonathan 103
Eliot, T.S. 164
Elizabeth II, Queen 327
Epiphany 149
Erasmus 250
eremitic monks 162
eternal life 66, 100, 185
ethical dilemmas 312–13
the Eucharist 124–5
Evangelical Alliance (1846) 264
evangelicals 212
evangelism 289
Evangelists (Gospel writers) 9, 82
the Exile 62, 64
the Exodus 60, 62, 119
extemporary prayer 144

facts and faith 311–12
faith 187–8
feminist theology 267
First Vatican Council (1869-70) 201, 202
fish symbol 133
forgiveness 13, 102, 130, 142, 190
form criticism 81
'four last things' 101–7
Fox, George 165, 214
Francis of Assisi, St 163
Fraser, Dr Giles 186
Freud, Sigmund 308, 309
future, predicting 328

Galileo Galilei 306, 307
garden tomb 40, 228
Gaudi, Antoni 237, 238
Genesis 58–9, 75, 99, 302, 307–8
Geneva Bible 89
Gentiles (non-Jews) 66, 108, 197

globalization 271–3
God, Christian experiences of 107–9
Good Friday 28, 105, 150
Good Samaritan parable 12, 66
Gospels
    apocryphal 83–4
    canonical 76–7
    synoptic 65–6, 80, 123
Gothic architecture 232, 233, 236, 237
Great Schism (1054) 200, 205
Greek cross 132
Gregorian chant 245, 253
guilt 186
Gutenberg Bible 89

Habitat for Humanity 291–2
Hagia Sophia, Istanbul 227
Hardy, Thomas 252
heaven 106–7
Hebrew scriptures, see Old Testament
hell 102–5
Herbert, George 254
'high church' worship 212
Hitler, Adolf 104–5, 128
Hobbes, Thomas 101
Holgate, Archbishop 250
holiness 165, 185
    three marks of 187–90
Holman, Bob 327
Holy Communion 122–8
holy places 223–39
Holy Spirit 97, 98, 138, 151
Holy Week 150
hope 188–9
hospice movement 101, 292
Human Genome Project 305, 326
Hume, Cardinal Basil 107
humility 311–12
    epistemological 158
hymns 246–9